THE ANALOGICAL READER

Perspective taking is a critical component of approaches to literature and narrative, but there is no coherent, broadly applicable, and process-based account of what it is and how it occurs. This book provides multidisciplinary coverage of the topic, weaving together key insights from different disciplines into a comprehensive theory of perspective taking in literature and in life. The essential insight is that taking a perspective requires constructing an analogy between one's own personal knowledge and experience and that of the perspective-taking target. This analysis is used to reassess a broad swath of research in mind reading and literary studies. It develops the dynamics of how analogy is used in perspective taking and the challenges that must be overcome under some circumstances. New empirical evidence is provided in support of the theory and numerous examples from popular and literary fiction are used to illustrate the concepts. This title is part of the Flip it Open program and may also be available Open Access. Check our website Cambridge Core for details.

PETER DIXON is Professor Emeritus at the University of Alberta, Canada. He has authored or coauthored over 100 articles and chapters on topics such as attention, problem solving, motor control, and word and discourse processing. He has worked collaboratively with Marisa Bortolussi on the empirical study of literature.

MARISA BORTOLUSSI is Professor Emerita at the University of Alberta, Canada. She has taught French, Spanish, and comparative literature. Her first publications were on Hispanic literature, including a book on children's literature. With Peter Dixon she coauthored *Psychonarratology* (2002) and numerous articles on the empirical study of literature.

THE ANALOGICAL READER

A Cognitive Approach to Literary Perspective Taking

PETER DIXON
University of Alberta

MARISA BORTOLUSSI
University of Alberta

Shaftesbury Road, Cambridge CB2 8EA, United Kingdom

One Liberty Plaza, 20th Floor, New York, NY 10006, USA

477 Williamstown Road, Port Melbourne, VIC 3207, Australia

314–321, 3rd Floor, Plot 3, Splendor Forum, Jasola District Centre, New Delhi – 110025, India

103 Penang Road, #05-06/07, Visioncrest Commercial, Singapore 238467

Cambridge University Press is part of Cambridge University Press & Assessment, a department of the University of Cambridge.

We share the University's mission to contribute to society through the pursuit of education, learning and research at the highest international levels of excellence.

www.cambridge.org
Information on this title: www.cambridge.org/9781009344159
DOI: 10.1017/9781009344203

© Peter Dixon and Marisa Bortolussi 2024

This publication is in copyright. Subject to statutory exception and to the provisions of relevant collective licensing agreements, no reproduction of any part may take place without the written permission of Cambridge University Press & Assessment.

First published 2024
First paperback edition 2025

A catalogue record for this publication is available from the British Library

ISBN 978-1-009-34418-0 Hardback
ISBN 978-1-009-34415-9 Paperback

Cambridge University Press & Assessment has no responsibility for the persistence or accuracy of URLs for external or third-party internet websites referred to in this publication and does not guarantee that any content on such websites is, or will remain, accurate or appropriate.

*To our cats, Reggie and Coco,
who didn't help at all*

Contents

List of Figures		*page* ix
List of Tables		x
List of Boxes		xi
1	Introduction	1
	Importance of Perspective Taking	2
	Toward an Interdisciplinary Account of Literary Perspective Taking	9
	Goals and Anticipated Contributions	10
	Book Overview	13
2	An Analysis of Perspective and Perspective Taking	17
	Defining a Perspective	17
	Defining Perspective *Taking*	26
	Perspective Taking As Analogy	33
	Summary and Conclusions	39
3	Perspective Taking in Life	40
	Mind Reading	40
	Perspective Taking and Empathy	58
	Neuroscience of Perspective Taking	70
	Summary and Conclusions	78
4	Perspective Taking and Literature	80
	Processes Related to Perspective Taking	81
	First-Order Textual Features	89
	Second-Order Textual Features	99
	Perspective Taking and the Narrator	110
	The Reader and the Character	116
	Summary and Conclusions	121
5	Processing Components of Perspective Taking	122
	Retrieval of Personal Knowledge and Experience	123
	Construction of Similarity	132
	Analogical Inferencing	138

Perspective-Taking Dynamics	142
Summary and Conclusions	150

6 Challenges to Perspective Taking — 151
Available Information — 151
Variations in Perspectival Resonance — 159
Perspective and Character Complexity — 163
Individual and Contextual Differences — 165
Summary and Conclusions — 174

7 Evidence for Analogy in Perspective Taking — 176
Measuring Perspective Taking — 176
A Perspective-Taking Questionnaire — 179
Experiment 1: Cultural Knowledge — 181
Experiment 2: Tracking Remindings during Reading — 186
Experiment 3: Priming Prior Experience — 193
Summary and Conclusions — 201

8 Conclusions — 203
A Theory of Perspective Taking As a Process of Analogical Inferencing — 203
What Are the Benefits of Perspective Taking? — 207
Future Empirical Directions — 212
Closing Remarks — 215

References — 217
Index — 250

Figures

2.1	Structure of the perspective-taking analogy	*page* 37
5.1	Event-driven analogies	143
5.2	Evaluation-driven analogies	145
7.1	Mean PTQ score as a function of story	184
7.2	Mean PTQ score as a function of remindings and reading orientation condition	191
7.3	PTQ score as a function of reminding and image strength	192
7.4	Mean PTQ score as a function of story and prime condition	198
7.5	Relation between PTQ and retrieval strength	199

Tables

7.1	Perspective-Taking Questionnaire items	*page* 180
7.2	Distribution of participant sessions across design in Experiment 2	190

Boxes

7.1 Priming tasks in Experiment 3   *page* 196
7.2 Strength items for retrieval tasks in Experiment 3   197
7.3 Strength items for control task in Experiment 3   197

CHAPTER I

Introduction

Perspective taking is believed to be a central component of reading literature. It is critical to responses that make reading meaningful and enjoyable, such as the feeling of being transported into another world, identification with and empathy for characters, vicarious emotion, and a sense of heightened awareness and understanding. Therefore, any analysis of these processes must include perspective taking in a central fashion. Perspective taking is also crucial for interpersonal interaction in real life, and many of society's persistent problems can be traced to an inability to understand how others think and feel. An intriguing and as yet unanswered question is whether skillful perspective taking on the part of readers carries over to real life or vice versa. Before this question can be answered, though, it is necessary to examine the relationship between the two. One of our theses is that they are fundamentally related: Perspective taking in literary reading depends on the same processes that are involved in real-life social interaction. To date there is no systematic study of literary perspective taking that avails itself of the decades-worth, rich body of psychological research on perspective taking in real life. Thus, in this book we take up that challenge and draw from that research to inform our study of perspective taking in literature.

A second thesis is that perspective taking in both life and literature entails making a personal connection between oneself and the perspective-taking target, be it another individual or a literary character. As we relate in succeeding chapters, this personal connection is an essential component of understanding another's perspective and is based on making use of one's own personal knowledge and experience. Our theoretical analysis is that this use of personal experience is at its core a process of constructing an analogy between some aspect of one's own life and that of the target. As we describe in Chapter 2, such an analogy entails finding corresponding relationships rather than mere superficial similarity. Thus, in order to understand what it means to take a perspective, we need to understand the process of analogical reasoning and its processing components. These two ideas – that literary perspective taking is like perspective taking in life and that both depend on personal analogy – provide the core message of this book.

In this introductory chapter, we discuss the importance of perspective taking, both in reading literature and in real life, and describe our goals for this book in more detail. We close with a roadmap of what we will cover in the balance of the book.

Importance of Perspective Taking

Importance of Perspective Taking in Literature

Engaging with fictional minds may well be the single most important determinant of literary enjoyment. How-to-write-fiction manuals explain what every writer and every lover of fictional narratives knows: Although good stories consist of many components – including intriguing plot and setting, witty or revealing dialogue, evocative descriptions, and effective tropes and symbols – the principal element responsible for maintaining readers' interest, for that "getting lost in a book" experience, is engaging characters. Literature is fundamentally about human experience. That is what we, as readers, crave and what narrative plots are about. Arguably, it is narratives about unfamiliar human experiences lived by memorable characters that satisfy our curiosity and attract us the most. However, it is not so much what characters do that piques our interest as what drives their actions: why they do what they do, how they reason about themselves and others and the world around them, and how they experience their reality. In other words, we are interested in their motives, goals, aspirations, desires, fears, and decisions – in short, their minds.

Barring perhaps experimental fiction that sets out to violate traditional storytelling norms (Richardson, 2015), fiction is about the functioning of minds and patterned on real minds (Palmer, 2004). Important as other aspects of narrative are, they are effective only insofar as they enhance that human element. Well-crafted, suspenseful plots are crucial in spy and detective fiction but it is the devious and masterful minds of its characters that excite us. Eerie, foreboding environments are a staple of gothic horror, but it is the sensations and thoughts of characters caught in those environments that generate emotion in us. People read fiction for the enjoyment it imparts. For some, that enjoyment may be the aesthetic pleasure afforded by elegant or poetic language and artistic style, others may thrive on the intellectual stimulation of philosophical content, and still others may seek to satisfy their curiosity about social problems, historical issues, or cultural scenarios. Naturally, these motivations and forms of enjoyment are not mutually exclusive, but intrinsic to all of them is the human dimension. Without engaging characters, style and philosophical or historical content would be insufficient to keep readers turning the pages of a novel.

However, the enjoyment derived from engaging with characters may be only one explanation for the allure of fictional narratives; it may be that there is an actual need that drives people to seek out reading experiences. Literary critic Zunshine (2006) argued compellingly that the allure of fiction lies in its potential to engage and challenge our mind-reading tendency, which she equates with theory of mind. Echoing evolutionist arguments, she claims that we enjoy reading fictional minds because interpreting "observed behavior in terms of underlying mental states" (p. 7) is a natural human propensity. Daily acts of interpretation such as figuring out what "makes others tick," what could have led so-and-so to do this or that, guessing "what was she thinking?", or trying to infer if the look on someone's face is indicative of scorn or simply surprise are a natural, fundamental ability we have developed as a species for navigating our social environment. They constitute the basis of all our interactions: gossip, judicial procedures, managerial communication, and earnest endeavors to better understand others. Given this natural tendency, it is entirely plausible that the enjoyment of reading fiction is owing to "the cognitive rewards of pretend play" and the opportunity to "try on" different mental states (p. 17). Narrative fiction exposes minds and invites us, metaphorically, to enter into them, thus affording us the opportunity to exercise this natural tendency. Activating our mind-reading faculty to decipher characters' minds as they evolve throughout the story could be a form of satisfying a need. Exercising this cognitive skill might result in enhanced interpersonal skill in real life.

Based on our own pleasurable reading experiences, we can reasonably take for granted that engaging with fictional minds is enjoyable for readers. What is less obvious is what that process of engagement entails or what other effects it might engender. In this book, we argue that if reading fiction is immersive or absorbing, it is because it affords the opportunity to involve the self through an extended comparison between the reader and characters. In other words, it is not just the need to objectively understand other minds that constitutes the pleasure of engaging with fiction minds, but the involvement of oneself in that process. Readers bring to the text their own lives and experience, with all the knowledge and doxastic baggage that that entails. Fictional texts often present characters very different from ourselves, in very unfamiliar situations. How we evaluate, judge, and interpret characters is a function of how we deal with the challenge of relating the unfamiliar to our own knowledge and experience, how we bridge the gap between the two. In this book, we argue that this active process of identifying and constructing relations between the reader and the characters constitutes the core of perspective taking, and we describe the precise nature and mechanism of that process.

Importance of Perspective Taking in the Real World

The ability to understand the perspective of other people is unquestionably a fundamental social skill (e.g., Piaget, 1932; Davis, 1983a). There is evidence that the skill leads to a more favorable judgment of others (Epley et al., 2002), produces feelings of sympathy and compassion for the target (Davis, 1983a; Batson et al., 1989), contributes to moral reasoning (Kohlberg, 1976), inspires empathy and altruism (Batson et al., 1997), and reduces aggression (Richardson et al., 1994) and stereotyping (Galinsky & Moskowitz, 2000) by virtue of greater empathy. It has also been shown to improve an advantaged social group's evaluation of a disadvantaged group, thereby increasing the former's understanding of the latter, improving intergroup relations (Galinsky & Ku, 2004; Cakal et al., 2021), and increasing willingness to engage in intergroup contact (Wang et al., 2014).

Given the myriad of interpersonal contexts that require the ability to understand and consider others' points of view, one can easily imagine how a deficiency in this general competency could impede or damage interpersonal relations. Social scientists with an evolutionary bent – anthropologists, psychologists, biologists – have argued that over time, humans have developed a variety of cognitive and emotional capacities as adaptive measures for survival in collective, social environments (Buck, 1984; Dunbar, 2006). Several interrelating and partially overlapping terms have been coined to refer to these skills: mind reading, perspective taking, theory of mind, simulation, and empathy. Given their potential evolutionary basis, these skills are plausibly a part of the genetic makeup that ensures our social survival.

However, despite what our long evolutionary history might suggest, it does not appear that we have mastered the skill of perspective taking. Research in several fields has led to the conclusion that humans can be notoriously poor perspective takers and that it is difficult to overcome our own egocentric perspective. There is evidence that humans are not born with the skills required to take another's perspective easily but rather develop them over time and to differing degrees (Epley & Caruso, 2009). Perspective taking is not a simple, measurable skill that reaches maturity and can be applied unfailingly in all situations. It is rather a complex, effortful, cognitively demanding process, the adequate execution of which is far from guaranteed. It is this unreliability that led Epley and Caruso (2009) to conclude that "the only general conclusion one can render is that the ability to accurately adopt someone's perspective is better than chance but less than perfect" (p. 298). Further, it depends on a wide range of personal and contextual variables. In particular, cognitive processes such as decision making, working memory, moral reasoning and judgment, attention, inferencing, and critical and analogical thinking are pivotal.

Because perspective taking is such an important aspect of social competence, yet so difficult to master, it is hardly surprising that interest in the topic has attracted attention both in popular and academic circles. Perspective taking has been the subject of countless self-help articles, books, and blogs that attempt to describe what it entails and what the many factors are that influence our ability to successfully infer, consider, reason about, and understand another person's perspective or state of mind. As any cursory web search reveals, the same issues have also been the object of intense scholarly scrutiny in fields as varied as evolutionary psychology (de Waal, 2008), history (Kohlmeier, 2005; Chapman, 2011), ethnography (Naaeke et al., 2011), psychotherapy (Day et al., 2008), developmental psychology (Bailey & Im-Bolter, 2020), social psychology (Mead, 1934; Sevillano et al., 2007), psycholinguistics (Barnes-Holmes et al., 2004), neuroscience (Ruby & Decety, 2004), education (Abacioglu et al., 2020), business management (Platt, 2020), philosophy (Nussbaum, 2001; Currie & Ravenscroft, 2002), and empirical literary studies (Hakemulder, 2000; van Peer & Maat, 2001; Weingartner & Klin, 2005; Dore et al., 2017; Salem et al., 2017; Creer et al., 2019), among others.

However perspective taking may be conceived and whatever it may entail, there is no shortage of advice on how to acquire it. The internet abounds in "self-help" blogs: For example, our last simple Google search for "perspective taking" (in December 2021) brought up more than 3.5 billion hits, a large proportion of which were dedicated to providing advice and even exercises to strengthen perspective-taking skills in children and adults in order to help autism, improve intimate relationships, succeed in business, and so on. In developmental psychology and educational circles, children's role taking and theory of mind are often treated as fundamental skills that can be taught to children through a variety of games and activities. Numerous popular books on perspective taking present the skill as the solution to social harmony. For example, Dalai Lama and Cutler (1998) discussed the importance of mastering strategies often associated with perspective taking – such as overcoming egocentric biases, prejudices, and stereotypes – in order to achieve happiness in a troubled world. Writing from within the field of public policy, Molix and Nichols (2012) advocate the necessity of taking the perspective of Muslims in order to understand radicalization. By extension, the lack or failure of this ability is blamed for many personal, socio-cultural, and political problems. For example, Sillars (1998) studied how misunderstanding others' perspectives could adversely affect close relationships. This is perhaps justified: Many of the agonizing human crises that persist in our twenty-first century – such as xenophobia, racism, homophobia, and misogyny – bespeak intolerance or indifference at best. It is no wonder that we seek solutions to societies' perspective-taking failures.

Can Literature Promote Perspective Taking in Everyday Life?

Given our thesis that real-life perspective taking shares processes with literary perspective taking, it is natural to ask: Can literature help us improve our perspective-taking abilities? It is commonly claimed that literature has the power to affect readers and sometimes effect changes in society. A famous example is Lincoln's alleged remark to Harriet Beecher Stowe that she was the "little lady who started this great war" (Kane, 2013, p. 20) with her novel *Uncle Tom's Cabin* (Stowe, 1891/2021). The publication of *A Christmas Carol* (Dickens, 1843/1992) is said to have revived the diminished "Christmas spirit" (Standiford, 2008) and to have led to an increase in charitable donations, especially among members of the wealthiest class. It has been claimed that children's stories published in 1923 containing achievement imagery were positively correlated with economic growth up to 1950; similarly, it has been argued that achievement imagery in Spanish and English literature of specific periods was also related to economic growth in those same countries (McClelland & Winter, 1969). If true, we might hypothesize that the effect is due to readers' connection with characters' goals and achievements.

Many have suggested that literature provides a tool for solving problems of perspective taking in society. How engagement with fictional minds affects readers beyond the immediate reading experience is a question that has interested not just literary specialists but also social and political authorities for centuries. Literary history is replete with examples of prohibited fiction and of works banned out of fear of their ability to change readers' perception, to alter minds, and to be a threat to established norms. Book banning in the USA is a recent example of the same fear. On the positive side, it has always been assumed that literature "opens our eyes" to new dimensions of human reality, sharpens our understanding of human nature and behavior, and in this sense widens our mental horizons. An age-old belief in literary studies is that transporting readers into other times, situations, and circumstances allows them to experience characters' plights and minds; thus, literature expands readers' horizons, allegedly sharpening their ability to understand reality from other points of view. Hayawaka (1990) claimed that literature could profoundly change readers by enabling them to experience many different "alternative lives and personas" (p. 1). Hakemulder (2000) argued that reading fiction could make readers more sensitive to, understanding of, and empathetic toward others' distress. Nussbaum (2001) expressed the conviction that fiction can help us better connect to real minds. Gottschall (2012) urged us to "read fiction and watch it. It will make you more empathic and better able to navigate life's dilemmas" (p. 198). Sommer (2013) suggested that intercultural novels "may encourage readers to change perspective, to cope creatively with clashes of mind-set ... and to become more sensitive, as mind readers, to the variability of cultural norms and expectations" (p. 171).

Empirical scholars have provided modest support for these claims. On the basis of some psychological findings, Mar and Oatley (2008) conjecture that reading fiction "may be helpful for reducing bias against out-group members" and could train us to "extend our understanding toward other people, to some extent embody, and understand their beliefs and emotions" (p. 181). There is some evidence linking exposure to fiction and social ability (Mar et al., 2006; Johnson, 2012). For example, fiction reading has been found to be related to performance on an empathy task (Mar et al., 2009; Djikic et al., 2013), suggesting that it may increase empathy in general. However, the task used to measure empathic capacity – the Reading the Mind in the Eyes Test – is limited to a single component of perspective taking, and it is possible that the direction of causation is reversed: Empathy leads to an interest in reading fiction. Johnson (2013) provided some evidence that reading fiction reduces prejudice against and increases empathy for other ethnic groups. Kidd and Castano (2013, 2016) found evidence that reading literary texts (as opposed to popular fictional texts) improved performance on theory-of-mind tasks (although this result is not always replicated). As we discuss further in Chapter 8, the generality of the effects on these improved performance measures is still unknown.

Firm belief in the power of fiction to strengthen understanding and tolerance of others, and ultimately to improve society, has inspired some individuals to promote fiction for social purposes. After the Second World War, Jella Lepman, founder of the International Board of Books for Young People, believed that children's literature could lead to the creation of a better world insofar as it could increase readers' understanding of the plight, life, and worldview of others (Lepman, 1969; Pearl, 2007). With this goal at heart, her organization promoted the production of books about the experiences of children in remote and troubled parts of the world and the distribution of these to children of the Western world. Literary stories have been hailed for their ability to promote moral development (Vitz, 1990). More recently, former Barack Obama adviser William Bennett strongly recommended the inclusion of fiction in the school curriculum for the same reason. His bestseller *The Book of Virtues: A Treasury of Great Moral Stories* (Bennett, 1993) had a powerful impact in pedagogical circles. In it, he argued that exposure to literary classics can build moral character in children, presumably because readers take the perspective of the heroes and assimilate their ethos: Reading "[g]ood stories [that] invite us to slip into the shoes of other people is a crucial step in acquiring a moral perspective. Stories about friendship require taking the perspective of friends" (p. 269). In Latin America, publishing companies such as Ediciones Ekaré have emerged to promote children's picture books that focus on the dire plight and suffering of poor and marginalized children in order to foster understanding, altruism, and, ideally, social change.

Intuitively, optimistic claims about the power of fiction make sense. Were it not for literature, we might never imagine the plight of an abused child in rural post-revolutionary Mexico, the terror experienced by ethnic minorities during the Rwanda genocide, the mental anguish that led victims of the Spanish Civil War to spontaneous violence, the self-loathing that southern American Black people experienced after the Civil War, or the despair of refugees in their new host environments to which authors such as Rulfo, Jensen, Matute, Chopin, and Thompson-Spire exposed us. This literature "opens our eyes" in the sense of allowing us to experience new realities and arousing emotions, and these experiences could potentially change our attitudes. If it is in fact true that engaging with fictional minds makes readers better perspective takers, then we have good reason to rejoice that literature provides the solution to many of the world's current problems. A work that depicts our shared humanity with "the other" and allows us to experience reality from that character's perspective could arouse our empathy and alter whatever biased perceptions we may harbor. Optimistic faith in the power of fiction to make us better people by enhancing our perspective-taking skills is understandable from a creative and academic perspective; the livelihoods of authors and publishers and the existence of university literature programs are grounded on faith in the enlightening, transformative power of literature. Evidence that fiction has such power would certainly cement the role of literature programs in the humanities as an indispensable social and educational necessity. So important is perspective taking for social survival, and so dangerous the painful lack of it in the world around us, that understanding how it can be promoted should be a social and political priority. Therefore, it is crucial that we understand how perspective taking in literature occurs and how it is related to perspective taking in the world. Without such basic knowledge of the underlying processes, we would be at a loss to make serious recommendations about how to use literature to effect such social changes. Our goal with the present work is to further the development of this knowledge.

Toward an Interdisciplinary Account of Literary Perspective Taking

Optimistic intuitions aside, the truth is that we know very little about how readers engage with fictional minds, let alone the longer-term effects of that engagement on readers; perspective taking is really still a little-understood aspect of literary response (Caracciolo, 2013; Dore et al., 2017). In fact, there is a dearth of evidence as to whether perspective taking is even required for engaging with fictional minds and for meaningful reading experiences (Currie, 2020). We believe that an interdisciplinary approach can help us advance our understanding of how we go about making sense of characters. Such an approach combines research on literary response with psychological evidence on real-life perspective taking as well as knowledge and understanding of cognitive processing. Psychological research on perspective taking in real life, while emphasizing its vital importance for social survival, also imparts some less optimistic caveats that obligate us to rigorously examine how literary perspective taking works, what kinds of texts promote it best, what kind of readers are most or least successful at it, what factors may enhance or inhibit it, and what mental processes it actually entails. Literary and empirical studies of literature have examined a variety of components assumed to be central to perspective taking; however, they have been largely uninformed by this wealth of relevant research on perspective taking in everyday life. To date, evidence on the impact of perspective taking during the reading of any given narrative on life is scant. There is limited evidence that a history of reading fiction is correlated with the capacity to experience empathy and social acumen (Mar et al., 2006). However, as Hogan (2003) spelled out, no life activity such as reading can be "torn out of a large network constituted by many other life practices" (p. 1); this requires the examination of other variables. Although some behavioral impact has been found immediately after literary reading, much of this is inconclusive (Koopman, 2015), and there is no evidence of the long-term effects of taking characters' perspectives. Given the findings of psychological studies, there is good reason to suppose that perspective taking in literature is subject to as many constraints as in real life, and it may not be as unequivocally successful as might be assumed. Until we have a solid grasp of the cognitive mechanisms of perspective taking in reading, we are not in a position to draw the grandiose conclusions that reading literature improves people's ability to willingly put aside their own views to consider how others perceive reality, or that this ability has broad, generalizable effects on behavior. Furthermore, it may well be the case that reading literature does not so much affect real life as the contrary; that is, meaningful reading is a function of the skills and conditions upon which real-life perspective taking depend. We hope that a detailed understanding of perspective taking in literature and life will help resolve these issues and that the present work contributes to this understanding.

Goals and Anticipated Contributions

Advancing our understanding of what perspective taking is and how it functions in the context of reading literary fiction is the main goal of this book. Understanding how readers engage with characters' minds during the reading process is a first step to understanding how the reading experience affects the mind. There are many reasons for investigating this issue.

First, the research could be of enormous benefit to educators at the primary, secondary, and post-secondary levels. We have seen how important activists and educationalists have earnestly endorsed the optimistic belief in the power of fiction. However, there are not many reliable follow-up studies. Furthermore, bold claims such as Bennet's (1993) have been seriously criticized. One argument is that there is no necessary correspondence between what is in a text and what a reader might get out of it

(Narvaez, 2002). Life circumstances, as well as individual and collective variables, such as upbringing, personal biases, inclusion in racist pockets of society, or in-group affiliation, might inhibit successful perspective taking (Cakal et al., 2021). Pedagogical strategies could be informed by a knowledge of what those variables are and how their influence might be overcome, for example through particular kinds of interventions. Understanding what text variables might be the most effective in promoting perspective taking might be helpful for the purposes of establishing curricula, informing teachers' pedagogical strategies, and enriching library holdings. Understanding "the psychological dynamics triggered by literary characters may help scholars and teachers use literature more effectively to prompt reflection on ethical and social issues" (van Lissa et al., 2016, p. 45).

Second, a serious investigation into the effects of literary perspective taking is important for its social relevance and could be of interest to authors, editors, and booksellers. It seems especially warranted given the astounding proliferation of fictional works published every year throughout the world. In spite of pessimistic predictions, fictional narratives have proven to be a staple of life. Warnings of the doomed fate of the novel have been uttered by prominent philosophers, literary critics, and writers in almost every decade of the twentieth century. Ortega y Gasset (1925) was one of the first to cast a dire warning with his publication of *Decline in the Novel*, a thought Benjamin (1930/2019) fueled in *Crisis of the Novel*. Echoes of these early alerts were sounded in the 1950s and 1960s by Kayser (1954) and Robbe Grillet (1963). Sukenick (1969) even wrote a story entitled "The Death of the Novel." Some feared that existing structures, techniques, and styles would run their course, not imagining perhaps that novelistic innovations could develop. Cultural studies programs in North American universities have purged literature courses from their course offerings on the belief that visual media is preferred to the reading of literature, and that media genres and technology will finally quell the thirst for literary fiction, a prediction whose weakened note still sounds in our current century (Ballatore & Natale, 2016). Yet, judging by publication statistics, the novel thrives; this is a social and cultural reality. Technology and media advances such as Kindle and the free, downloadable works of the Guggenheim Library have, if anything, made the selection and acquisition of literary works simpler and cheaper. Defying the ominous forecasts, new voices keep emerging all over the world as authors continue to select fiction as a means of communication with audiences. Far from a dead form of a bygone age, fictional narratives continue to draw the attention of both reviewers in print and online media and readers who engage with their works. In spite of the proliferation of movies and video games, readers still seek reading experiences. The enduring and thriving fiction industry is an economic and social phenomenon. It is therefore important that we come to a better understanding of how different kinds of literature affect readers' minds. This includes understanding whether readers necessarily adopt a perspective, and if they do, if it is spontaneous or requires more complex processing; whether the perspective they adopt is uniform, single, and lasting; and what types of fiction more successfully spark it, and why or how.

Third, an in-depth study of literary perspective taking is of particular interest to literary scholars. Perspective taking is crucial for understanding the three basic components of literary communication: the author, the text, and the reader. It is important for the author because fostering perspective taking is an obvious goal in writing fiction. Good writers of fiction aim not just to entertain but also to communicate some perspective(s) on some aspect of life, the world, or reality. Words and expressions such as "authorial intention," "theme," "message," and "meaning," elusive and hotly debated as they are, all refer to this deeper, epistemic level of the text. Whatever an author may wish to communicate is refracted through a complex web of interconnected perspectives of the narrator and the characters woven into the work; thus, understanding how a fictional text communicates requires drawing inferences about the relationship of these voices and perspectives. Perspective taking is important for understanding the text because to fully appreciate the story one must understand not just what is told but how it is told. Writers have at their disposal a well-equipped toolbox of strategies and techniques for conveying the workings of characters' minds. Some may enhance perspective taking, while some may inhibit it. Finally, perspective taking is important for understanding the reader because the text as it is crafted is a mine of potential inferences that readers can draw about the perspectives of the narrator, character, and author. Knowledge about how real readers respond to literary characters could thus help advance the field of narrative studies.

Fourth, an understanding of the features that make fictional works most likely to promote perspective taking could be of invaluable use to group therapists of different stripes. In the USA, and no doubt other countries, individuals charged with discriminatory behavior are often required to take special courses in empathy and bias recognition and control (Zaki, 2014). This research could facilitate instructors' selection of works for group discussion that might help their enrollees understand the perspective of minorities or refugees.

Fifth, we believe that our contributions to the study of how readers process fictional minds can advance psychological studies of real-life perspective taking. Under the general rubric of "mind reading," research on theory of mind, theory theory, and simulation theory investigates how individuals make sense of other minds, but this field only provides a facile explanation of what a perspective is and what it means to take one. In essence, the process psychologists describe hinges on a very basic form of self–other analogy. We argue that the process involved in establishing relations between self and others is much more complex. Our expanded theoretical analysis of perspective taking draws on cognitive psychology to more precisely define a "perspective" and on psychological analogy theory to more fully describe the process of establishing self–other connections.

Sixth, we argue that the current approach will illuminate the role of perspective taking in the fields of discourse and narrative processing. Although researchers have commonly argued that perspective taking is a central component of the development of story-world situation models (e.g., Black et al., 1979; Mulcahy & Gouldthorp, 2016; Creer et al., 2019), there has been little investigation into the mechanics and prerequisites of this process beyond the analogy with visual point of view. Indeed, classic analyses of the structure of stories (e.g., Mandler, 1984) seem to presuppose perspective taking in the reader's understanding of the "main character's" plans and goals. However, circumstances, reader characteristics, and texts under which this transpires have not been studied. The analogy-based analysis we present takes into account fundamental cognitive processes such as memory and inference that are crucial for understanding how perspective taking occurs (or does not occur) in narrative processing.

Book Overview

In Chapter 2, "An Analysis of Perspective and Perspective Taking," we provide a critical review of how the terms "perspective" and "perspective taking" have been understood in both literary studies and social, personality, and cognitive psychology. We explain how current definitions of the term "perspective" and the process of "perspective taking" are too broad in what they implicitly encompass, and we identify the components that should be excluded in the interest of clarity and precision. In this chapter, we also provide a conceptual and theoretical analysis of what perspective taking involves. In particular, we argue that a perspective is an interpretation of evaluations and that perspective taking depends on the construction of an analogy between the evaluations of the character and those of the reader. This analysis provides the background for our critiques of research on perspective taking in life and in literature in subsequent chapters.

Although our ultimate goal is an analysis and theory of perspective taking in literature, an important insight is that perspective taking in reading literature is subject to the same factors and constraints and may depend on the same types of processes as perspective taking in real life. In Chapter 3, "Perspective Taking in Life," we review research in social and personality psychology that is applicable to literary perspective taking and can help us advance our understanding of how readers make sense of fictional minds. Under the general umbrella term of "mind reading," theory of mind, theory theory, and simulation theories offer competing explanations of how individuals make sense of other minds. We argue that a more rigorous application of analogy theory provides the basis for a more coherent analysis. We also consider the problem of empathy and how it is related to mind reading. Our analysis is that empathy should be thought of as emotional perspective taking, and we apply our analogical inference approach here as well. Finally, we consider the neural bases of perspective taking and discuss how different brain networks may be related to the components of perspective taking by analogy.

All fiction writers write to be read; presumably, this means that they write in a way that will be understood by their readers. This entails following, playing with, or introducing textual conventions that will be appreciated by and make sense to their readers and that will also guide readers in their interpretive responses. One of these interpretive responses, it has been argued, is the taking of characters' perspectives. Studies of literary response have also associated other responses with perspective taking, including identification, empathy, and transportation. In Chapter 4, "Perspective Taking and Literature," we review these processes and argue that our analysis of perspective taking provides new insights into what these must entail. In the second part of the chapter, we examine the relationship between text features and perspective taking. We review both the theoretical accounts of specific textual features believed to induce perspective taking and the empirical evidence for the effect of these techniques on perspective taking. We conclude that there is little clear evidence for a simple causal relation between features and the cognitive responses. However, based on deeper analyses, we argue that elaboration is central to perspective taking in narrative. Elaboration in many cases requires the reader to use their own personal knowledge and experience to enhance their representation of the story world and the characters. The activation of this information then provides the basis of forming perspective-taking analogies.

In Chapter 5, "Processing Components of Perspective Taking," we discuss the processing components that underlie the perspective-taking analogy that we articulate in Chapter 2. This analysis makes it clear that the retrieval of personal knowledge and experience is critical, and we review some of what is known about episodic retrieval and how it can be used in this context. In forming an analogy, one must be able to identify how elements of the story world are related to corresponding elements in one's own experience. As we describe, that relationship entails finding a sense of similarity constructed through attention, interpretation, and inference. Finally, we discuss the mechanics of analogy formation per se and describe the notion of a structural mapping between the reader and the character that underlies the perspective-taking analogy. We close out Chapter 5 with a discussion of perspective-taking dynamics. This includes an illustration of how perspective taking can be driven by the events of the story world or evaluations of the character. As we make clear, perspective taking is an ongoing process that can unfold in a variety of ways over the course of reading a narrative.

In Chapter 6, "Challenges to Perspective Taking," we elaborate on the difficulties that may arise in perspective taking. These depend on individual, contextual, and textual variables. Among the individual factors are motivation, cognitive skills and capacities, and empathic dispositions. Variations in the situation and context, such as available information and feedback, can affect perspective taking. Specific difficulties include: the failure to identify relevant personal knowledge and experience, inconsistent and conflicting perspectives, problems reconciling a character's perspective with the reader's own evaluations, and/or the relationship of the reader's cultural background to that of the character. Subtleties in the text, such as multiple perspectives, unreliable perspectives, and multiple perspective-taking targets, pose their own challenges.

In Chapter 7, "Evidence for Analogy in Perspective Taking," the penultimate chapter, we outline new empirical evidence for our approach. In particular, the core assumption in our view is that perspective taking depends on an analogy to personal knowledge and experience on the part of the reader. As support for this view, we demonstrate that perspective taking in literary reading covaries with the availability of such memories. In the first experiment, participants read narratives that involved either familiar or unfamiliar cultural and social schemas. Our prediction was that it would be more difficult to take a character's perspective when the events of the story world do not make sufficient contact with the reader's own experience (as they would with unfamiliar social schemas); this finding was obtained. A second experiment examined the use of prior knowledge and experience as it unfolds in the course of reading. In this case, readers identified places in the text where prior experience or imagery was activated and then rated that experience on its intensity. The result was that when participants focused on remindings, the number of such remindings predicted perspective taking. Moreover, more intense remindings tended to be associated with greater perspective taking. In a third experiment, we manipulated the availability of relevant personal knowledge more directly: Before reading a story, participants were asked to think about a prior experience that either was or was not related to the experience of the character. As we predicted, priming relevant prior experience in this way promoted perspective taking. These three experiments generally support our claim that perspective taking depends on the analogical connection between the reader's personal knowledge and experience and the events of the story world.

In the final chapter, "Conclusions," we review the framework for perspective taking that we have developed in the book and highlight what we feel are the most important elements. In that context, we return to the questions raised in this introductory chapter about the relationship between perspective taking in reading literature and perspective taking in real life and suggest some conclusions. We also outline future directions for further empirical research.

CHAPTER 2

An Analysis of Perspective and Perspective Taking

The term "perspective taking" consists of both a noun – "perspective" – and a gerund – "taking." Therefore, to understand the term, one must first define what constitutes a *perspective* and then what it means to *take* one. In this chapter, we will first present an analysis of "perspective" and "perspective taking." In doing so, we will provide an overview of the cognitive processes involved in assessing perspectives; we will then introduce our theory of perspective taking as analogical inferencing.

Defining a Perspective

The term "perspective" can refer to either a physical or psychological state. In the physical sense, it refers simply to an observer's actual viewing or sensing location. This is one's perceptual perspective. The psychological meaning of the term is more difficult to define; terms such as "vantage point" or "position" are metaphorical extensions that allude to a person's mental state. We have argued that psychological perspective can be related to perceptual perspective under some circumstances (Dixon & Bortolussi, 2019). However, in general, psychological and perceptual perspectives are distinct. Neither literary studies nor the psychological research on mind reading offers a clear working definition of the psychological sense of the term. In literary studies, conceptualizations of the term "perspective" are typically vague and refer to either very general subjective mental states or, more broadly, worldviews or ideology (Uspensky, 1973; R. Fowler, 1982b). Such definitions are now recognized as being too broad to be useful (Lanser, 1981; Chatman, 1986). Lanser (1981) argued that a perspective is a relationship that is "difficult to grasp and codify" (p. 13). We believe, on the contrary, that it is only difficult to grasp if one casts the definitional net too wide.

Some psychological studies on perspective taking conceived "perspective" in terms equally as vague and overarching. For example, Nickerson

(1999) defined it in terms of knowledge, including "beliefs, opinions, suppositions, attitudes, and related states of mind" (p. 737). More recently, Cakal et al. (2021) suggested that a target's point of view includes thoughts and views of the world. We argue that these definitions are problematic because they imply an all-encompassing totality – an all-or-nothing state that draws in everything a person thinks, believes, and feels. Thus, they are too broad and imprecise. In order to attain greater terminological precision, it is worth reflecting on what properties suggested by the current definitions in both fields need to be excluded.

What a Perspective Is Not

Concepts such as "worldview," "ideology," and "mental state" have been evoked in literary studies and mind-reading theories to define a perspective. However, these terms imply that a perspective is determinate, unitary, stable, and, in some cases, defined a priori. We now consider why that is an oversimplified and unhelpful way to think about the concept.

Not Autonomous and Determinate

Since this book is about how readers interact with fictional minds, in particular how they relate to views and feelings inscribed in or suggested by the text, it is important to clarify the notion of "fictional minds." An obvious but fundamental difference between real and fictional minds is that real minds have an autonomous existence tied to a real brain with real neural activity. Such a preexisting mind serves as a backdrop against which a target's evaluations of the world could potentially be verified. Real-life communicative interactions allow for the disambiguation of uncertainty about another person's mind, including feelings and emotions. Thus, a target can answer a perceiver's questions or make disclosures or confessions, others may provide additional information, and body language may make the target's mindset obvious (Leudar & Costall, 2009). Fictional characters, in contrast, do not have preexisting, autonomous minds that authors somehow capture in their entirety; they are schematic imaginative projections, as are all aspects of story worlds (see Ingarden, 1931/1973b). As narratologists well understood, fictional characters constitute a collection of signs: attributions, ascriptions, and descriptions (Margolin, 1990). Thus, there is no existing backdrop against which to assess the validity of one's interpretation. The author's mind cannot be that backdrop because authors cannot give life to full-fledged, fully determined, embodied entities. As a result, readers are left to draw inferences about characters' mental states and to fill the textual gaps. Whatever inferences they draw about the unstated aspects of textual minds are potentially independent of the author's conception of their characters; thus, in a fundamental sense, characters are reader constructions.

In spite of this fundamental difference between literary characters and real people, there is a sense in which real-life minds are also like literary minds: Although *potentially* discoverable, a perceiver trying to understand another real mind may find it difficult to comprehend at a practical level due to the paucity or distortion of the available information. Often there is no opportunity for the kind of communication that would be illuminating or there may be compelling reasons to doubt the information so gathered. Thus, there are many situations in which one is left wondering what goes on inside another's mind that might explain some unexpected behavior, and the perspective of a real person may appear just as indeterminate as that of a fictional character. In other words, both real and fictional perspectives depend on a web of inferences on the part of the perceiver or reader. In both cases, we are left to resort to what is effectively guesswork: inferencing (Ickes, 2003) and reasoning about the content of the target's mental and emotional states (Goldman, 2006; Barlassina & Gordon, 2017).

Not Unitary and Stable
Not only are perspectives not autonomous, they are also not unitary and stable generalizations that capture everything about a target's views. Individual evaluative judgments of a character may be clear but there may be many variations, exceptions, and other complexities that make a consistent, unitary description impossible. In literary texts of any complexity, a character's perspective is rarely conveyed in terms of simple, clear-cut worldviews, belief systems, or whatever one might understand by "ideology." In fact, this is not different from real-world views and ideologies, which can also be inconsistent and indeterminate. For example, Marxism is an ideology but one that has splintered into various offshoots; any left-leaning individual may have a different understanding of what it means or may endorse parts of convergent versions. Similarly, a Republican congressperson can identify as conservative but believe in a number of issues associated with liberal ideology, such as LGBTQ rights and Black Lives Matter. Readers of fiction may distill many views, possibly contradictory ones, into a simple, unified global perspective on the part of a character, but that inference is a construction, not necessarily an a priori, textual given. Indeed, other readers may arrive at quite different views of what that perspective is. Similarly, in real life, other individuals may appear

schematic: Perceivers may only discern glimpses of someone's evaluations and these could well constitute a seemingly inconsistent, unnamable whole. Inferential attempts to characterize that whole in terms of a simple position, mental state, or belief system could amount to misinterpretations or inaccurate reductions. Further, in real life and in longer narratives, perspectives are dynamic and can undergo many fluctuations and modifications. Indeed, the point of many stories concerns how evaluations and perspectives change over time. In real life, our eagerness to hold someone to a specific position on an issue can fail to consider that the person's doubts are small, but important, ideational developments.

Therefore, rather than a unitary and stable view, a perspective must be piecemeal and dynamic, based on some collection of potentially inconsistent positions, each of which reflects an evaluation of something. These evaluations may conflict in one way or another and may change over time. Any perspective that is based on such evaluations is consequently incomplete and may change as new information becomes available.

What Is a Perspective?

Although psychological research offers us no simple definition of a perspective, it has typically cast a much more focused net, thereby laying the groundwork for a more robust definition of both the noun and gerund. The key insight in real-life perspective-taking research is that a perspective is based on an "evaluation" (Nickerson, 1999; Galinsky & Moskowitz, 2000; Galinsky & Ku, 2004; Eyal & Epley, 2010; Wondra & Ellsworth, 2015) or judgment (Epley, Keysar, et al., 2004). Nickerson (1999) examined how participants judge whether others share their own evaluations. Eyal and Epley (2010) and Galinsky and Ku (2004) examined self-evaluation and how that compares to how they evaluate others. Epley, Keysar, et al. (2004) investigated the extent to which participants thought other uninformed participants would share their assessment or evaluation in an experimental task they were asked to perform. These considerations lead to the view that a psychological perspective should be defined in terms of evaluations – that is, how the character or individual reacts to, judges, or assesses various aspects of their world.

However, our analysis is that simply saying that a perspective consists of evaluations is incomplete; after all, people commonly speak of "a perspective" in a unitary sense and readily contrast perspectives as if they were a single thing. Consequently, we propose that a perspective should be conceived of as an *interpretation* that applies to some sufficiently numerous set or subset of evaluations. This is consistent with arguments about what a perspective is not – a complete, stable, unitary whole – while incorporating the psychological insight that perspectives are based on evaluations. This view reconciles the sense that there must be, at some level, an identifiable perspective with the observation that the information about perspectives (i.e., the evaluations themselves) is incremental and potentially inconsistent. Thinking of perspectives as interpretations emphasizes the constructive role of the individual.

Properties of a Perspective
With these ideas about the nature of a perspective in mind, we can outline several dimensions on which perspectives may vary: generality, coherence, and explicitness. These properties become important in considering how perspectives are used in perspective taking.

Generality. A perspective, as an interpretation of evaluations, may exist at different levels of generality. To take an example from literature, in *A Christmas Carol* (Dickens, 1843/1992), Scrooge has a fairly general "bitterness at the world" perspective. This encompasses separate evaluations, such as an impatience with charity requests and disdain for family gatherings. At other times, a perspective may be more specific. For example, Scrooge suggests that money is necessary for happiness. Although this perspective unifies a number of different evaluations in a relatively consistent manner, those evaluations pertain to only some aspects of his worldview. In other words, a perspective is a generalization of a variety of evaluations, and it may be more or less inclusive. Another way to describe this dimension is with respect to the scope of the evaluations it entails: A general perspective will subsume a range of different evaluations, while a more specific perspective only subsumes a few. For example, the perspective "I don't like social gatherings" could cover a wide range of evaluations, from "Christmas with the family is unpleasant," to "I feel awkward at big parties," to "I don't like loud bars." Other perspectives might have a more limited scope, such as "I like birthday parties"; in this case, birthday parties comprise only a small number of personally experienced events.

Coherence. As we noted, a perspective is more than simply a collection of evaluations; it is a general interpretation of a set of such evaluations that are more or less coherent. For example, the perspective "I don't like social gatherings" might be a plausible interpretation of a range of evaluations of activities such as cocktail parties, backyard barbecues, and pub nights, but it might not apply to family get-togethers and soccer games. Thus, the perspective would have relatively little coherence. In contrast, the perspective "I love animals" might have high coherence if the individual likes cats, dogs, birds, wild animals, and so on with little discrimination. Because a perspective covers a range of evaluations, it can vary in consistency or coherence. When a perspective is coherent, it can be used to make inferences about other evaluations that are unstated. For example, if the perspective "I love animals" is assumed to be coherent, then one can infer that the individual would like an iguana. On the other hand, inferences based on a less coherent perspective would be less reliable. For example, if the perspective "I don't like social gatherings" is minimally coherent, it might be difficult to predict whether the individual would be interested in attending a birthday party.

Explicitness. A perspective serves to integrate evaluations into a more global reaction to some aspect of the story world or real life. In literature, the evaluations or the perspective may be stated more or less explicitly in the text. For example, in the initial part of *A Christmas Carol* (Dickens, 1843/1992), Scrooge has the perspective that the world is hostile to him. This is stated in so many words: "No wind that blew was bitterer than he ...." Later, Scrooge clearly indicates a general animosity toward Christmas: "Every idiot who goes about with 'Merry Christmas' on his lips, should be boiled with his own pudding, and buried with a stake of holly through his heart." At other times, perspectives might need to be inferred from character behaviors or other aspects of the narrative. As a simple example, in the presence of the Ghost of Christmas Present, Scrooge listens to the cheerful banter of the Cratchit family; from this exchange, the reader could infer that Bob Cratchit loves his family. The same considerations apply to perspectives in real life: Sometimes evaluations or perspectives may be stated explicitly by an individual, but more often they need to be inferred on the basis of behavior or other comments.

To summarize, on our analysis, an individual's or character's perspective is an interpretation or generalization of a collection of evaluations that are sufficiently numerous and coherent. It may vary in *generality* (i.e., how inclusive the perspective is); *coherence* (i.e., the extent to which all of the apparent evaluations support the perspective); and *explicitness* (i.e., the degree to which the perspective is identified in the text or by the perspective-taking target). In the context of fiction reading, because characters are not autonomous entities, their perspectives must often be inferred by readers on the basis of the character's evaluations, which may also have to be inferred if not sufficiently explicit.

Inferences in Identifying Perspective
As alluded to earlier, a central aspect of this conceptualization is that a perspective depends on a network of inferences on the part of the reader or observer. To begin with, the reader would need to identify evaluations that have a common theme. For example, consider the perspective of Scrooge's nephew in *A Christmas Carol*: In his interview with Scrooge early in the story, he persists in claiming that it would be good for Scrooge to visit on Christmas; later, at a gathering, he argues that he feels sorry for Scrooge. From these evaluations, one might infer that his nephew is generous and charitable. In this instance, we want to distinguish particular evaluations from the more general perspective that provides a thematic interpretation or summary of those evaluations. Evaluations reflect particular reactions, while perspectives unify those reactions in some manner.

Inferring this interpretation is trivial if it is stated explicitly, as we described earlier. However, an interpretation of a set of evaluations might need to be inferred by the reader or observer. Even here, though, the reader or observer need not generate this unifying interpretation consciously; it may be enough simply to be aware of a degree of consistency among evaluations that are apparent in the text. For example, in *Harry Potter and the Philosopher's Stone* (Rowling, 1997), there are multiple instances in which Harry reacts angrily when anyone casts aspersions on his parents (whom he never knew) and spends extensive time gazing at a magical mirror that shows his parents. The reader might easily see how these behaviors are broadly consistent without attempting to form an explicit verbal label for Harry's attitude.

A critical component of one's perspective is that it is based on evaluations derived from one's previous knowledge and experience; for example, fear of the dark may be related to some event in one's past or past events of which one may have knowledge. As we describe more fully in the next section, this has implications for perspective taking: For example, in real life, to understand a target, an observer may need to understand why the target evaluates aspects of the world in a particular way; this amounts to inferring the causes of the evaluations. With respect to literature, readers generally assume that the evaluations of a character are justified by events in the story world. Sometimes these justifications are explicitly mentioned. For example, in his encounter with the Ghost of Christmas Past, Scrooge expresses a joyful evaluation of his old mentor and "cried in great excitement: 'Why, it's old Fezziwig! Bless his heart; it's Fezziwig alive again!'" The subsequent text provides a justification for this evaluation with a description of his generous and warm actions. Moreover, the reader might infer that Fezziwig's behavior was systematic and habitual. In other instances, the justification for an evaluation must be inferred on the basis of weaker cues. For example, in "The Office" (Munro, 1996), the narrator expresses the view that writing is undervalued as a profession and the reader is left to infer what previous events might justify this evaluation. Kotovych et al. (2011) referred to these inferences as "narratorial implicatures," that is, inferences that are licensed by the assumption that the narrator is espousing reasonable and justified views. In this case, one may infer that the narrator suffered experiences in which her talent was in fact not supported or appreciated.

An additional complexity is that some narrators are unreliable, and readers need to draw more inferences about what aspects of their story are reliable and what they may not be telling us (or what they may not understand about what they tell us, as in the case of a child or an adult with intellectual disabilities) or what they may be consciously misrepresenting to us. For example, in Dávila's (2013) story "Detrás de las rejas" ("Behind Bars"), a young woman, orphaned at a young age and raised by a domineering, much older aunt, gets caught in a love triangle after falling in love with an unemployed bachelor who is also romantically involved with the aunt, presumably for her money. Narrating from within a mental institution to which her aunt allegedly confined her in order to live with the lover, the narrator-protagonist expresses her incredulity with respect to her situation through a series of evaluations of her aunt's, her lover's, and her own behavior. The reader is left to interpret which evaluations are objective and which the product of her own delusion.

When a perspective (i.e., a unifying, general interpretation of a set of evaluations) is sufficiently coherent and general, it can provide a basis for inferring other subsequent evaluations. For example, when we know that Scrooge is miserly (a general perspective), we can infer a range of other evaluations such as that he prefers not to spend money on nice meals, home furnishings, and other creature comforts. Such an interpretation thus provides a basis for understanding the subsequent description of his material circumstances. When such inferential processes successfully contribute to one's understanding of the story world, that provides additional evidence for the perspective, making it more coherent. However, when additional evaluations are found in the text that are inconsistent with a general perspective, coherence decreases; with enough inconsistency, the reader may abandon the perspective as a useful interpretation of the character's evaluations. For example, in *The Lathe of Heaven* (Le Guin, 2008), the initial chapters might lead the reader to infer that the main character's perspective is passive and fatalistic in that he does little to protest any imposition on him. However, further events suggest that such an inference is simplistic and that the character's perspective is one of principled coexistence with others and the world around him. Presumably, this change in the reader's understanding of the character's perspective occurs because the initial interpretation does not cohere with subsequent evaluations.

A related issue arises when a character's evaluations change over the course of the work. In that case, the reader must identify the perspective change and, perhaps, why it occurs. As an example of this dynamic, consider the story "The Mask of the Bear" (Laurence, 2010), in which an adult narrator recounts how at the age of ten she, her mother, and her aunt judged her grouchy, ill-mannered, socially awkward grandfather as a mean, unfeeling, hostile, and irredeemable force to be scorned and avoided. As we witness the grandfather's behavior, we share the women's judgment. However, when the grandmother dies at the end of the story and the grandfather unexpectedly expresses his appreciation of her for the first time, the narrator's mother and aunt begin to wonder if there was a deeper level to the grandfather, an insecurity and need for affection that no one had previously understood. A revelation at the very end deals a powerful blow to our previous resonance with the female character's perspective: Many years later at a museum, the sight of a Haida bear mask makes the narrator realize that once "the mask had concealed a man" (Laurence, 2010, p. 91). The mask is an apt metaphor of the grandfather's inner life that had escaped everyone's comprehension and a reminder of how we often misjudge on the basis of externals. This evaluation is inconsistent with the narrator's perspective as it is developed in the first part of the story and it might be difficult to reconcile with the interpretation of the patriarch character as uncaring. This conflict might be resolved if it is inferred that the narrator's own perspective on the father has changed.

In general, it would be a mistake to describe a single, static perspective for a character because a change in perspective, and how it is signaled by a decrease in coherence, is often the point of the story. An interesting example of the interplay between coherence and dynamics is found in *A Christmas Carol* when Scrooge, who presumably has a highly systematic and coherent disdain for generosity early on, expresses distinct and novel evaluations later in the story in his encounters with the ghosts that gradually make this perspective less coherent. For example, he remembers Christmas greetings fondly ("Why was he filled with gladness when he heard them give each other Merry Christmas ...?"), expresses remorse at threatening a caroler ("There was a boy singing a Christmas carol at my door last night. I should like to have given him something"), and regrets his treatment of Bob Cratchit ("I should like to be able to say a word or two to my clerk just now"). These small changes in evaluations ultimately culminate in a change in perspective as Scrooge comes to embrace the spirit of Christmas entirely. This suggests a shift from one coherent perspective (bitterness) to another at the conclusion of the story (generosity).

Defining Perspective *Taking*

Now that we have a more nuanced account of what constitutes a perspective and the kinds of inferences required to determine one, we are in a stronger position to analyze what it means to "take" one. In our view, what needs to be understood is the process that allows a reader or perceiver to make a personal connection to the perspective of a character. This criterion allows us to eliminate some trivial and uninteresting senses of "perspective taking" and focus on what we hope is a more insightful analysis. As with the term "perspective," we first describe what should not count as perspective taking, and then we turn to an analysis of what it must instead entail.

What Perspective Taking Is Not

Consensus about the precise import of the term "perspective taking" is often lacking, and thus our understanding of what it means to take a perspective is murky at best. De Graaf et al. (2012) correctly pointed out that there is no consensus on the meaning of the term. Both in literary studies and real-life research, conceptualizations of the gerund "taking" are often grounded in loose metaphors such as "seeing through the character's eyes," "standing in someone's shoes," "putting oneself in the place of another" (Galinsky & Ku, 2004, p. 595), and so on. In keeping with these metaphors, taking a perspective is often associated with different aspects of the relation between the reader and the character in literary studies: exposure to a target's mind (e.g., narrators' explanations of what characters think and feel or an individual spelling out personal thoughts and feelings), comprehension (understanding what a text says about what a character thinks or feels), shared perspectives (agreeing with a character), and the perception of trait similarity (also described as the basis of identification; Surtees & Apperly, 2012). Some of these same relations are assumed in the psychological research as well. For example, the claim that perspective taking entails knowing what others know (Nickerson, 1999) or the explanation that perspective taking is "the ability to entertain the perspective of another" (Galinsky & Moskowitz, 2000, p. 708) imply comprehension; otherwise, what one entertains could be something far removed from the target's state of mind. Summarizing previous research in discourse processing, Mar (2004) noted that readers understand a narrative's events "by assuming the perspective of a character," which entails "mentally representing his or her emotional states" (p. 1416). The shared-perspectives assumption is also supported by some psychological research that has shown that the perception of similarity traits facilitates perspective taking in some limited circumstances (Gerace et al., 2015). (However, other research has shown the limitations of shared similarity for perspective-taking purposes; Batson et al., 2005; Hodges, 2005.) Each of these interpretations is discussed in what follows. We argue that these descriptions of the reading experience do not fully capture the "personal connection" component of perspective taking and that there is much more involved in terms of cognitive processing than these explanations suggest.

Not Mere Exposure
In literary studies, sometimes perspective taking is associated with exposure to fictional minds (Leech & Short, 1981). Metaphorically, exposure makes us "see through the character's eyes." On this view, we take a character's perspective by virtue of tracking what the text tells us about what characters see and how they think, feel, and act. Capote's (2013) *In Cold Blood* presents us with two ruthless criminals who brutally murder an entire family. We become witnesses who follow their actions and who are made to see the world through their calloused, degenerate minds. In O'Connor's (1955) "A Good Man Is Hard to Find," we follow The Misfit as he orders the murder of a grandmother's family while he indulges her in conversation before ordering her murder as well. Here, too, the narrative describes the helpless victims from the criminal's perspective. However, in spite of witnessing the story-world events and secondary characters from the criminals' physical vantage and being told what they think and feel, it is unlikely that most readers will actually resonate with their perspective, that is, their evaluations of the situations and events of the story.

As another example, the disturbing story "We So Seldom Look on Love" (Gowdy, 1997) profiles a professed necrophile who tells us about her attraction to dead bodies and, in explicit detail, recounts her sexual experiences with them. She explains how she shared her experiences with a boyfriend she did not love until he committed suicide, after which she enjoyed an erotic encounter with his corpse, only to get caught in the act by the authorities. The story exposes her mental states and how she thinks and feels, so we are exposed to her perspective. However, it seems to us that this is unlikely to make readers establish a close connection to the protagonist.

Our interpretation of these examples is that mere exposure to a character's actions, speech, and thoughts is an insufficient criterion for perspective taking because it fails to capture some deeper sense of what it means to "take" another's point of view. In particular, a crucial component of interacting with characters is the way a reader relates personally to them. As we discuss in Chapter 4, the immorality of the characters in these examples might be an impediment to taking their perspectives and personally relating to them. However, the critical point is that equating perspective taking with mere exposure neglects that critical constructive component of establishing a relationship between the character and the reader.

This is similar to what happens in real life: Simply being exposed to information about an individual's thought processes or motivations does not imply that one will take that individual's perspective. Jury members in the Derek Chauvin case saw a video that exposed them to the officer effectively killing George Floyd as he maintained his knee on the victim's neck, and they heard evidence from witnesses of the officer's refusal to comply with requests to desist (Xiong et al., 2021). The evidence to which they were exposed clearly points to his racist mentality and criminal intention. As the world followed the trial, we hoped that no member of the jury would take that perspective but rather that they would all distance themselves from and condemn it.

Thus, with respect to both fiction reading and real life, merely witnessing or being exposed to another's perspective does not – indeed, in the cases provided here, hopefully would not – lead to a "taking" of it.

Not Simply Comprehension
Associated with mere exposure is a second limiting sense of perspective taking: simple comprehension or knowledge of a character's views and actions. Clearly, we cannot take a perspective if we do not understand how or what another person thinks or wants. However, such a comprehension requirement is also insufficient to produce a deeper relationship between the individual and the comprehender. One reason has to do with the potential for some degree of distance between characters' or individuals' view of morality and our own. We know that the murderers in Capote's

novel need money and that The Misfit and his cronies need a vehicle. We understand that these relatively trivial objectives drive their heinous behavior. We understand that Chauvin intended to use extreme force. Nevertheless, we do not take the morally deviant characters' or officer's perspective in a deeper, moral sense: We do not agree with, share, adopt, endorse, or accept their view of the world. On the contrary, we judge, repudiate, and condemn it, no doubt because our moral compass leads us to assess the world differently. For the deviant characters, their victims are inconveniences to be eliminated; for us, they are helpless, hapless, and innocent human beings. Thus, understanding a perspective, even deeply, does not necessarily entail taking that perspective.

An example of the simple comprehension of perspective comes from Gernsbacher et al. (1992). They investigated how readers processed the description of emotions in short texts. They found that readers were quicker to process target sentences that included an emotion term that matched the emotional state of the character. Under the conditions of the study, this suggests that the emotional state of the character is tracked and included in the reader's representation of the story world. In this sense, the readers have comprehended the perspective of the character. However, we would not say that readers have taken the character's perspective; they simply have available the emotional state of the protagonist, which subsequently aids in the comprehension of the relevant emotion term. Although readers *may* have taken the character's perspective, the simple reading time difference found in the study fails to demonstrate the personal connection that we believe is crucial.

Not Shared Evaluations
A third sense of what it might mean to take a perspective has to do with shared or matching perspectives. Having stated that comprehension is an inadequate criterion because understanding does not preclude rejection, one might then suggest that agreeing with or sharing another's perspective is sufficient to take it. However, we argue that if a person or reader already holds a view, belief, attitude, or opinion that matches that of another individual or fictional character, then nothing is "taken." Shared perspectives can be thought of as mirror images that involve a recognition of sameness; in some cases, this may be automatic or at least easily achieved. In contrast, the gerund "taking" suggests additional cognitive effort to make sense of the other's perspective. In particular, one of the main arguments of this book is that perspective taking requires forming a deeper connection with the target that relates their evaluations and

experiences to one's own. Such a connection is based on a particular use of one's stored repertoire of knowledge and experience that makes another's evaluations acceptable or understandable. Simply recognizing that one's evaluations match those of the target would generally not require this use of knowledge and experience.

Our argument is that taking a character's or individual's perspective means that we share not only that character's or individual's evaluations but also the reasons and justifications for those evaluations. For example, we might regard Barack Obama as an honorable and intelligent public figure. Presumably, we share this evaluation with Michelle Obama. However, we would not say that we have taken Michelle Obama's perspective because there is no reason to think that the justification for her evaluation is identical to our own. To take an example from literature, in the first portion of *A Christmas Carol*, Bob Cratchit likely regards Scrooge as a miserly and bitter man, a perspective that the reader may share. However, we have not taken Cratchit's perspective; Cratchit's justification for such an evaluation is presumably based on extensive experience that is not shared by the reader. Although we understand and agree with the character's perspective, we would not describe that as "taking" that perspective unless there is a greater, personal connection to the character's basis for that perspective.

Another problem with the shared-perspective criterion is that it can also work the other way: There may be situations where one can take a perspective even though one holds antagonistic views. For example, we may strongly condemn sexist behavior, yet recall that in our younger years we watched *Three's Company* without railing against its sexism. This might allow us to make a personal connection to a friend or relative who still holds sexist views (consonant perhaps with those expressed in the TV show), as we understand how we too were products of our age, caught up in societal biases. This allows us to take the target's perspective by making a connection to our own comparable experiences, establishing a correspondence between our evaluation and its cause and the friend's or relative's.

A few literary examples will further illustrate the point. In the story "Celia Behind Me" (Huggan, 1943/1995), an adult narrator recounts how in elementary school she participated in bullying a classmate. Most readers of the story are probably not, and never have been, active bullies, and may strongly disapprove of bullying. However, one may acknowledge some situation in which one engaged in some different form of unkind behavior, attitudes, or thoughts that hurt someone. Thus, one could take the protagonist's perspective by relating it to such personal experiences. As another example, the story "In the Moonlight" (Maupassant, 1903) is about an overtly misogynistic priest who, at the sight of a happy young couple one beautiful moonlit evening, is struck by a sudden epiphanic awareness of his own misguided evaluation of romantic love and, presumably, of lost opportunities. As readers, we may react with great disdain toward the country priest's discriminatory attitude toward women in general. Yet we may be able take his perspective by recalling related epiphanies that we have had in our own lives. This can establish a reader–character connection that is the basis of perspective taking. An important point that these examples raise is that to take a perspective is not necessarily to come to agree with it; that would amount to simply developing similar views. What constitutes a "taking" of that position is the additional cognitive processing undertaken to establish a personal connection between us and the target based on a functionally similar relation between the evaluation and its cause.

Not Perceived Similarity
Related to shared perspectives is perceived similarity or homophily. Recalling the work of Rogers and Bhowmik (1970), Eyal and Rubin (2003) defined homophily as "the degree to which people who interact are similar in beliefs, education, social status, and the like. It can be objective or subjective. It is subjective when it concerns our perception of how similar we are to a target person" (p. 80). Objective homophily includes traits such as age, gender, and demographics. Empirical evidence shows that when given the choice, we prefer to interact with those we perceive to be more like ourselves and that communication is more effective when source and receiver share attitudes and beliefs (Rogers & Bhowmik, 1970; Norton et al., 2003). In similarity or attraction theory, people are more attracted to others they perceive as similar, and trait similarity drives the selection of friends and romantic partners (Berscheid & Walster, 1969; Byrne, 1971). There is evidence that objective similarity positively affects the propensity to model a character's behavior (see Slater & Rouner, 2002). It has also been isolated as an important cross-cultural communication variable. For instance, research has shown that members of a group who perceive out-group members as having similar values manifest lower social distance toward them (Rokeach, 1979) and that greater perceived similarity of belief or values leads to closer ties between nations and more effective cross-cultural communication between social groups (Johnson et al., 1989). Some health research has shown that

objective homophily between readers and protagonists of health messages influences aspects of readers' beliefs about cancer (de Graaf, 2017). (For a review of this research, see van Krieken et al., 2017.) Similarly, the term homophily is also used in relation to identification in media studies: The greater the perceived similarity between viewers and television characters, the greater the identification (Eyal & Rubin, 2003).

Intuitively, perceived similarity with a target should increase perspective taking and empathy. However, this intuition has been disclaimed in some noteworthy studies (e.g., Batson et al., 2005; Hodges, 2005). The studies found evidence that contradicts intuitive common sense: First, similarity only affected empathic concern, not empathic accuracy, and second, perceived similarity did not increase empathy. Slater and Rouner (2002) explained that homophily does not necessarily affect liking of, or lead to identification with, a character, and that it is not as effective as emotional involvement in increasing the persuasiveness of a message. Some kinds of similarities, such as age, gender, or demographic traits, may be insufficient to override other kinds of differences, such as religious or political beliefs, while at times dissimilarity engenders attraction (Singh & Soo Yan, 2000). (For a review of research on the limits of trait similarity influence on perspective taking, see Batson et al., 2005.)

As well, homophily cannot be used as an account of perspective taking when we succeed in taking a perspective of one with a very different background. One of the traits of good literature is that it allows us to adopt the perspectives of characters whose existential traits are very dissimilar to our own. As Carroll (2001) explained, "characters very often surprise us just because their imagination is beyond simulation by average viewers, listeners, and readers" (p. 315), and this is typically what readers of fiction expect. Although we share nothing with horses in terms of physical appearance, dwelling, tastes, and so on, we can still take the perspective of the horse in Sewell's *Black Beauty*. An android in a science fiction work and an elf in a fantasy novel are similar examples of this phenomenon. For example, in the novella *Piel* (*Skin*) (Barceló, 1989/2021), the narrator describes the life of androids in imagined dystopian surroundings as they are exploited and discarded by humans. As readers, we share no physical, demographic, or lifestyle traits with the androids, and yet we come to feel that we have more in common with them than with the human characters in terms of attitudes and feelings. Again, we believe that this is because we come to form a deeper connection with the characters that overrides superficial differences. In these examples, demographic and personality trait similarity might be to a large extent irrelevant; as readers we are able to perceive similarity in difference – that is, we can identify a personal connection between the androids and ourselves, despite the lack of superficial homophily.

What Is Perspective Taking?

To summarize, taking a character's perspective is more than just following what happens to that character as the story exposes us to what that character thinks or feels or does; it is more than simply understanding motivations, beliefs, or emotions; it is more than holding similar views; and it is more than simply recognizing some obvious similarity. In particular, these ideas miss what we regard as critical to perspective taking: the process of actively making a connection between a character or individual and one's self. Davis et al. (1996) laid the groundwork for understanding how that connection works. Unsatisfied with previous explanations, they sought answers to the question of what observers actually do when instructed to take a target's perspective: For example, do they expend more effort interpreting cues or do they recall similar instances from their own past? They concluded that observers create a representation of the target that closely resembles their own self-representation. Other psychologists have come to endorse this basic insight. Nickerson (1999, p. 737) theorized that we imagine another's perspective by using "one's own knowledge as the primary basis for developing a model of what specific others know." Epley and Caruso (2009, p. 303) explained that in the absence of role-playing instructions, participants "start by using themselves as a default, or guide," using their own evaluations as a starting point, and that deliberate reasoning, attention, and motivation are required to overcome that basis when one realizes that it is insufficient.

These ideas share the common theme that perspective taking entails using one's own knowledge and experience to draw a deeper, analogical connection with the target. This connection ties one's own life to that of the target and allows us to understand in a personal way the basis for the target's evaluations. In the following section, we formalize this analysis.

Perspective Taking As Analogy

Our argument is that the personal connection in perspective taking has the form of an analogy: The perspective-taking target or character is seen as similar by analogy to the observer or reader. This conception solves the problem of understanding how the reader can take a perspective even though they are unlike the character or disagree with the character. In particular, forming a perspective-taking analogy depends on the use of the reader's prior knowledge and experience in a way that is hinted at but not fully developed in prior discussions of what it means to take a perspective. In this section, we first describe the mechanics of analogical inference that form the basis of our analysis; we then lay out this idea of perspective taking by analogy in some detail. In Chapter 5, we consider the cognitive processes and dynamics that must underlie this notion of perspective taking more fully.

Analogy Theory

Fundamentally, an analogy is a comparison. In more technical terms, an analogy is formed when elements from a source domain are mapped onto a target domain. A domain is an area of knowledge or understanding. The source domain is the more familiar, better-understood domain; the target is the domain a person wishes to understand. A mapping is an alignment of source and target elements so that knowledge of the source helps elucidate the target (Hogan, 2011). Simple analogies establish an isomorphic, one-to-one correspondence between elements of the two domains. Structure mapping, or structure alignment theory, stresses that analogical mapping is guided by higher-order relations (Gentner, 1983). In particular, the relation between elements in the source domain mirrors the relation between corresponding elements in the target domain. Reinforcing this idea, other researchers have specified that analogies are strongest when the relations are identical and the elements have many identical attributes (Holyoak & Thagard, 1989).

A classic illustration of these ideas is the analogy between (the Bohr model of) the atom and the solar system. The elements of the atom consist of the atomic nucleus and the orbiting electrons; the elements of the solar system consist of the sun and the orbiting planets. While the elements of each domain are dissimilar (e.g., a planet is very different than an electron), the relations among the elements are comparable: Both the planets and the electron orbit around a central body (the sun on one hand and the nucleus on the other). Further relational similarities apply as well: Gravity, which keeps planets in orbit around the sun, is comparable to the atomic electrostatic force, which keeps the electrons in orbit around the nucleus.

Gentner et al. (2001) provided a literary example of an analogy taken from the ancient Mesopotamian epic of *Gilgamesh* (Anonymous, 1200 BCE/1994). Upon the death of his beloved friend Enkidu, the hero Gilgamesh hovers over his friend's corpse, "swooping down over him like an eagle, / and like a lioness deprived of her cubs / he keeps pacing to and fro" (p. 125). At first glance, the two sides of the comparison have nothing to do with each other: One involves humans, the other animals; one involves the death of a friend, the other maternal attention to her brood. Clearly, it is not individual elements – hero, corpse, lioness, brood – that allow the two domains to be connected. Rather, the relational similarity exists at the level of emotional parallelism; in both cases, one may infer, there is an emotion of intense protectiveness and bonding. The critical element in our application of this theoretical account of analogical inferencing is the mapping of a relation between the source and target domains. It is not necessary that the elements of the domains be similar in any simple way; instead, what is crucial is that the relation among elements in one domain maps onto the relation among elements in the other. Thus, Gilgamesh is not like a lioness, but rather his feelings about his friend correspond to the lioness's feelings about her brood. As we develop in the rest of this section, identifying this connection across domains is a key part of perspective taking.

The Perspective-Taking Analogy

With these basics in mind, we can begin to flesh out a theory of perspective taking as a form of analogical inferencing. Readers' relationship to characters can be described in terms of source, target, and mapping. The target, or less familiar, domain is the character and their life in the story world; the source, or more familiar, domain is the reader and their repertoire of knowledge and past experience. Mapping entails finding the correspondence (i.e., the personal connection) between the experiences and evaluations of the character and those of the reader or observer. As we outline in more detail in Chapter 5, we hypothesize that finding a perspective-taking analogy involves first identifying some form of similarity between the source and the target, in terms of either the evaluations or the justifications for those evaluations. A relational structure is then constructed so that evaluations of the target are seen as corresponding to those of the reader or observer, and the justifications for those evaluations are also seen as similarly corresponding. As in the examples earlier, the analogy between the reader and the character depends not simply on similarity between the reader and the target but on the mapping of relations in the reader's experience onto the relations in the target's world.

As we noted earlier, we understand a perspective to be an interpretation of a set of evaluations of people and events in either the reader's or the character's world. A part of perspective taking involves seeing some similarity between the evaluations of the character and the reader's own evaluations of situations in their world. However, in our analysis, the perspective-taking analogy encompasses not just the evaluations themselves but also the basis of those evaluations – that is, why do the reader and the character feel the way they do? We assume that, normally, a reader's own evaluations can easily be justified on the basis of personal knowledge and experience; the reader can retrieve from memory episodes that provide a basis for the evaluation. For example, if one holds the evaluation, "I don't like going to hair salons," there is likely to be some incident in the person's past experience that justifies that evaluation; that is, there is a justification relationship between the past experience and the evaluation. The key element in our theory of perspective taking is that readers share not only a comparable evaluation with a character but also a comparable basis for that evaluation. Since both the reader's and the character's evaluations are justified by previous events, the reader can identify a similarity relationship between those justifying events as well. A missing link in the study of the process of literary perspective taking is thus the analogical inference that allows the reader to make these connections.

The structure of this perspective-taking analogy is illustrated in Figure 2.1. At the top-left are the evaluations of the character that make up their perspective. At the right are reader evaluations that are seen as similar in some way. Both the evaluations of the character and those of the reader are justified by personal knowledge and experience – by the reader's knowledge and experience in the real world and by the character's experiences in the story world. The essence of the analogy is that the justification for the character's evaluation is analogous to the justification for the reader's evaluation.

As an example, consider taking the perspective of Harry Potter in the initial chapters of *Harry Potter and the Philosopher's Stone* (Rowling, 1997). Harry regards it as unfair that his aunt and uncle ignore his birthday (in contrast, at least, to their doting on his cousin's). While it is very unlikely that the reader's childhood was anything like Harry's, it may be quite possible for the reader to retrieve memories of treatment by parents or relatives that they thought was unfair in some other way. For example, they might have missed out on a recreational trip in the same way that Harry is typically excluded from trips to the zoo. Thus, the reader may be able to identify some form of similarity between their evaluation of that event and Harry's. To construct the analogy, the reader would identify the similarity

Perspective Taking As Analogy

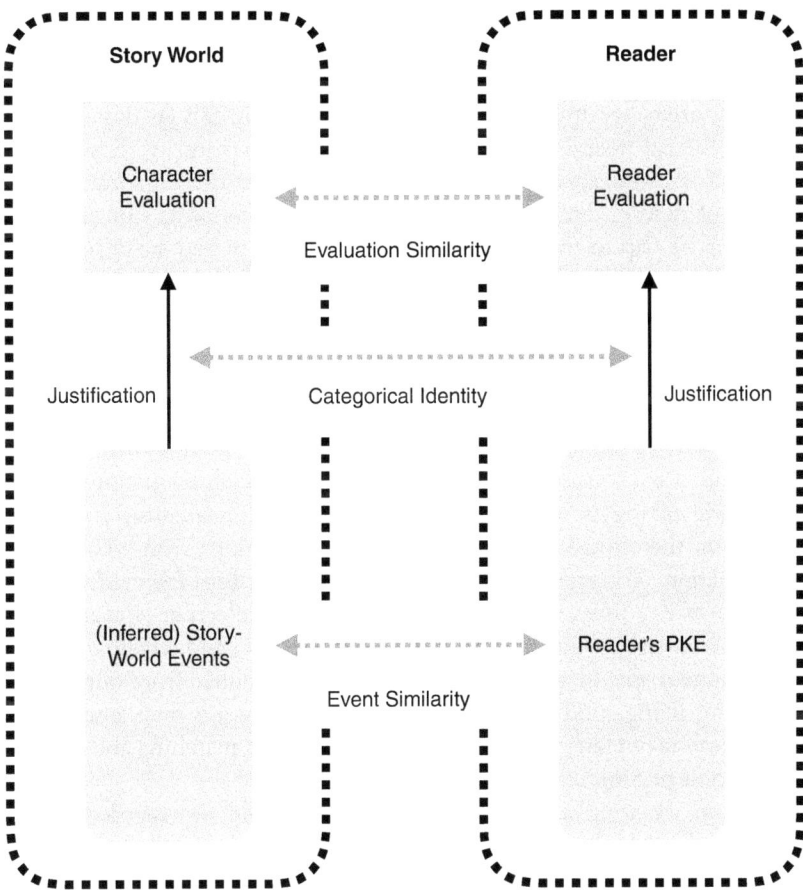

Figure 2.1 Structure of the perspective-taking analogy. PKE = personal knowledge and experience.

between some of the events that justify Harry's evaluation and those that justify their own (presumably much more limited) sense of unfairness. The analogy consists of the mapping of the justification relation between the two domains: the reader's personal knowledge and experience and Harry's world in the novel. The justification for Harry's attitude is seen as analogous to the justification for the reader's attitude.

The analogy structure depends on three links between the reader and the character. First is the similarity relationship between the evaluations. Similarity indicates that the evaluations share some feature or label. In the previous Harry Potter example, both Harry's evaluation and the reader's evaluation share a feature of "unfair treatment by a family member." Although these two evaluations could differ in many respects, the similarity arises because they could both be labeled in this fashion. Second is the similarity relationship between the events that justify those evaluations. As with the evaluations, similarity means that there is some feature or level of description in which those events are the same. For example, both Harry's trip to the zoo and the reader's activity may be desired and seen as deserved by some criteria. Finally, there is the relationship between those events and the evaluations: For both reader and character, the prior events provide a justification for the unfairness evaluations. The analogy is thus that there is corresponding justification for the corresponding evaluations.

As we have described earlier, though, a perspective is more than a single evaluation; it is a consistent interpretation of a *set* of such evaluations. Thus, perspective taking is more than finding a single, analogously matching evaluation; there must be a set of matching evaluations with a consistent interpretation. To expand on the previous example from *Harry Potter and the Philosopher's Stone*, one can find in the story a collection of evaluations that have a common interpretation of Harry resenting and rebelling against his aunt and uncle. In addition to typically being excluded from outings, he dislikes his living conditions, resents his uncle taking his mail, and so on. Readers can take Harry's perspective if they can form matching analogies to a significant portion of those evaluations.

In sum, we argue that perspective taking should be regarded as the product of analogies between the evaluations and experiences of the character or target and those of the reader or observer. As we discuss more extensively in Chapter 5, the notion of similarity here is quite flexible. Sometimes analogy formation might be triggered by closely related traits, circumstances, or evaluations in the reader's and character's experience. However, more abstract senses of similarity can be used to identify relationships between evaluations and experiences that are superficially disparate. This obviates any necessity to think of perspective taking as trait similarity or shared views and allows one, under the proper circumstances, to take perspectives of characters or individuals who are very different. Further, the perspective-taking analogy provides a formalization of the intuitive notion that perspective taking requires a personal connection between the reader and the character, and it makes clear how the personal knowledge and experience of the reader is crucial. As we describe in Chapters 3 and 4, the notion of perspective taking as analogy provides a common but implicit basis for many theoretical proposals about perspective taking in life and literature and provides new insights into these phenomena.

Summary and Conclusions

In the present chapter, we have outlined a conceptual analysis of perspective and perspective taking and have described an interpretation of perspective taking as analogical inference. A perspective was defined as an interpretation of a reasonably coherent set of evaluations. A perspective is not autonomous and determinant and not unitary and stable. Perspective taking was understood as requiring a personal connection between the reader or observer and the perspective-taking target. This personal connection implies that perspective taking cannot be mere exposure, simple comprehension, shared evaluations, or just perceived similarity. Instead, we argue that perspective taking is best understood as an analogy in which evaluations of the target, and the justifications of those evaluations, are seen as comparable to those of the reader or observer.

The main goal of this book is to advance our understanding of what perspective taking is and how it functions in the context of reading literary fiction. Our belief is that the present analysis of perspective and perspective taking allows one to arrive at a more sophisticated understanding of perspective taking in any given situation. A crucial component of the pleasure of reading fiction lies in the ways in which readers react to, interact with, and make sense of fictional characters. Readers come to the text as individuals, bringing to it their own specific life experience and their own individual idiosyncrasies. There they encounter characters with life experiences and idiosyncrasies attributed to them, who can be very different from the readers. Whether readers succeed in establishing such a connection may depend on different qualities of the reader and on properties of the text. How readers engage with characters' minds during reading is a first step to understanding how the reading experience affects the mind. Research on real-life mind reading provides a wealth of knowledge on the factors that affect how people approach other minds that can shed valuable light on how readers approach characters' minds. Literary studies provides a wealth of knowledge on textual factors that affect a reader's representation of the story world, such as artistic genres, styles, and techniques. This research is examined in the next two chapters with a view to developing a coherent interdisciplinary and empirical framework for studying the text–reader interaction that produces perspective taking.

CHAPTER 3

Perspective Taking in Life

As we noted in Chapter 2, we believe it is important to stress the commonality of perspective taking that occurs in reading literature and that which occurs in real life. In particular, the theoretical analyses and evidence on perspective taking in life strongly suggest that similar constraints apply to reading literature. In the present chapter, we review some of these ideas and evidence and describe how our analysis of perspective-taking-by-analogy applies. We also briefly discuss how these issues have been treated in literary studies. There are three areas of investigation that we consider here: mind reading, which is the process of identifying and understanding the state of another's mind; empathy, which is the experience of emotions that correspond to another's situation; and the neuroscience of perspective taking, including the neural circuits and brain regions that are thought to underlie these processes.

Mind Reading

Closely related to perspective taking, in both fiction and real life, is the process of explaining and predicting the mental states and behavior of others. Indeed, there can be no perspective taking without the ability and effort to understand the state of another's mind. However, understanding this process is complicated by terminological and conceptual inconsistencies. For example, different umbrella terms have been used to refer to the broad and unspecified set of abilities by means of which human beings make sense of others. Some of the most common – mind reading (Eyal & Epley, 2010), mentalizing (Launay et al., 2015), mind-modeling (Stockwell & Mahlberg, 2014), mindblindness (Michlmayr, 2002), and mind misreading (Whalen et al., 2012) – are used for unfamiliar situations that require guesswork; the latter two stress the possibility of false or inaccurate attributions of others' mental states. Hutto (2011) reserved the term "mind reading" for the automatic, embodied responses based on "fairly reliable access to another's state of mind by means of their expressions" (p. 282) and the term "mind guessing" for situations where "we are forced to speculate or theorize about the state or contents of another's mind" (p. 282). We would argue, though, that this usage is unsatisfactory because "reading" suggests effort, not automaticity; thus, in fact, mind guessing is implicit in the term "mind reading." Instead, we use the metaphorical term "mind reading" for the general process of trying to figure out what goes on inside other people's heads.

Conceptually, mind reading is often used to refer to our "social cognitive abilities, whatever characteristics they may have" (Hutto, 2011, p. 278). As such, it has been the subject of substantial research and theorizing. Two main approaches dominate the research on mind reading: theory-based and simulation-based accounts. Both offer explanations of how we identify another person's mindset or perspective. Controversies abound within each theoretical camp, and a complete summary and analysis of these issues is not central to the purpose of this book. (However, for a thorough review of the issues, see Goldman, 2006.) In this section, we briefly describe the fundamental issues of two theory-based accounts – theory of mind and "theory theory" – as well as simulation conceptualizations. Our overall assessment of these accounts is that mind reading depends on perspective taking and that our analysis of perspective taking as analogy provides insight into many of these ideas.

Theory of Mind

Theory of mind is a topic of longstanding interest to philosophers (Michlmayr, 2002) but is far from a unified theory. This led Apperly (2012) to conclude that "the appearance of consensus on what theory of mind is, and how we should study it, is misleading" (p. 826). However, some basic principles are shared. More specifically, theory of mind first came to refer to the assumption that human beings normally have a "concept" of mind (including beliefs, desires, hopes, intentions, and so on) and the understanding that another person's mind is possibly different from their own (Hutto, 2008). Since then, it has generally come be equated with an "understanding of others' mental states," including emotion recognition (Wimmer et al., 2021, p. 2). On the acknowledgment that understanding others' mental states involves more than simply knowing that others have different mindsets, the term is now used to refer to "the knowledge and skills that allow us to infer mental states such as goals, intentions, and beliefs" (Hoyos et al., 2020, p. 1).

The term "theory of mind" was introduced in the field of primatology by Premack and Woodruff (1978) who wondered if chimpanzees had an ability to identify mental states in their conspecifics. Following the research of Wimmer and Perner (1983), the concept became the focus of extensive research programs in developmental psychology; this work often used the so-called false-belief paradigm. In its basic form, this task required children to predict another's behavior regarding a hidden object based on the belief that that individual might be presumed to have about the object (Wimmer & Perner, 1983; Baron-Cohen et al., 1985). In a classic version of this task, children see an object, such as a chocolate, which is placed first in a specific locale before a witness, the puppet Maxi, and then switched to a different locale after Maxi leaves the room. The children are then asked where Maxi will look for the chocolate when he returns. Results indicate that before the age of four, children generally assume that Maxi knows what they themselves know, that is, where the chocolate really is. This is taken as a demonstration that these children do not have the concept of a mind that others' knowledge and beliefs are different from their own; they do not have a theory of mind in this sense. In particular, the young children do not appreciate that Maxi must have a false belief about the location of the chocolate. Subsequently, some researchers examined the lack of false-belief capacity in autistic children (Leslie & Thaiss, 1992; Sodian & Frith, 1993; Happé, 1994; Samson et al., 2004).

Conceptual issues revolve around the acquisition and development of theory of mind. An early explanation was that theory of mind is innate (Carruthers, 1996). One version of this conceptualization was based on a modular view of the human mind. On this account, the mind has a genetically determined module for reasoning about mental states, and it is the development of this module that enables children to identify false beliefs (Leslie et al., 2004). However, this view fails to account for the continued development of theory of mind: Theory of mind is not an optimal state that one attains once and for all with the mastery of false belief (Apperly et al., 2009; Apperly, 2012) but rather something that individuals develop and achieve to varying degrees. Simply put, some are better at it than others because of "varying conceptual sophistication, varying capacity to deploy those concepts in a timely and contextually appropriate manner, and varying motivation to do so" (Apperly, 2012, p. 835). These discoveries are important for the basic facts they underscore: that understanding other minds is more complex than simply knowing that others have different mental states; that it depends on cognitive and social abilities that vary across individuals; and that these abilities are not always guarantors of successful mind reading.

Another view is that theory of mind is linked to particular semantic and syntactic skills in language development (Slade & Ruffman, 2005; Milligan et al., 2007). These linguistic approaches are based on the argument that to be functional, a theory of mind must enable one to verbally explain another's mental state, and this in turn requires the construction of propositions about those states. Thus, propositional representations of the nature of another's beliefs would be needed. For example, a proposition such as "Maxi thinks that the chocolate is in the cupboard" would be needed to solve a false-belief task. However, there is good reason to doubt that this is the complete story. For example, infants have demonstrated some recognition of others' intentional mental states, and this has been seen as proof that theory-of-mind skills predate language acquisition skills (Scholl & Leslie, 1999; Onishi & Baillargeon, 2005). Another argument is that some children with advanced linguistic skills do poorly on theory-of-mind tests (Siegal, 2011) and, conversely, some who display poor grammatical skills still pass the false-belief tests. *As an alternative to specific linguistic skills, Hutto (2008, 2011), based in part on evolutionary and phylogenetic reasoning, advanced a* "narrative-practice hypothesis" in which theories of mind are a learned competence acquired through listening to narratives about other people's motives and reasons. On this view, mind-reading competence must be examined in concrete social contexts in which children acquire human interaction competencies that enable them to attribute other kinds of beliefs or reason about others' mental states (Leudar & Costall, 2009).

More relevant to our purposes is the continued development of mind-reading abilities beyond success in simple versions of the false-belief task (Carpendale & Chandler, 1996; Miller, 2009; Devine & Hughes, 2013). Instead, subsequent research framed theory of mind as a developmental process in which reasoning about mental states becomes increasingly more sophisticated. In this line of thinking, the acquisition of semantic and syntactic skills plays a crucial role (Hoyos et al., 2020). Launay et al. (2015) defined theory of mind as "the ability to understand the recursively embedded mind states of other people" (p. 6). Such mentalizing skills range from simple to more complex levels of embedded beliefs. Level 1, mastered during childhood, involves the ability to believe that someone else has a belief. Level 2 would involve a belief that someone has about another's belief. Level 3 would involve a belief about a Level 2 belief, and so on. False-belief tasks of traditional theory-of-mind research, he explained, only test Level 2 mentalizing, that is, the ability to recognize that someone else can hold beliefs that differ from one's own. However, competence for Levels 4–5 continues to develop through the end of adolescence. This makes clear that mastery of more complex mentalizing requires abilities beyond the simple possession of the concept that others have beliefs or intentions different from one's own.

This analysis has led to the design of methodologies to examine the development of mentalizing first in older children and then in adults. One of these is the Strange Stories Test, designed to test for understanding of more complex mental states such as misunderstandings, deception, satirical intent, and so on. In early uses of this task (Happé, 1994; White et al., 2009), participants were asked first to read twenty-four short vignettes that depicted social scenarios and then explain the character's behavior based on their mental states. Later versions limited the number of vignettes to eight scenarios that depicted examples of double bluff, misunderstandings, deception, and white lies. Another was the Silent Films Test, in which participants first viewed brief silent film clips depicting some character's behavior and then had to use their own beliefs and desires to explain that behavior (Devine & Hughes, 2013). The advantage of these story-based methods is that they can test mentalizing skill for embedded levels of mental states in adults. The results showed that "there is significant individual variation in mentalizing competencies in adults, with the upper limit varying across fourth to sixth order intentionality" (Launay et al., 2015, p. 7). The fact that adults have different levels of mentalizing skill suggests that the skill is not a distinct, "modular," cognitive ability but is rather contingent upon other cognitive capacities. For example, it may be "an emergent property of underlying aspects of executive function such as memory, causal reasoning, and inhibition" (Launay et al., 2015, p. 6). Higher levels of executive capacity (Apperly, 2012), as well as social competence (Devine & Hughes, 2013), are presumably required for more complex mind reading, especially in unfamiliar or ambiguous situations, and both of these vary across individuals.

A major component of performance on theory-of-mind tasks is the executive function of inhibitory control: the ability to quarantine one's own knowledge, beliefs, and desires in attempting to understand another's mental states. Failure to accomplish this is known as the "egocentric bias." Children's inability to bracket out their own states of mind is one of the factors that leads to lower theory-of-mind skill. However, Piaget (1959) noted that although adults are better at these tasks than children, they are by no means masters of the skill. Subsequent findings in social and personality psychology have lent abundant empirical support to this intuition that adults have difficulty suppressing their own egocentric perspective (Perner, 1996). Failure to quarantine one's own point of view can take many different forms. These include the "curse of knowledge" (Camerer et al., 1989), the "illusion of simplicity," the "false-consensus effect," and the "failure-of-consensus effect" (Nickerson, 1999). Kahneman and Tversky (1973) suggested that the ready availability of one's own perspective may make it difficult to consider the existence of other possibilities. A useful concept in this context is the idea of "naïve realism" (Ichheiser, 1949) in which one believes one sees the world as it really is while others who hold differing views do not. Based on this idea, Pronin et al. (2004) provided evidence for an "introspection illusion" in which one believes that one's own judgments are correct and grounded in reason. While adults generally possess theory-of-mind abilities, more subtle egocentric biases are difficult to overcome and constitute one of the greatest challenges to objective inferencing about others' mental states.

There is yet another major shortcoming of theory-of-mind research: It minimizes the process by which another's mental state is identified. It is one thing to note that there is a requirement of understanding that others have a mental state different from our own, but it is another to say what that mental state is. We suggest that the process that is often implicit in theory of mind is one of analogy formation. Specifically, in order to identify another's mental state, there must be some form of analogical comparison of observers' and targets' knowledge. Recently, some researchers have begun to describe and empirically test the idea that analogical comparison is central to theory-of-mind acquisition (Hoyos et al., 2020). In our view, there must be an analogy between what the target knows in their situation and what the observer would know in a corresponding situation. For example, the participant in a classic false-belief task must make an analogy between Maxi's knowledge and what their own knowledge would be in a corresponding situation in which they did not see the chocolate moved. The reasoning might be: "If I were outside of the room, I would not have seen the chocolate moved. Therefore, I would not have updated my belief about its location." Indeed, Dunbar (2006) defined theory of mind as "the ability to read or imagine how another individual sees the world" (p. 172), effectively defining it as perspective taking. The required analogical inference is not typically elaborated in classical research on theory of mind. On our account, analogical reasoning is a fundamental component of mind reading, as well as of perspective taking more generally, but, as we describe later in this chapter, it involves more than just a comparison of visual, objective knowledge.

Theory of Mind and Literary Studies
Literary scholars have not typically differentiated between different theories of mind reading and often use different terms interchangeably. The work of literary researchers with a cognitive bent has been broadly concerned with mental state attributions and conflates theory of mind and mind reading. Zunshine (2006) claimed that cognitive psychologists use the terms "theory of mind" and "mind reading" interchangeably, and she proceeded to define theory of mind as "our ability to explain people's behaviour in terms of their thoughts, feelings, beliefs, and desires," that is, the ascription of "certain mental states on the basis of … observable action" (p. 6). Kidd et al. (2016) echoed this view: For them, theory of mind was the "ability to infer and understand others' mental states" (p. 43). Assuming that we are biologically wired to interpret others' intentions, Whalen et al. (2012) argued that we need a theory of mind to understand others' actions "in terms of the mental states (i.e., thoughts, feelings, and goals) that we can reasonably attribute to them" (p. 301).

In their very general treatment of theory of mind, literary scholars have also overlooked important developments in real-life mind reading. In particular, they have often failed to acknowledge the specific cognitive capacities required to make sense of other minds and the limitations of those capacities. Just as individuals misread other minds in everyday situations, it is entirely possible that readers misread characters' "minds" for the same reasons: Readers may have limited capacity for discerning embedded levels of beliefs, difficulty in overcoming egocentric biases, and limited individual cognitive competencies that affect their ability to draw inferences about the content of another person's mind.

Harrison (2017) noted that the term "theory of mind" is often used to describe "how readers model minds in the context of reading" (p. 30); this implies that it entails the ability to maintain "a working model of the characteristics, outlook, beliefs, motivations and consequent behavior of others" (Stockwell & Mahlberg, 2015, p. 132). Characters' mental states are only as "nuanced" as allowed by the textual cues that form the building blocks of our mental representation of the story world; thus, the mental representation of characters' mental states overlaps with narrative processing and comprehension more generally. Consequently, a robust theory of literary perspective taking must take into account readers' text processing capacities.

Theory Theory

"Theory theory" is an account of mind reading based on the idea that our everyday knowledge of psychology is a theory we use to predict and explain others' mental states (Morton, 1980). Also known as "folk psychology" theory, it is a tacit body of knowledge consisting of basic psychological principles about mental states and how they relate to human behavior (Lewis, 1966; Churchland, 1991; Stich & Nichols, 1992). The assumption is that if we can navigate our way in the social world, we must possess an intuitive theory of how and why others act. As Hutto (2008) explained, this body of knowledge is put to the service of "predicting, explaining, and explicating intentional actions by appeal to reason" in order to understand what motivates a target's actions (pp. 2–3). Folk psychological concepts can consist of propositional attitudes marked by "that-clauses" such as "if P wants X and knows that X can be obtained by Y, then P will engage in Y" (Heal, 1996). For example, one may know that if a person is hungry, they can alleviate that hunger by having something to eat. In turn, if someone is observed having a snack, one uses this knowledge to work backwards to the inference that the person must be hungry. A set of propositions such as this relate beliefs, intentions, and desires to behavior in a systematic way. This provides a common-sense psychological explanation of the social world that rests on a mastery of platitudes or lore about causal relations between mental states, sensory stimuli, and behavior (Stone & Davies, 1996). Generally, it is assumed that this folk psychological knowledge is automatically activated when it is relevant in a given context. (An important subtlety is that this folk theory is inevitably probabilistic; a related behavior is only *likely* to occur rather than being inevitable. Thus, the relevant backward inference depends on Bayes' Rule and the associated base rates; one must know, for example, how likely the behavior is a priori in order to correctly infer the related mental state. Baker et al. [2011], among others, have developed some of the implications of this insight.)

As with theory of mind, there are competing accounts of how a folk psychology theory is acquired. Nativists endorse an "inherited theory-theory" account in which it assumed that this knowledge is innate; humans are born equipped with principles about basic folk psychological rules

(Carruthers, 1996; cf. Fodor, 1987). Other theory theorists stress that this knowledge is learned through different forms of experience. Some have compared the child to a little scientist who develops and revises or changes theories about other minds, developing an understanding of mental states based on observation (Carruthers, 1996; Wellman et al., 2001; Bonowitz et al., 2012; Hoyos et al., 2020). In addition, children can listen to others talk about mental states, exposing them to a consistent set of rules that form the basis of a more developed theory (Hutto, 2008). (However, for a critique of the child scientist view, see Goldman, 2006.)

We suggest that a folk psychology could also be developed by applying self-knowledge to others. Because one's own mental states and their relation to one's own behavior are generally available, using self-knowledge provides a great deal of knowledge that one could use to develop behavioral rules. However, using such knowledge requires applying a form of analogical inferencing: The target is assumed to be like oneself to the extent that the rule one can generate from personal experience also applies to the target. For example, I reason that if I want to eat when I'm hungry, then someone else who is hungry will also want to eat. This form of inference would thus make an analogical connection between the target and the observer and would be tantamount to perspective taking as described in Chapter 2.

A critique of theory theory that is relevant to our purposes is that even if this account works well under mundane circumstances, it can be more problematic in unusual or ambiguous situations. Folk theories are only "generalities about beliefs, perceptions, emotions, projects, etc. as broad classes" (Heal, 1996, p. 78). However, in unusual, more complex, or ambiguous situations, such generalities or stereotypical knowledge are likely to be insufficient, and deeper cognitive processing would typically be required (Botterill, 1996; Perner, 1996; Stone & Davies, 1996). We argue that the folk psychology rules would often have to be adapted to the current context (cf. Heal, 1996) and that this adaptation may have the form of an extended analogy. For example, if one has a causal rule that describes a behavior following a mental state, this could be extended by applying analogous qualifiers to the behavior and state. Thus, "hunger → eat" could become "minimal hunger → snack" or "sweet craving → eat dessert." Such a process is by no means a simple or automatic response and may require some subtle, knowledge-based judgments. For example, how is "sweet craving" like "hunger"? And what behaviors would be analogous to "eat" under such circumstances?

Critiques aside, theory theory does provide an advantage over accounts based on the concept of theory of mind: It provides an explicit description of how the observer identifies the state of mind of a target. However, as in our analysis of theory of mind, a realistic theory theory depends on analogy: Analogs between the self and others might be used in acquiring general rules, and analogical inferencing would be required to adapt any general rule to a specific set of circumstances. Understood in this sense, the analogical use of personal knowledge and experience comes into play both during the acquisition of a folk theory of behavior and during the application of the acquired rules. If, in certain circumstances, a given rule does not readily apply, then one must adapt it through further analogical inferencing. On balance, we believe it is unreasonable to assume that this knowledge could be used in an automatic fashion.

Theory Theory and Literary Studies
In cognitive and empirical literary studies concerned with reader–character interaction, scholars commonly refer to theory of mind rather than theory theory. However, to the extent that theory of mind is typically understood as a form of mind reading, the idea that readers read fictional minds by drawing on their store of folk psychological knowledge is implicit. Thus, theory theory is one explanation of how that mind reading occurs.

One theory-theory concept that seems applicable to fiction reading is the "little scientist," mentioned earlier: the idea that children construct and subsequently revise theories of human behavior in the face of new data. In particular, adult readers may revise their understanding of (fictional world) behavior based on reading experience. Studies of novice and expert readers have demonstrated that seasoned readers become familiar with the literary conventions associated with the types of works they read, and this familiarity affects their interpretation of the text (e.g., Bortolussi & Dixon, 1996; Sommer, 2013). We surmise that as readers of fiction acquire expertise through the reading of different works, they revise and update their understanding of character depictions, altering their response to particular kinds of characters. The more familiar certain types of characters become, the easier it may be to draw analogical connections. For example, a reader who is unimpressed by Beowulf's bragging might, upon reading Homeric and other epics, come to appreciate it as a genre convention that highlights heroes' merited recognition. We can hypothesize that readers' acquired understanding of this behavior facilitates taking a boasting character's perspective.

Although the concept of a folk psychology may be useful for formulaic narratives, it falls short of explaining literary response in general. Even fiction that highlights the universal human condition through well-known themes (such as love, hate, loyalty, or betrayal) may present these human experiences in historical, cultural, and social environments that may require readers to adapt their folk psychological understanding in new ways. Presumably, this adaptation requires more extensive analogies to their personal knowledge and experience. Because stories and novels typically present complex characters whose behaviors and states of mind require substantial inferencing and interpretation, the application of a simple folk theory would require deeper inferences and processing. Presumably, this additional processing is part of what makes literature interesting and challenging.

Simulation

The final account of mind reading and perspective taking we discuss is simulation. Etymologically, the verb "simulate" means to imitate or feign. As defined by a standard dictionary, a "simulation" is "the imitative representation of the functioning of one system or process by means of the functioning of another" (Webster, 1989). Computer simulations, for example, can model the weather or the piloting of a plane. Simulations comprise a simulator and the thing simulated. A simulator is "a device that enables the operator to reproduce or represent under test conditions phenomena likely to occur in actual performance" (Webster, 1989). Important in this definition are the words "represent" and the concept of reproduction under test conditions. Parts of this simulation metaphor seem intuitive: Simulators are individuals (perceivers) who engage in the process of simulating, that is, representing, imitating, replicating, or mirroring another person's – the target's – mind. The "device" that runs the simulation is the perceiver/simulator's mind. Thus, human minds are both the vehicle for, and object of, simulation. Unfortunately, metaphors are only imprecise heuristics that can lead us astray (cf. Kuhn, 1962). Conceptualizations of how simulation works have led to decades-long controversies, a host of competing explanations, and not a little obfuscation.

Generally, simulation is "the hypothesis that we predict, understand, and interpret others by putting ourselves in their place, that is to say, by adopting their point of view" (Carroll, 2001, p. 306). An antecedent of current simulation theory in psychology has been traced back to developmental psychologist Piaget (1959), who equated simulation with a form of role playing that allegedly helps children overcome their egocentric views. On this understanding, simulation is a form of imitation, and role playing is a form of perspective taking. In its more recent configuration, simulation theory emerged in the field of philosophy of mind as a challenge to theory of mind, intended to provide a more viable alternative of how we go about making sense of and construing others' minds (Gordon, 1986; Heal, 1986). More specifically, simulation theorists argued that mind reading is driven not by any theory but by a process that requires the active use of one's own mind to imitate a target's state of mind in order to predict that person's behavior. The idea that simulations are run "offline" is central to simulation theory; that is, we use, or "reuse" (Carruthers, 1996), our own decision-making apparatus not for the purpose of personally acting on a decision but only to explain and predict the target's mental state and behavior. In Carroll's (2001) words, when we go offline, we "decouple ... our mental system from our active system" (p. 308). Simulation theory assumes that in trying to understand another's state of mind, "we input their relevant beliefs and desires into the black box of our own offline cognitive/conative system and then consider the output as a predictor of their behavior" (p. 307). To use Perner's (1996) example, I imagine being in the target's position – a dark alley – and I pretend to believe a nearby person is going to mug me, pretend I'm scared and want to run away, and so on. Thus, Perner argued that simulation relies solely on imagining pretend states and on using one's own mind as "an analogue model (in the sense of having a relevantly similar causal structure)" (p. 91). He noted that this was close to reasoning by analogy in which one uses "knowledge about [oneself] ... as a typical specimen of the human species" (p. 92).

A core issue with this conceptualization is that there is no clear sense in which the human mind possesses a separable decision-making system to which one can input information; all we have is a network of neural processes integrated with our own autobiographical and semantic knowledge and behavior. Simulation theories assume that we can take those neural processes, abstract them away from the inputs and outputs with which they are normally associated, and then reuse them on a hypothetical set of inputs one has imagined. There is no good reason to assume that this is possible. Moreover, this explanation presupposes a state of isomorphic similarity between, or accurate mirroring of, the minds of the simulator and target. We think that such an ideal state is unlikely to be achieved.

In particular, a contentious issue is how we come in the first place to know the target's beliefs and desires that are to be inputted into the simulator's mental apparatus. Philosophers and psychologists have resorted to other metaphors to explain the process, the two most prominent ones being "transfer" and "transformation." In arguing for a transfer metaphor,

Goldman (1995) maintained that the perceiver/simulator is the springboard for drawing inferences that are then attributed to or projected onto a target. As simulators, we start by imagining or pretending to be in the target's shoes and then we "consider what we should do if we had the relevant beliefs and desires" (Goldman, 1995, p. 81). Transfer is thus a construction metaphor: Projection starts with ourselves "as detectors of [another's] intention" (Carroll, 2001, p. 308) and extends outwards as we "cantilever" (Stone & Davies, 1996) away from the self in order to understand the target's beliefs and actions (p. 128). For Davis et al. (1996), this causes the target to be more "self-like" because it "alters the cognitive representation of the target . . . to more closely resemble the observer's own self-representation" (p. 714).

Others have relied on the transformation metaphor. Gordon (1996) vigorously disputed the transfer analysis in which "we make inferences from what we ourselves would do in the imagined circumstances to what the other will do" (p. 15). He regarded such inferences as a type of conceptual judgment and argued instead that simulation is nonconceptual. As an alternative, he proposed a transformation metaphor in which one undergoes an "imaginative transformation into the other" (p. 15). By taking on the other person's psychological traits, we become, metaphorically speaking, the target of simulation (Gordon, 1996; Barlassina & Gordon, 2017). In this case also, the self takes on the attributes of the target. This view assumes that we somehow just know another person's mental state. However, replicating or reproducing another mind is beyond our human capacity unless the target's mental states are clearly communicated in an explicit manner. Therefore, our analysis is that taking Gordon's inherently idealistic transformation metaphor literally would amount to resorting to telepathic mysticism.

Both the transfer and transformation metaphors rely on some ill-specified forms of imagination. Gaesser and Schacter (2014) described "episodic simulation" as simply the imagination of an event. Escalas (2007) was more specific, referring to mental simulation as "the imitative mental representation of some event or series of events, including rehearsals of likely future events, fantasizing about less likely future events, realistically re-experiencing past events, or reconstructing past events while mixing in hypothetical elements" (p. 422). (Interestingly for our purposes, this latter view acknowledges the role of personal memories, which we believe is central to perspective taking.) Simply stating that we imagine being in a target's situation leaves unanswered the question of how such a process works. In situations that are similar to previous experience, simulation may operate by retrieving details from one's own past. However, if the situation to be imagined is unfamiliar, this may not be so simple, and other strategies would be needed to construct a simulation.

Our perspective-taking-by-analogy approach provides one account of how to simulate based on prior experience: As described in more detail in Chapter 5, we take the perspective of a target by constructing a perspective-taking analogy. The analogy would then be used to reconstruct the target's situation from elements of prior experience adapted to the target's context (cf. Schacter & Addis, 2007). For example, suppose the perspective-taking target hits someone in anger, but the perceiver has never done that. The perceiver may be able to simulate that action by adapting an experience in which they struck an inanimate object in frustration. In such an analogy, the object corresponds to the target's victim, and the frustration corresponds to their anger. One of the implications is that the beliefs and actions of the target would not need to be identical to one's own beliefs and actions but rather simply be analogous. The major difference between our account and simulation approaches is that we use a consistent analysis of what transfer entails rather than a vague metaphor. Moreover, our account goes beyond the simple self–other analogy of simulation, in which the target is assumed to act in a similar fashion as the simulator, and allows for the possibility of a deeper, more abstract relationship.

One of the important issues with which simulation theorists have had to grapple is the problem of egocentric biases. To construct a simulation, we draw inferences about a target's decision by relying on our complement of background knowledge, beliefs, desires, and emotions. This suggests that it may be difficult to bracket out one's own perspective; failing to do so can result in inferences that are often very different from how the target might feel or act (Dennett, 1981, 1987; Michlmayr, 2002; Goldman, 2006; Hutto, 2008; Ohreen, 2015). (For a review of debates on this issue, see Epley & Caruso, 2009.) Goldman (2006) recognized that because we can never cease to be ourselves, "our default procedure is to mind read in a fundamentally biased, egocentric fashion" and that "we project our own conceptual, combinatorial, and even ontological dispositions onto others" (p. 176). Applying traits of the perceiver to the target, or traits of the target to the perceiver, can lead to egocentric misattributions such as wishful thinking, the attribution of idealized properties of the target to the self. This is especially pertinent in difficult, ambiguous, enigmatic situations, where clear signs or adequate information regarding the target's situation, psychology, and history are unavailable. Imagining how we would feel or act in such a situation could rely on two types of inferences: those that generate attributions of mental states and those that generate hypothesis to explain behavior. Both can be inaccurate or incorrect.

These limitations of simulation models have led some to endorse information-based accounts of mind reading. For example, Nichols et al. (1996) argued that although offline simulation theories assume that "the subject's information about the domain is irrelevant" (p. 46), they in fact depend on knowledge and information. On the basis of the experiments they reviewed, they concluded that it was unclear if subjects had different decision-making systems, inputted the wrong pretend state, or used different judgment criteria, all of which strongly suggest that simulation may not be a viable account of mind reading. Epley, Keysar, et al. (2004) argued that simulation will not be undertaken at all in cases where the other person's perspective may be considered inaccessible, as in the case of outgroup members. Borrowing Tversky and Kahneman's (1974) anchoring and adjustment heuristic, Epley, Keysar, et al. provided evidence that perspective taking is a process in which people start by "initially anchoring on their own perspective and only subsequently, serially, and effortfully accounting for differences between themselves and others until a plausible estimate is reached" (p. 328), and proposed that "in the absence of sufficient motivation for accuracy, people are likely to terminate adjustment once a plausible estimate is reached," a process referred to as "satisficing" (p. 334). This suggests that the egocentric bias may be trumped in the interest of expediency and convenience and that expediency and convenience trump the deeper search for accuracy.

Given the limitations of pure theory-theory- and simulation-based accounts of mind reading, others have endorsed a blended theory-theory /simulation account (Nichols et al., 1996; Perner, 1996; Epley, Keysar, et al., 2004; Goldman, 2006; Barlassina & Gordon, 2017). These accounts recognize that all mind reading cannot be explained solely in terms of one or the other mechanism, and that different strategies come into play in different situations. For example, if the situation is reasonably stereotypical, inferences based on theory theory may suffice; however, in more ambiguous or novel circumstances, one may need to simulate based on the available information.

Simulation and Literary Studies
On an intuitive level, it is easy to understand how the simulation metaphor is appealing in the context of literature: It captures important aspects of literary production and reception. Aristotle first recognized that literature presents not replicas of reality but rather models of some aspect of human

experience (Aristotle, 400 BCE/2013). The simulation analogy captures this important insight. Like computer programs, literary works model or simulate in the sense that they provide an approximate imitation of some aspect of real-life situations. Flight simulators recreate some components of the airplane flight environment (e.g., weather conditions) in test conditions propitious to training and testing. Likewise, narrative fiction imitates aspects of human life – predicaments, relationships, emotions, behaviors, and worldviews – exposing readers to novel experiences in the comfort of their safe reading spaces. Simulators, such as flight simulators, enable the user to observe potential outcomes. Similarly, fiction allows the reader to observe and vicariously test new possibilities, limits, and consequences. Throughout literary history, writers of different stylistic stripes have regarded themselves as programmers of literary simulations. For example, some realist and naturalist writers, like Zola, inspired by positivist and determinist ideas, likened themselves to scientists in a lab, regarding their narratives as opportunities to explore human behavior in controlled situations (Mack, 1997). Modernist writers, many inspired by Freud, modeled the functioning of the psyche through the use of introspective techniques (Mack, 1997).

With respect to literary reception, the simulation metaphor is less effective. That fiction can present novel experiences is obvious, but the complexities of how readers process that novelty and the ensuing results of that processing exceed simple simulation explanations. Goldman (1993a) assumed that fiction triggers perspective taking; he hypothesized that reading either a history book or a novel could lead to "imaginatively assuming one or more of the other person's mental states" and that these mental states become the inputs that trigger "further states that (in favourable cases) are similar to, or homologous to, the target person's states" (p. 141). Empirical scholars of literary response have often cast the age-old simulation metaphor and its purported perspective-taking effects in terms of the offline, transfer, or transformation versions of simulation theory. Mar and Oatley (2008) not only maintained that fiction serves to "model and abstract the human social world" (p. 173) but also went a step further, extending the simulation analogy to readers who engage in a "simulation of experience" (p. 183). In particular, Oatley (1999) explained that readers use their own minds (more specifically, their own personal decision-making or planning processors) to make sense of fictional entities. This account recalls the transfer metaphor involving pretending and imagining: Readers represent a character's situation by imagining what they themselves would do in similar situations and then project or transfer that scenario onto one or more characters. Oatley added that readers can run the processor offline, either forwards to predict character's future actions or backwards to infer their intentions. Some literary applications of psychological theories also conflate simulation with identification in a way that is reminiscent of Gordon's (1995) transformation metaphor: Readers represent a character's situation and mental states by imaginatively merging with that character, thereby transcending the self–other barrier. Mar and Oatley (2008) proposed that as a result of running the planning processor, "a reader generally identifies with a protagonist" and "essentially enters another mind" (p. 182). Djikic et al. (2013) claimed that "literature encourages us to become others in imagination" (p. 44). In both cases, perspective taking would be the result of simulating, or imagining, characters' minds.

However, we argue that this reader-as-simulator account is schematic and incomplete. We describe three limitations here: the assumption that perspective taking via simulation occurs automatically without regard for the reader or the text, the omission of constraining factors and variables, and the lack of specificity concerning the process underlying perspective taking. First, simulation may not always occur. Tan (1994) argued that "the reader does not imagine him or herself to be the protagonist, but witnesses what befalls the latter" (p. 173). Currie (1995) challenged the assumption that readers of fiction necessarily take a character's perspective through simulation; he argued instead that readers may adopt a distanced, critical, or reflective mode. Similarly, Carroll (2001) argued that readers do not feel empathy by simulating characters' mental states because they view the story world from the outside, not as participants, and Coplan (2004) maintained that readers do not simply simulate or empathize but have their own "thoughts and feelings about the overall theme and messages of a narrative" (p. 149). Even though simulation accounts acknowledge the role of the text (e.g., Mar & Oatley, 2008), they do not identify the text features that trigger simulation (Meskin & Weinberg, 2003; Vermeule, 2011). Second, knowledge concerning mind reading in real life has not been incorporated into empirical studies of literary response (as noted by Zunshine, 2006). As described previously, these include limitations in attention, motivation, executive (inhibitory) control, memory, and the ability to track embedded levels of perspective. Finally, a third limitation is that the nature of the simulation process is ill specified (Meskin & Weinberg, 2003). Often, the term "simulation" is used without definition (Nijhof & Willems, 2015) or is simply associated vaguely with forms of imagination. For example, van Krieken (2018) wrote that readers of a particular story "can safely simulate hearing the sounds and seeing the sights that are part of mass shootings" (p. 21); this suggests only that they imagine those sounds and images. Used in this sense, simulation becomes a dead metaphor. Furthermore, developments within psychology to identify the mechanisms involved in simulation (such as satisficing, anchoring and adjustment, or analogical inferencing; Hoyos et al., 2020) have not been incorporated into studies of readers' reactions to fictional characters.

We propose that the simulation metaphor can be made more concrete by conceptualizing it as a form of analogical inferencing. As we discuss further in Chapter 5, we argue that simulation depends on the recruitment of memory of one's prior experience in the service of understanding a new situation. This prior experience is then adapted by analogy to the current context. Because humans do not have a mental "simulation" processor, only a network of neural processes associated with personal experience and knowledge, it is important to adequately account for the conditions under which that stored personal repertoire is activated, how the knowledge is used, and the kinds of self–other analogies it might elicit. Our theory of analogical inferencing provides a framework for describing simulation as perspective taking, both in literary processing and in real life.

Conclusions about Reading Real and Fictional Minds

Critical analyses of both theory- and simulation-based accounts of mind reading have highlighted their inadequacy as general and complete explanations of how we go about trying to make sense of other minds. In our view, one of the main problems is that both are predicated on a form of simple analogical thinking based on simple similarity: I think I can understand another's mindset because I believe all minds are alike in some fundamental ways (theory of mind and theory theory) or because I believe another individual's human experience is similar enough to mine to result in the same behavioral outputs (simulation). The problem is that reliance on simple analogies of this nature presupposes idealized simulators and situations in which things happen "as they rationally ought to" (Stone & Davies, 1996, p. 136). In simple, ceteris paribus scenarios (e.g., if A wants X and knows that doing B will achieve X, then A will do B; Hutto, 2008) or in common or familiar situations, simple similarity inferences may suffice. However, neither life nor literature always conforms to stereotypical patterns. Instead, they often put people in unfamiliar, complex, ambiguous social and cultural situations that can be perplexing, if not incomprehensible. Consequently, neither the knowledge that others have different mental states, nor a tacit body of folk psychological understanding of mental states and behaviors, nor the assumption that mental states will result in prescribed behavioral outcomes will be sufficient. In contrast, our theory elaborates a more complex description of perspective taking by analogy, elements of which are implicit in theory- and simulation-based accounts of mind reading. We argue that taking a perspective involves drawing on personal knowledge and experience to retrieve evaluations that match the target's, not in terms of superficial similarities but on the basis of deeper structural relationships. In this sense, perspective taking, when it occurs either during the reading of fiction or in real life, may not be "accurate," but nevertheless represents an effort to personally connect to other minds.

Perspective Taking and Empathy

Consistent with other authors (e.g., Gerace et al., 2015), we argue that empathy is a form of perspective taking. Like perspective taking in general, empathy is a vital requirement for social interaction: It is a hallmark of humanness, associated with nobler sentiments such as sensitivity, compassion, altruism, generosity, friendship, and moral reasoning, all of which affect human interactions, from personal relationships to international cooperation. Because we can all agree about the benefits of empathy, it is surprising that agreeing on what precisely it is has been so difficult. In fact, academic attempts to define and describe empathy are so divergent that one scholar lamented that "the word empathy sometimes meant one thing, sometimes another, until now it does not mean anything" (Reik, 1948, p. 357). Eisenberg and Strayer (1987) concluded that "there is no correct definition of empathy, just different definitions" (p. 5). Ellison (2021) pointed out that in 2019 alone, more than 2,000 articles on empathy were published and that at least forty-three different definitions of the term have been identified, "ranging from basic shared emotions to more lofty mixtures of concern and kindness." It is no wonder that some have gone so far as to recommend we simply abandon the term (Decety & Cowell, 2014).

One point on which there is much agreement is that the emotions of perceiver and target need not be the same. Regan and Totten (1975) defined empathy as "reacting emotionally to cues transmitting the emotional experience of others" (p. 855). According to this view, both the stimulus and the reaction are of an emotional nature but the nature of the emotional reaction is unspecified. Later definitions have been consistent with this view. In their definition of empathy as "an emotional response that stems from another's emotional state or condition and that is congruent with the other's emotional state or situation" (p. 5), Eisenberg and Strayer (1987) added one detail regarding the nature of the reaction: It must be *congruent* with the target's. This suggests that the reaction need not be the precise emotional equivalent of the target's. For some, empathy is more generally "a vicarious sharing of affect" (Nichols et al., 1996, p. 59). Devine and Hughes (2013) noted that empathy "requires someone to generate an appropriate emotional response to another's mental state" (p. 989); presumably there could be more than one "appropriate" emotional response.

Many researchers of literary reception have also noted that emotional reactions are often central to the enjoyment of literature (e.g., Raney, 2006). Foremost among these reactions is empathy. Indeed, empathy is studied far more than other emotional reactions, both in more traditional literary investigations (Burke, 2006, 2011; Keen, 2007; Palencik, 2008) and in empirical work (van Peer, 1997; Oatley, 2002; Coplan, 2004; Oatley et al., 2006; Kotovych et al., 2011; Fong et al., 2013; Kidd & Castano, 2013; Koopman, 2015, 2016; Oatley, 2016). Nevertheless, in literary studies the understanding of this phenomenon is confounded by the same problems we have reviewed in psychological research: Discussions of empathy suffer from terminological and conceptual confusion about what is actually meant by the term.

In this section, we first review three main issues: the lack of precision regarding the relation of empathy to mind-reading theories (theory of mind, theory theory, and simulation), the blurred boundaries between empathy and related emotions such as sympathy, and the controversy regarding the role of cognition. We then explain how our theory of perspective taking resolves these issues. To foreshadow, our analysis is that emotions should be construed as types of evaluations; thus, finding analogous emotional evaluations in the service of understanding a target's mental state, or perspective, constitutes empathy. In effect, to empathize, one finds in one's personal experience emotional evaluations that are analogous to those of the target; based on this analogy, one develops a personal connection to the emotional experience of the target.

Empathy and Mind Reading

Mind reading in general has been described as a form of empathy (Goldman, 2006; Zaki, 2014). However, the relation of empathy to mind reading and perspective taking is fraught with controversy. For example, empathy has been conceived as either a requirement (Lamm et al., 2007), a mechanism (Decety & Jackson, 2006), a goal (Langkau, 2020), the causal trigger (Lamm et al., 2007), or the effect of perspective taking (Davis, 1980; Batson et al., 2002; Decety & Jackson, 2006). Others proposed revising mind-reading theories to accord a more prominent role to empathy. For example, Shanker (2009) argued that theory of mind is erroneously conceived as "an autonomous cognitive capacity, as opposed to being part of a more general ability for reflective thinking and empathy" (p. 697) and concluded that affect plays a pivotal role in the development of theory of mind. Along similar lines, de Waal et al. (2006, 2016) proposed that theory of mind is only part of a system whose core is "hard-wired empathy" and that empathy plays the most significant part. He added that empathy is more vital to survival than knowing what people are thinking. In philosophy of mind, empathy is often presented as a rival alternative to theory of mind (Bavidge & Ground, 2009). For others, theory of mind includes empathy (Black et al., 2021). With respect to the effect of mind reading and perspective taking, some dispute the claim that they lead to feelings of greater emotional proximity or sharing of a target's emotions (Buck, 1984). Given these conceptual inconsistencies, it is not surprising that many of the same problems we have reviewed in the sections on mind reading are also central to empathy research.

One of these is the question of whether empathy is learned or innate. As Black et al. (2021) explained, apart from some neuroatypical individuals, people have the "biological capacity" for empathy. However, having the capacity does not mean it will always be used. As we saw in the previous section, other researchers argue that mind reading and empathy are learned: The extent to which individuals understand others' emotional states is a function of their evolving, situated knowledge and experience, not some natural ability hardwired into us. For example, Buck (1984) argued that understanding others' feelings is to a large extent the product of cultural norms and consists of the "appropriate application" of culturally acquired skills (Sharrock & Coulter, 2009, p. 87). For example, the failure to learn that certain gestures in some cultures are signs of friendliness and encouragement and in others signal vulgar insults would obviously lead to a misinterpretation of the corresponding emotion.

As with other mind-reading theories, successful empathy is often conceptualized, controversially, in terms of accuracy. This seems to be implied by Goldman (1993b): He described empathy as a process in which a perceiver first imaginatively assumes a target's mental states, either through direct observation or indirect explanation, and then inputs those pretend states into their emotional response system (as opposed to the decision-making system) to produce genuine emotional outputs. Later accounts more explicitly equated empathy with successful mind reading: For example, it was defined as "one's ability to accurately infer the specific content of another person's covert thoughts and feelings" (Ickes & Simpson, 1997, p. 251). However, as we described earlier, accuracy cannot be the critical ingredient in the experience of empathy. Further, the absence of absolute standards by which to measure empathic performance makes accuracy difficult to assess. The perceiver's imagination of a target's mental state could be discrepant with the target's actual state of mind and therefore more of a naïve fiction than an accurate correspondence. For example, the ability to draw accurate inferences about another's thoughts and feelings depends on "the extent to which an observer can create a complex and fleshed-out representation of the other person" (Myers & Hodges, 2008, p. 282). However, creating a full representation requires adequate knowledge, which, as the authors add, is rarely available. Ickes (1993) identified other factors that can affect mental state inferences, such as the history of the perceiver's relationship to, and desired future relationship with, the target; presumably, friends have greater information about each other than strangers and may be more motivated to understand them. Thus, the representation must be constructed from available cues that are, even for the most motivated and attentive individuals, only an "incomplete and ambiguous guide at best" (Myers & Hodges, 2008, p. 281). The lack of empathic accuracy could be due to "imperfect strategies" that lead to incorrect inferences about a target's thoughts and feelings (p. 282).

Others have argued that empathic accuracy is not even necessary for the purposes of everyday interactions. Moment-by-moment, thought-by-thought inferencing accuracy about another person's mental state is not required to be socially successful and "good enough" accuracy suffices (Myers & Hodges, 2008). There are two reasons for this: First, perceivers generally do not verbalize their inferences, and therefore targets cannot be offended by inaccurate perceptions; second, if the inferences were not central to the immediate interaction, they would not really matter. With respect to literary response, it is not at all clear what it would mean to react with accurate empathy to characters' emotions. As we discuss further in Chapter 4, fictional characters have no independent existence beyond the mind of the reader, and there is no way to interrogate the character about what they are actually feeling (cf. Dixon & Bortolussi, 2001).

Some psychologists have argued that not only is empathic accuracy improbable, it can also be undesirable. For example, Batson (1995) demonstrated that when research participants felt empathy for individuals, they made decisions that were partial to those individuals, even if those decisions conflicted with their moral principles. The ability to accurately read minds can also be put to nefarious advantage, such as influencing, manipulating, or controlling the target's mind (Michlmayr, 2002) or lead to the adoption of a target's negative traits (Galinsky et al., 2008). Ickes and Simpson (1997) reviewed the empirical evidence on the injurious or damaging effect that empathic accuracy can have on close relationships and explained how it can "hurt relationships when perceivers arrive at insights about the target's thoughts and feelings that cause one or both partners to experience pain or distress, thereby shaking their confidence in the relationship" (p. 225). In other words, there are times when it is best to resist knowing what a target is thinking or feeling, a tendency they call "motivated inaccuracy" (p. 228). Similar comments have been made with respect to literary response (Carroll, 2001; Currie, 2020). Currie (2020) proposed that fiction arouses "non-empathic emotions and other states which independently contribute to ... good outcomes" (pp. 52–53). Also, there may be situations in which it is undesirable for readers to empathize with a character's negative traits.

Descriptions of empathy in literary studies are also commonly confounded with mind-reading concepts, notably theory of mind, simulation, and perspective taking. Kidd and Castano (2013) cast empathy in terms of theory of mind, distinguishing between "affective theory of mind" and "cognitive theory of mind," with the former linked to empathy (p. 377). For some, empathy is a form of mental simulation "whereby I try to put myself mentally in the place of another and imagine what he is perceiving or perceived from his time space location" (Hüln et al., 2009, p. 48). Dymond (1950) described perspective taking in terms reminiscent of the simulation transfer account, as "the imaginative transposing of oneself into the thinking, feeling, and acting of another" (p. 343). In contrast, Oatley's (1999) description is more in line with the transformation metaphor; he argued that we do not just sympathize, "we become that person" (p. 446). Langkau (2020) understood empathy in terms of perspective taking, that is, "taking over the target's perspective in order to feel with them" (p. 3). Furthermore, research in literary studies confounds empathy and perspective taking with two other ill-defined processes: identification and transportation (Bal & Veltkamp, 2013; Johnson et al., 2013). (The relation between perspective taking and these processes is discussed further in Chapter 4.) As we discuss later, thinking of empathy as a perspective-taking analogy with emotional evaluations eliminates the need for these other mentalizing terms.

The Empathy/Sympathy Distinction

Empathy is popularly contrasted with sympathy. Originally both were considered forms of "feeling with," and the notion of projection was initially attributed to both emotions. (In this case, the concept of projection was inspired by the term "einfühlung," coined by Vischer [1994] to describe the aesthetic experience of projecting oneself into an object of beauty.) Smith (1759) regarded sympathy as a moral feeling in which an observer imaginarily entered into another body. Empathy was considered the experience in which one identifies with someone "and then transfer[s] positive emotional attitudes" to that person (Thagard & Shelley, 2001, p. 346). Now, sympathy and empathy are considered distinct reactions. Empathy is typically understood as feeling *with* another person, as opposed to sympathy, which is described as a feeling *for* another person, such as feeling concern, pity, or sorrow for another person (Eisenberg, 1988; Currie, 2020). Feeling for another implies the maintenance of a sense of separation from the target (Decety & Jackson, 2004), while empathy is thought to be the vicarious experience of feeling what another person feels (Langkau, 2020). In this sense, empathy is in effect a form of merging. This view of empathy as a sharing of the same emotion implies an accurate reading of a target's emotional state of mind, which, as discussed earlier, is typically not feasible.

While this distinction between empathy and sympathy may seem superficially clear, upon further reflection it is quite murky. Some psychologists continue to use the terms indistinguishably. For example, Frick (2018) claimed that emotional or affective perspective taking "imply empathic thoughts and the ability to *feel for* someone else" (p. 2; italics in original), although "feeling for" is typically associated with sympathy. Similarly, Zillmann (2006) maintained that empathy entails a reaction to another's state, which can be for or with the target. The for/with distinction suggests that the emotions of perceiver and target are similar in the case of empathy (Eisenberg & Strayer, 1987). However, this idea has proven to be untenable. Instead, others, like Coplan (2004), have argued that the emotions need only be congruent. Indeed, it would be odd to claim that the emotions are always similar. For example, we do not personally go into mourning when we witness someone suffering the loss of a loved one; in this case, we may feel concern or pity for the person experiencing the loss.

Further complicating the sympathy/empathy distinction is that both can overlap or be confused with other emotions. Scheler (1954) distinguished empathy, which he regarded as the emotional intuition of another's feelings, from several related emotions: copathy, mimpathy, transpathy, and unipathy. Nevertheless, the term "empathy" continues to be associated with a host of different emotional experiences. For example, Preston and de Waal (2002) understood empathy to include "emotional contagion, sympathy, cognitive empathy, helping behavior, and so on," arguing that they all share "aspects of their underlying process and cannot be totally disentangled" (p. 4). From these conceptualizations we can conclude that empathy is not a specific emotion, but rather an emotional reaction to a target's emotional state of mind, and, presumably, the emotions experienced by a perceiver will vary with the context.

Developments in emotion research have highlighted the complexity of any given emotion. The basic-emotions theory suggests that there a few simple, easily identifiable and categorizable states that are governed by separate psychological systems (e.g., the "sad" system). However, this view is simplistic. In his novel *Swann's Way*, Proust (1922/2009) reflected on the complexity of emotions: "For what we suppose to be our love or our jealousy is never a single, continuous and indivisible passion. It is composed of an infinity of successive loves, or different jealousies, each of which is ephemeral, although by their uninterrupted multiplicity they give us the impression of continuity, the illusion of unity." Thus, emotions are not simple and homogenous but rather a complex interaction of several different, even contradictory feelings. Lending support to this literary master's assertion, cognitive psychologists Wondra and Ellsworth (2015) explained that any emotion is really "a variety of emotional experiences that shade into each other with no clear boundaries" (p. 417). This would suggest that emotion detection and attribution are not always simple, automatic, or accurate. On the basis of these insights, we can infer that empathy similarly is not a simple, homogenous, or specific emotion.

The same sympathy/empathy confusion is also found in literary studies. For some, the distinction is clear, and empathy entails "sharing the feelings of the character . . . not for the character" (Cohen, 2001, p. 256), but for others the distinction is less clear. In spite of the feeling for/with distinction, "empathy . . . is sometimes seen as one of the components of sympathy" (Caracciolo, 2013, p. 27). Bal and Veltkamp (2013) hypothesized that sympathizing with a character increases transportation, which is responsible for increased empathy. Johnson et al. (2013) referred to "affective empathy" as "an individual's ability to feel for another" (p. 306). There is now some recognition that the distinction is arbitrary because "these reactions are likely to co-occur" (Koopman, 2015, p. 3); one can at the same time share the same emotion as another person and pity that person. As we discuss later, we argue that empathy should be thought of as an emotional evaluation that is analogous to that of the target. This implies that the relation between the target's and the perceiver's emotions will vary with the nature of the analogy, and that the empathy/sympathy distinction is unneeded.

Empathy and Cognition

The contribution of cognition to empathy has been the subject of much debate. Empathy is sometimes reduced to a purely emotional experience in which the perceiver either shares the target's emotion (Eisenberg & Strayer, 1987) or reacts to it (Batson, 1991). Others have conceived of empathy in purely cognitive terms, as a discerning of the target's mental state, without an emotional component (Wispe, 1986). Generally, though, there seems to be widespread recognition that empathy involves both emotion and cognition. For example, in many cases empathy requires understanding, assessing, interpreting, or judging the target's circumstances (Hoffman, 1984; Davis, 1994; Nickerson, 1999; Currie & Ravenscroft, 2002; Goldman, 2006; Zillmann, 2006). Eisenberg et al. (1997) referred to the "cognitive component of empathy" as "the capacity to understand others' internal states" (p. 73). Similarly, Hoffman (1979) argued that empathy also depends on individual cognitive capacities. This combined emotional/cognitive line of reasoning stresses the importance of "understanding" and knowledge and has been widely accepted (see, for example, Currie, 2020; Coplan, 2004; Decety & Jackson, 2004; Zillmann, 2006; Lamm et al., 2007; Cakal et al., 2021). That a cognitive appraisal of a set of circumstances is necessary to experience emotion makes intuitive sense. An example will illustrate the point. If I see someone crying, I might be concerned about their plight; without further information, though, my concern is unlikely to be congruent with the emotions of the target. Further, if I know that the person has a history of melodramatic reactions that earned them the qualifier "crybaby," I might feel not pity or concern at all but rather annoyance. Thus, one's interpretation and reaction depend on situational and prior knowledge.

In some research, memories are a source of information that is used to assess a target's circumstances. For example, Hoffman's (1984) "direct-association" account of empathy explained that the perception of another's emotion triggers recollections of situations in which that emotion had been experienced. Eisenberg and Strayer (1987) challenged an account of empathy based on simulation, stressing that "people empathize not because they have put themselves cognitively in another's place, but because they have retrieved relevant information from their memories" (p. 9). Similarly, Nichols et al. (1996) modified the simulation account, arguing that "emotions are at least partially the product of beliefs or memories" in the sense that beliefs or memories serve as inputs that produce emotional states as outputs (p. 69). The authors further argued that empathy occurs "when the subject is reminded of events in her past similar to those of the object of empathy" (p. 61). In this sense, past memories serve as a type of information that affects one's inferences and responses. The example they provide is of a friend telling someone of the death of their dog: The listener empathizes upon remembering "analogous past experiences," which need not be conscious (p. 61). The recognition of the role of personal knowledge and experience stored in memory accords with our theory of perspective taking by analogy. We argue that drawing on analogical personal memories for the sake of understanding another's mental states is a comparable form of personal connection to the target. Indeed, we would regard this as perspective taking.

An important theoretical development incorporates empathy into an appraisal theory of emotion (Moors et al., 2013; Engen & Singer, 2013). In keeping with Smith's (1759) insight that feeling for others is linked to how we approve of their emotions, Wondra and Ellsworth (2015) defined emotion in general as "based on how we evaluate [the target's] situations" (p. 411). On this understanding, they argued that empathy occurs when "the observer appraises the target's situation the same way as the target" (p. 418). If the appraisals are different, they argue, there is no empathy: "if the observer appraises the target's situation differently, then a different emotional experience occurs" (p. 418). An example they provide to illustrate their point is that of a conference attendee seeing a colleague walk to the podium, unaware that their shoe is dragging a strand of toilet paper; the observer feels embarrassment, while the colleague does not. They conclude that what the observer experiences is not empathy but some other vicarious emotion. In this example, the emotions of observer and target are not congruent. As discussed later, we share this view that the cognitive evaluation of the circumstances is a critical component of empathy.

The role of cognition in emotion and empathy is also an issue in literary studies. Dodell-Feder and Tamir (2018) defined empathy in reading as "emotion sharing." However, van Krieken et al. (2017) understood that identifying a target's emotions involves a cognitive component and differentiated affective empathy from "cognitive empathy" defined as the "recognition of another person's mindset" (p. 10). Others also maintained this terminology. For example, Tal-Or and Cohen (2010) distinguished between "affective empathy," or feeling affinity toward a character, and "cognitive empathy," or "adopting the character's goals and point of view within the narrative" (p. 404). Others have explicitly stressed the crucial role of cognition (e.g., van Peer, 1997). Nussbaum (2001) argued that "emotions are appraisals or value judgments" regarding, for example, another person's "flourishing" (p. 4). This is not to deny that emotions can have a bodily component, but, as Nussbaum explained, this "does not give us reason to reduce their intentional/cognitive component to nonintentional bodily movements" (p. 25). Van Lissa et al. (2016) maintained that empathy "is a complex, multidimensional construct, which involves both affective, sympathetic responses to others' emotions and cognitive perspective taking" (p. 44). Along similar lines, Jumpertz and Tary (2020) cogently argued that "empathy presupposes knowledge about the agent a reader identifies with" (p. 122).

Empathy As Analogical Emotions

We argue that many of the issues in understanding empathy in life and literature are resolved by an analysis of empathy as emotional perspective taking by analogy. Our view of perspective taking is that it entails matching evaluations of the target to analogous (but not necessarily identical) evaluations in one's personal knowledge and experience. In the "cognitive appraisal" theory of emotion, emotion is a form of evaluation or reaction to something or some situation. Thus, appraisal theory maps emotions directly onto our account of perspective taking, and we will use the term "empathy" to refer to perspective-taking evaluations that involve emotions. For example, in order to feel empathy for a target, one would take the target's perspective by finding an analogous (not necessarily superficially similar) emotion from one's own life. Using a perspective-taking analogy (as described in Chapter 2), the evoking circumstances of that recalled emotion would be mapped onto those of the character. This provides a personal connection to the target's emotion, even if the analogous emotion is not identical. In other words, our analysis suggests that empathetic accuracy is not a critical concern; instead, we stress that it is the personal connection to one's own knowledge and experience that is important. This is consistent with arguments that empathy is triggered by similar relevant memories (Davis, 2006) and requires a perceiver to "have some past experience that is relevant to the target's state or situation" (Wondra & Ellsworth, 2015, p. 416).

This can be illustrated with an example from literature. In the concluding segment of *A Christmas Carol* (Dickens, 1843/1992), Scrooge feels joy from providing gifts to the needy Cratchits. In order to take Scrooge's perspective (and empathize with him), the reader would need to find a comparable emotional evaluation from an analogous experience. A reader might, for example, remember the joy from providing a highly appreciated gift to a friend or relative. Although the real-life and fictional circumstances of the joy emotion are clearly not identical (the reader is presumably not a miser, or rich, and the recipient not in dire straits), the reader may be able to see how they are analogous in certain respects. In particular, corresponding emotions that are identified in this way can vary in intensity or other features as long as readers can form the analogy. Therefore, empathy can be more precisely defined as emotional perspective taking, in which there is an analogical match between the emotional evaluation of the character and that of the reader, both justified by the circumstances and prior events. An advantage of this conceptualization is that it associates empathy with the mechanisms that underlie all mind-reading concepts; we argue that the fundamental processes in generating empathy are effectively the same as those involved in perspective taking in general.

Other scholars have lent theoretical support to this interpretation in the context of reading literature. Oatley (2002) maintained that "as we assimilate a story, our emotions are our own, not those of a character" (p. 43). He explained that "the vicissitudes that occur to the protagonist-agent tend to elicit emotions of a personal kind" (p. 40) and that emotions occur as readers "construct their own versions of the story," which includes "activation of emotional autobiographical memories that resonate with story themes" (p. 41). In stating that readers' emotional responses are connected to schemas (already formed systems of appraisal about objects), Palencik (2008) also suggested that fiction elicits emotion via recalled experience. Burke (2011) also believed that the main effect of literature is to constantly prime memories through its suggestiveness. To bolster his view, Burke cited Hogan (2003), who argued that "our emotional response to a work develops out of a particular set of primed memories" (p. 161) that "guide our realization or concretization of that work" (p. 150). (There is some debate, though, about the nature of the relation between emotion and memory. Hogan [2003] argued that readers' evoked memories trigger emotion, while Bower [1981] and Forgas [1992] suggested that emotions prime memories.) Similarly, remindings, in which segments of text prompt the retrieval of prior experiences, are often associated with emotional valence (cf. Larsen & Seilman, 1988; Gerace et al., 2015). When such retrieved emotions are congruent with those of the character, they may suggest a perspective-taking analogy.

Thinking of empathy as emotional perspective taking by analogy has another advantage: It can account for those situations in which the emotion of the reader does not correspond to that of the character. In particular, when one has successfully created an analogy between the story-world situation and an experience in one's own personal knowledge and experience, one may also have emotional reactions to that entire remembered situation, even if the corresponding emotion cannot be experienced by the character. These are not analogous emotional reactions but rather emotional reactions to the analogous experience. For example, Stephen Leacock's story "My Financial Career" (Leacock, 1910/1911) tells of a shy young man who goes to a bank to deposit a modest sum, and in his nervousness makes a string of mistakes that cause him immediate embarrassment and humiliation. On our analysis, the reader forms an analogy with a remembered experience in which they committed some comparable unintentional faux pas. Although the reader may not have felt any embarrassment at the time, believing the errors were without incident, they might have later come to feel embarrassed after further reflecting on their mistakes and how they might have been perceived. Forming the analogy thus may lead the reader to feel embarrassment for the character.

Suspense may be another example. Readers may feel suspense in reading a story because, in the context of taking the character's perspective, they have successfully mapped the circumstances of the story world onto their own experiences in memory. The remembered emotional reactions to the situation as a whole could constitute suspense. For example, if the remembered experience included a fearful outcome, fear might be experienced while reading in anticipation of the analogous outcome in the story world. Such emotions may be experienced despite the fact that the character, not knowing the future story events, cannot experience the corresponding emotions. This analysis also explains why suspense is experienced even on rereading when one knows how the events of the story world are resolved (cf. Gerrig, 1989; Gerrig, 1993; Yanal, 1996; Carroll, 2013). In fact, knowing the resolution may make it easier to find an analogical match in memory and easier to retrieve the emotion-evoking experience.

In sum, understanding another's emotions requires an element of effort, imagination, and inferencing. On our account, the basis of empathy in all its complexity is a perspective-taking analogy, as described in Chapter 2. To succeed in building this analogy, the observer must be able to retrieve from personal knowledge and experience an emotional evaluation that analogously corresponds to that of the target. However, the corresponding emotions need not be identical and could even be quite dissimilar; what is critical is that the observer makes the personal, analogical connection to the target. The variations in the nature of the analogy and the particular emotion that is retrieved account for the complexity of relationships that can unfold.

Neuroscience of Perspective Taking

A variety of different neural mechanisms have been hypothesized to underly some of the processes related to perspective taking. Here, we briefly review work relating particular regions of the brain to some of our hypothesized components of perspective taking. These are the mirror network and its implications for mind reading, prefrontal cortical regions related to analogical inferencing, the default network and its relation to simulation, and so-called empathy circuits. We then turn to how neuroscience has been applied to perspective taking in literature. A principal goal of much of this research has been the localization of function: Where in the brain does the work of perspective taking occur? Our general view is that although the evidence on localization is ultimately important, it is unlikely to be definitive given our current state of knowledge. As is clear from our description of perspective taking in Chapter 2, there is a range of different processes involved, including autobiographical memory retrieval, identification of similarity, and analogical inference. Each is potentially independent of the others and unlikely to be localized in the same neural structures. Further, any one component of perspective taking is likely to depend on brain networks that involve widely dispersed regions that work together, and any given brain region is likely to be involved in a variety of different functions. This complexity is especially important in the context of narrative comprehension since this involves many other processes – word and sentence processing, mental model updating, forward and backward inferencing – that likely interact with components of perspective taking. Thus, although this neuroscientific evidence contributes to our understanding of these processes, simple, general conclusions about localization of function are probably unwarranted at present.

Mirror Network

An important neural network that is often discussed in the context of perspective taking is the mirror network. Research on mirror neurons dates to the work of Gallese et al. (1996). They described neurons in the ventral premotor region of macaque brains that had an intriguing property: They were observed to fire both when the monkey performed a motor action and when it observed another monkey performing the same action. Thus, they are "mirror" neurons in the sense that they replicate what happens in another brain. Since this discovery, there has been a flurry of speculation, often unsupported by strong evidence, about their existence and role in humans. In particular, a mirror network has been claimed to underlie mind-reading functions (such as the interpretation of others' actions) and empathy.

To support such accounts, one would need evidence, to start, that mirror neurons exist in the human brain. For ethical reasons, scientists may not perform the Gallese et al. (1996) experiment with humans because it would require implanting electrodes in the brain. However, several lines of evidence suggest that humans have neural networks that function similarly. For example, Fadiga et al. (1995) found that the electrical signals enervating the hand muscles were increased when participants observed hand movements and were simultaneously given transcranial magnetic stimulation to the motor cortex; such increases were not observed with visually comparable stimuli. Rizzolatti and Arbib (1998) argued that Broca's area in the frontal lobe is homologous to the monkey brain region in which mirror neurons were found and that this neural structure is used both for the perception and production of speech. Based on a meta-analysis of brain imaging data, Grezes and Decety (2001) found overlap in activation between action observation, execution, and simulation in four areas: the supplementary motor area, the dorsal premotor cortex, the supramarginal gyrus, and the superior parietal lobe. Related regions also seem to be involved in the simulation of action from different perspectives (Ruby & Decety, 2001). Such patterns of activation provide at least circumstantial evidence that a mirror network in the human brain functions akin to the mirror neurons in the monkey.

Crucially, there are several lines of evidence that the link between perception and action in a mirror network depends on an appropriate *interpretation* of the perceived action. For example, Umiltà et al. (2008) found that it was the distal goal of the action that mattered. In their study, a monkey grasped an object with two types of spring-loaded pliers: In normal pliers, squeezing the handle caused the mouth of the pliers to close; in reverse pliers, relaxing the grip caused the mouth to close. They found that the operation of the pliers was critical: A temporal pattern of activation was found in the mirror neurons associated with the hand closing even though the observed hand (with reversed pliers) was opening. In other words, the neurons responded to the pliers closing, not the hand closing. Further, the action has to be analogous to an action that the observer has performed: In an imaging experiment, Buccino et al. (2004) showed that activation in the network occurred when observing a person, monkey, or dog biting, but not when observing the dog barking. A potentially related finding was reported by Jellema et al. (2000): They found neurons in the superior temporal sulcus of the rhesus macaque that only responded to limb movements directed toward an object of attention. The implication may be that these cells are part of a network for understanding the action goals. Thus, mirror neurons do not seem to be implicated in a superficial form of imitation. These findings underscore the importance of understanding and interpretation in the functioning of mirror neurons.

The organization of the mirror network is likely to be complex. For example, van Overwalle and Baetens (2009) distinguished the mirror system proper (consisting of the anterior intraparietal sulcus and the premotor cortex) from a related mentalizing system (consisting of the temporoparietal junction, the medial prefrontal cortex, and the precuneus). The mentalizing system seems to be related to inferences concerning goals and beliefs. Chiavarino et al. (2012) proposed that the mentalizing system was important for understanding intentions. They argued that the mentalizing system itself consists of two subsystems: one that allows for the representation of mental states and one that employs abstract reasoning about intentions and their relation to other mental states. The representation subsystem seems to provide the basis of theory of mind (defined as the ability to understand that others have psychological states). (However, as we noted previously, that simple knowledge is insufficient for inferring what those mental states are.)

From the present theoretical perspective, we find it interesting that the functioning of mirror neurons, even in the original research with monkeys, requires a form of analogy: The observed hand is analogous to one's own hand, and the observer can presumably infer that moving one's own hand might achieve corresponding goals. The focus on the existence of mirror neurons tends to neglect the process of inference that allows such analogical correspondences to be identified. An important question is thus whether the putative mirror neuron network in humans is involved in the ability to form the more complex and abstract analogies that we argue are the basis of perspective taking.

Default Network

The default network refers to a set of brain regions that seem to be involved in imagining, future planning, autobiographical memory, and other functions. It was famously discovered as those regions that were active during "rest" periods in brain imaging studies – hence the term "default" network (Raichle et al., 2001). The brain regions involved in the default network are widely dispersed but are commonly taken to include the ventromedial prefrontal cortex, posterior cingulate cortex, retrosplenial cortex, inferior parietal lobule, lateral temporal lobes, and dorsal medial prefrontal cortex (Buckneret et al., 2008). It is likely that these regions and networks are involved in a range of different functions, and that the relative importance of the different components varies depending on the situation. However, an important idea for present purposes is that components of the default network are central to autobiographical memory and consequently crucial for the construction of the perspective-taking analogy.

According to Peters and Sheldon (2021), the network is used to retrieve and combine memories in order to simulate events. "Simulation" in this context involves developing a mental representation of a scenario by combining information about similar or related events stored in memory. Such simulated events might be part of retrieved previous experiences or might be involved in future thinking. (This use of personal knowledge and experience to engage in simulation is similar to our proposal of simulation by analogy that we describe more fully in Chapter 5.) Schacter and Addis (2007) described this as the "constructive episodic simulation hypothesis." The concept of episodic simulation is based on the notion that memory retrieval always involves reconstruction; they hypothesized that the same reconstruction mechanism is also used for future and imagined events. Gurguryan and Sheldon (2019) referred to the relevant portions of the default network as a core autobiographical memory area (see also Schacter et al., 2012). These ideas appear to be consistent with our view that elaboration of the story world is mediated by the analogical mapping of the readers' personal knowledge and experience onto the characters; importantly, we argue that the use of personal memory in this fashion is not limited to simple similarity. Consistent with this interpretation, the default network was found to be active when participants were told to imagine the perspective of another person (Buckner & Carroll, 2007).

Prefrontal Cortex

As discussed in Chapter 2, on our account, analogical inferencing is a central part of perspective taking. Several studies on this form of reasoning suggest that regions in the prefrontal cortex (and especially the left prefrontal cortex) may be critical. Examining patient populations, Waltz et al. (1999) found that the prefrontal cortex was critical for solving relational problems such as analogy. In an imaging study, Wharton et al. (2000) found that this region was preferentially activated when participants identified matches based on analogy rather than simple similarity. Thus, the left prefrontal cortex is likely to be more important in situations (such as literature) in which perspective taking entails identifying relatively abstract relationships. Further evidence for the functional importance of the left prefrontal cortex in analogy was found by Boroojerdi et al. (2001): When activation in this region was enhanced using repetitive transcranial magnetic stimulation, the response time to make the analogical matches was faster compared to a sham stimulation condition. Krawczyk (2017) concluded that although the left prefrontal cortex may be critical in analogical reasoning, other regions of the brain must also be involved, including those related to the retrieval of prior knowledge and working memory.

Empathy Circuits

Neuroimaging has also been employed to gain a clearer understanding of empathy. A key approach is the perception-action model of empathy (Preston & de Waal, 2002). Much like the mirror network discussed earlier, it is found that perception of a target's emotion activates the same neural network involved in the direct experience of that emotion (e.g., Dimberg & Thunberg, 1998). In particular, the model posits that an observer, upon perceiving a target's emotion, automatically generates a representation of the emotion, situation, and target, and this in turn "generates the associated *autonomic* and *somatic responses, unless inhibited*" (Preston & de Waal, 2002, p. 4; italics in the original). However, others have demonstrated that the observation of pain or distress in another person may or may not lead to empathic concern, and that an observer's response can depend on the motivation and information. For example, Lamm et al. (2007) found that the neural response was a function of whether one intended to take the target's perspective and the context of the target's reaction.

Singer (2006) described several studies examining the empathetic response to pain. For example, Singer et al. (2004) imaged the neural response of romantic partners when one partner received a painful stimulus and the other was merely informed that their partner received the stimulus. While some brain regions were activated specifically by the experience of pain, others were activated by either that experience or an indication that their partner experienced pain. Singer (2006) described these regions – the bilateral anterior insula and the anterior cingulate cortex – as an empathy circuit. Critically, the activation of the putative empathy circuits depended on the degree of empathetic concern for the target. For example, Singer et al. (2006) asked participants to observe still photos of people experiencing pain, and the activation in the empathy circuit was higher when the person in pain was liked by the participant. Although these studies provide a starting point for understanding emotional perspective taking, it is not clear how these affective responses are related to perspective taking more broadly. For example, would the empathetic experience of different emotions or evaluations operate similarly but involve different brain regions? More generally, we conjecture that the empathic connection between the observer and the target that mediates the experienced empathy depends on forming a perspective-taking analogy.

Neuroscience and Literary Studies

Apart from the neuroscience evidence in support of perspective taking in real life, researchers have also identified brain mechanisms that are specifically related to the processing of perspective while reading literature. In particular, we describe in the following subsections neural mechanisms related to "embodied" cognition in processing narratives and to the concept of mental exercise in perspective taking.

Embodied Cognition during Reading

Embodied cognition is the view that cognitive processing generally involves the retrieval and manipulation of sensorimotor information and that purely abstract mental representations are rare (e. g., Barsalou, 2008). Support for the importance of embodied cognition for processing literature comes from studies demonstrating that reading activates neural areas of the brain that overlap with those that are involved in performance and perception. For example, reading action words was found to activate the parts of the sensorimotor cortex involved in the performance of the corresponding action (Pulvermüller et al., 2005). The timing of the activation suggested that activation spread from language areas to the corresponding sensorimotor areas, consistent with the view that the motor activation was part of understanding the meaning of the words. Speer et al. (2009) similarly found that reading about actions activates the same areas of the brain as performing those actions. It is useful to note that the functions attributed to embodied cognition have something in common with the functions attributed to the mirror network described earlier: In both cases, a representation of an action on the part of the observer or reader is generated by the visual or textual depiction of that action by another.

However, patterns of activation indicative of embodied cognition are not always seen: For example, Tomasino et al. (2008) found effects of transcranial magnetic stimulation over the motor cortex only when readers were asked explicitly to "imagine yourself performing the action" (p. 1918) but not when performing silent reading. Similarly, Miller et al. (2018), when examining event-related potentials, found no limb-specific activation in response to the presentation of action words. One possible interpretation is that coactivation of related sensorimotor areas only occurs when the task or situation prompts the reader to deliberately use motor or sensory imagery; it may not occur automatically or obligatorily. Further, the spontaneous use of embodied representations while reading is likely to vary across individuals and texts. Evidence for this type of variation was found by Nijhof and Willems (2015). They examined activation in brain motor regions and mentalizing regions. Across individuals, activation in the anterior medial prefrontal cortex for mentalizing content was negatively correlated with motor activation for action content, suggesting that different processes were engaged depending on the text and the individual.

We conjecture that embodied cognition or imagery during reading is related to perspective taking because such representations are derived from perceptual experiences stored in autobiographical memory. In order to use this personal experience, an analogy has to be constructed between the reader's experience and the situation described in the text. For example, when the phrase "bare trees in winter" is mentioned in the text, the reader may draw on personal memories of bare trees. However, these would have to be adapted analogically to apply to circumstances described in the text by adding situational context, scaling the number and size of the trees, and so on. Presumably, this involves episodic reconstruction and analogical simulation, as mentioned earlier in our discussion of the default network and in Chapter 5. Given the appropriate textual cues, such perceptual analogies could form the basis of a more expansive analogy incorporating evaluations that we theorize lead to perspective taking.

Literature As Mental Exercise
Several authors have suggested that reading literature exercises the mental capacities related to social cognition and interpersonal interaction (e.g., Mar et al., 2006; Kidd & Castano, 2013, 2016; Pino & Mazza, 2016; Tamir et al., 2016; Willems & Hartung, 2017; Dodell-Feder & Tamir, 2018; Mar, 2018a, 2018b). Mar (2004) suggested that there may be a neural substrate for this transfer from literature to real life. For example, Mar (2011) examined sixty-three functional magnetic resonance imaging (fMRI) images and found overlaps between brain networks used to understand stories and those used to navigate interactions with others. To bolster the argument that improvement in one affects performance in the other, Berns et al. (2013) observed participants while they read a portion of a novel on nine consecutive days; they detected increased connectivity in parts of the brain associated with perspective taking and story comprehension, notably the left angular/supramarginal gyri and right posterior temporal gyri. This research would appear to offer support for the hypothesis that reading fiction may exercise the neural networks involved in perspective taking. In particular, the repeated engagement of cognitive processes involved in reading may lead to changes in neural networks that support those cognitive processes.

A similar hypothesis was investigated by Tamir et al. (2016). Participants in their study read a series of literary and non-literary passages while undergoing brain imaging; the passages varied in whether they described physical scenes vividly or described a person's mental content. They found that different parts of the default network were recruited during the reading of either vivid descriptions or mental content passages. They argued that "perhaps literary fiction improves social cognition to the extent that it requires readers to mentally construct social contexts" and that "such high-quality practice in simulation – or the capacity to experience realities outside of the 'here-and-now,' including hypothetical events, distant worlds, and other people's subjective experience – then translates into real-world consequences for readers' social cognition" (p. 216).

However, there are several reasons to suspect that exercising particular neural brain areas through reading is insufficient to achieve effects that carry over into real life. First, as we have seen, neural mechanisms in perspective taking are diverse and are commonly used in the service of a wide range of other tasks and situations. It would be surprising if spending a relatively small portion of one's life reading literature would provide significant improvement in such commonly used mechanisms. Second, how we infer mental states depends on a variety of personal and contextual factors: the amount of information available, the motivation to inhibit egocentric biases, the ease of retrieving personal knowledge and experience, and so on. It seems unlikely to us that more effective processing in specific regions of the brain would improve all of the personal cognitive abilities required for the perspective-taking task. Finally, fiction, as an intentional object, may provide more inference-constraining cues than does real life. This might mean that repeated reading might simply increase story comprehension proficiency without translating into increased life proficiency.

Summary and Conclusions

In this chapter, we have sketched some of the issues and evidence on perspective taking in life. We have attempted to clarify the relationship between several related terms: mind reading, theory of mind, theory theory, perspective taking, and empathy. We use "mind reading" as an umbrella term to refer to the inferences that individuals draw about other people's states of mind. Theory theory and simulation are two accounts of how mind reading can occur: To draw inferences about a target's mind, a perceiver can resort to either a commonly held folk "theory" about human behavior or use an offline simulation to imagine a target's state of mind. As we describe, both of these processes depend in part on different forms of analogical reasoning.

We followed this discussion of mind reading with an analysis of empathy and its relationship to perspective taking. This included a discussion of the relationship between empathy and sympathy. Although these concepts are sometimes distinguished as "feeling with" versus "feeling for," there remains a great deal of ambiguity about the distinction in particular cases. In this context, we described the "appraisal theory" of emotion in which emotions arise from a cognitive appraisal of one's own or a target's circumstances. Based on this idea, we propose that empathy consists of perspective taking by analogy in which the analogically corresponding evaluations consist of emotions.

Finally, we described the evidence on neural localization of processes related to perspective taking: the mirror network for mind reading, the default network for the use of autobiographical memories, the prefrontal cortex for analogical inferencing, and empathy circuits. Although it is useful to analyze how these processes are supported by neural mechanisms, our belief is that this evidence does not as yet provide strong constraints on our understanding of perspective taking.

CHAPTER 4

Perspective Taking and Literature

In the current chapter, we apply the insights garnered so far to the problem of taking the perspective of literary characters and narrating agents. In Chapter 2, we defined perspective taking in terms of evaluations, established what perspective taking is not, and developed a new account of the processes involved. In Chapter 3, we argued that mind-reading theories, which all imply perspective taking, depend on some form of analogical reasoning. Based on these insights, on our analysis, perspective taking should be understood as the construction of an analogy between one's own personal knowledge and experience and that of the perspective-taking target. In particular, readers establish an analogical connection between, on one hand, characters' evaluations of elements of their world and the reasons for those justifications and, on the other, their own analogous evaluations and justifications.

Constructing that analogy is far from simple. As discussed in Chapter 3, real-life perspective taking is effortful and constrained by a variety of personal and contextual challenges, and many of those challenges also apply to taking the perspective of a character in literature. In addition, literary perspective taking is limited by the ontological status of the character. Characters are imaginary, incomplete, and inconclusive creations with no real, preexisting autonomous mind to read or referent against which to measure one's "reading" or mental state ascriptions. An accurate understanding of characters' psychological states is only possible when those states are explicitly attributed or made unambiguously inferable in the text. Further, literary characters are often very different from the reader in terms of personality traits, life experiences, and even beliefs and attitudes. We argue that overcoming these difficulties entails the use of one's own personal knowledge in the construction of an analogical connection that makes the character more like the reader. An important question is how this elaborative, analogical, constructive process is prompted by the features of the text. The bulk of this chapter is devoted to this issue.

We begin with a discussion of two reading processes that are often connected to perspective taking in discussions of the processing of literary works: identification and transportation. In this discussion, we examine how they are related to our own view of perspective taking. Following this, we consider the role of textual features in guiding that process. We distinguish two types of features: First-order features are properties of the text that allow one to identify perspectives in the text and properties that have traditionally been assumed to lead directly to the reader taking the perspective of a character or narrator. Second-order features are indirectly related to perspective taking because they stimulate the elaborative processes that form the basis of an analogical connection between the reader and the text. After this discussion of textual features, we turn to the role of the narrator in perspective taking. Finally, the last topic in this chapter concerns the relations between the reader and the character that may motivate perspective taking.

Processes Related to Perspective Taking

We argue that perspective taking is a fundamental process in reading and appreciating literature, and is closely related to two other concepts that are commonly evoked in discussions of literary reader response: identification and transportation. The nature of that relationship has been disputed. For example, perspective taking has sometimes been described as the same as or part of identification (Hoffner, 1996; de Graaf et al., 2012); transportation has been hypothesized to be a mediating factor for perspective taking, although empirical results are inconclusive (Johnson, 2012; Bal & Veltkamp, 2013; Calarco et al., 2017). On our analysis, the elaborative, analogical inferencing at the heart of perspective taking is central to understanding these other processes. In particular, successful perspective taking, in our analogical model, produces the phenomenal sense of similarity that is symptomatic of identification, and the extensive elaborative processing needed to construct a perspective-taking analogy is a form of transportation.

Identification

Harding (1961) cogently argued that "identification" is an umbrella term that can refer to several very diverse experiences and processes. These could include fondness or admiration, emulation in the form of imitation, perspective sharing, and similarity recognition. He concluded that "the great difficulty about the term is to know which one of several different processes it refers to" (p. 141). Harding questioned whether the term is really applicable to all of these reactions and concluded that because readers' responses can encompass all of them and more, "no good purpose is served by blanketing them all with a term like 'identification'" (p. 142). The solution he offered was that we simply name the different processes for what they are: "empathy, imitation, admiration, or recognition of similarities" (p. 141). (We saw in the previous chapter that empathy is also an elusive concept.) Cohen (2001) echoed this view, adding that identification is often confused with other concepts, "such as parasocial relationships and fandom" (p. 249).

In many theories of identification in literary and empirical studies of literary response, the relationship between identification and perspective taking remains blurry. Is one the cause, consequence, or integral part of the other? For example, Ryskin et al. (2015) regarded perspective taking as a consequence of identification. To others, the terms appear to be synonymous. For example, Hoffner (1996) defined identification as a viewer's sharing of a character's perspective, and de Graaf et al. (2012) defined it as "an experience in which readers adopt the perspective of a character and see the narrative events through the character's eyes" (p. 804). In other cases, identification, perspective taking, and emotion are equated. For example, Busselle and Bilandzic (2009) noted that "identification is purported to be the adopting of the perspective and emotions of a character" (p. 338). Oatley (2002) stated that "identification and empathy are the same process" (p. 66). Salem et al. (2017) regarded identification as a measure of perspective taking. Tal-Or and Cohen (2010) linked identification to "a unity of perspective between character and viewer" (p. 413). Others detected a difference: For example, van Krieken et al. (2017) distinguished between cognitive, moral, and emotional identification. Cognitive identification is the *adoption* of another person's mindset, which they said consists of a "character's thoughts, expectations, aims, intentions, etcetera" (p. 10). Moral identification is the term they reserved for "a character's evaluations, attributions, memories, and desires" (p. 11). They argue that emotional identification is a form of emotional perspective taking referring to the adoption of another's feelings or feeling the same emotion as the character.

The language used in literary studies accounts of identification is reminiscent of the vague transformation or merging metaphor in simulation theories: becoming one with a character, adopting or taking on their goals and perspectives as if one were the character, or sharing the existence of the character. Freudian scholars such as Wollheim (1974) conceived of identification as the act of imagining oneself to be someone else, that is, imagining how another behaves and thinks. More recent scholarship echoes this idea. Oatley (1999) maintained that identification occurs when "we become that person" (p. 446); this entails that "the reader takes on the protagonist's goals and plans" (p. 445). Cohen (2001) described identification as the process that entails "imagining being the character" (p. 253). According to Spence and Efendov (2001), "In essence, to identify with a character means seeing the character's perspective as one's own, to share his or her existence" (p. 310). Writing about film reception, Tal-Or and Cohen (2010) maintained that viewers of films identify with characters and that this attachment entails the "experience of shifting identities" (p. 403) that leads viewers to adopt the characters' "goals and perspective on the narrated events" (p. 406). For Tal-Or and Cohen, identification is "based on a shared perspective between viewers and characters" (p. 407). Cohen (2001) associated identification with the experience of presence or the sense of being inside the story world. In his words, identification is "a mechanism through which audience members experience reception and interpretation of the text from the inside, as if the events were happening to them" (p. 245). He specified that identification "leads to imagining being the character ... as if he or she were inside the text" (p. 253). Interestingly, for Cohen, the merging of reader and character precludes judgments toward the character; he added that identification "does not foster any judgements that require treating a character as external to the self" (p. 254). As discussed in the previous chapter, though, the concept of identity merging is more effective as a metaphor than as a description of how readers really process other minds: A total merging of self and fictional other is in itself a fiction. Indeed, an experiment conducted by Salem et al. (2017) on the effects of four different perspectival techniques on the reader's perspective led to the conclusion that "absolute perspectivization," understood as "a complete shift of the perspective of the reader to that of the protagonist ... is not to be expected" (p. 16). (See also Radford, 1975; Walton, 1987, 1997; Nussbaum, 2001, for related arguments about the limitations of "merging" in identification.)

As an alternative to the merging metaphor, others regard identification as the transfer of attitudes about oneself to others (Thagard & Shelley, 2001). This is reminiscent of the simulation theorists' transfer process as discussed in Chapter 3 (e.g., Goldman, 1995; Stone & Davies, 1996; Davis et al., 1996; Carroll, 2001). However, as discussed in the previous chapter, both the transformation and transfer explanations still leave unanswered questions, such as what aspect of the stimulus triggers the transfer, what aspects of the self are transferred, and what mechanism enables it.

We believe that our framework provides a simple solution to the confusion that arises from navigating this labyrinth of conflicting conceptualizations. We concur with these researchers that there is a strong connection between the sense of a perceived alignment with the character, which is at the heart of identification accounts, and perspective taking. In particular, our account of perspective taking by analogy explains how this occurs. As we described in Chapter 2, a perspective is based on an evaluation of something or someone, and perspective taking entails finding analogically related evaluations from one's own experience. In our treatment, then, identification is the recognition of this connection between the reader and the character. When readers successfully construct a perspective-taking analogy, they have identified a relationship between some of their own experiences and those of the character, and they have identified how the character's evaluations are analogous to their own. Further, inferences may be used to fill out aspects of the character's experiences not described in the text based on their own experiences. As a result, reader and character overlap (rather than merge) in some respects, and the character becomes in effect more like (or more analogous to) the reader. Thus, in our analysis, the process of constructing the perspective-taking analogy produces the phenomenal similarity between the reader and the character that is commonly labeled "identification." Our focus on the process of analogical construction avoids the reduction of identification to general perception of superficial similarity.

An apt term that accords with our description of the analogical process is "personalization." Miller et al. (1993) used the term to refer to children's inclusion of personal memories in their retelling of a Peter Rabbit story. A similar effect with adult participants was found by Axelrad (1993): Parts of evoked personal memories were incorporated into the retelling of a James Joyce story. Axelrad argued that the retrieval of personal memories triggered by literary fiction led to greater engagement with the story, an important part of which is the appropriation of a work into one's autobiographical concerns. This accords with our idea that constructing a perspective-taking analogy involves the use of personal knowledge and experience and that this makes the reader and the character more alike. Previous accounts of identification imply the sharing of evaluations between reader and character; our model builds on this insight and incorporates it as a central processing component of perspective taking.

Descriptions of identification often imply homogeneity: the sense that identification is a fixed end product or a mental state that is attained. Stating that readers take on a character's mindset – goals, perspective, feelings – suggests that perspective is reducible to a coherent, homogenous, and unified worldview, general evaluation, ideology, or predominant emotion. However, complex literary characters are not reducible to a homogenous perspective. Further, the concept of homogeneity fails to capture the dynamic nature of the search for analogical correspondences between a character and a reader that, according to our analysis, enables perspective taking to occur. More plausible is a mode of processing that involves weaving in and out of rapprochement and distance, with the constant (re)evaluation, judgment, assessment, and interpretation that such a dynamic response entails. This is in line with Cohen's view that identification is "temporary and fleeting" and that therefore "it should be measured both in terms of intensity and frequency" (Cohen, 2001, p. 256).

For example, in Benito Perez Galdos's famous realist novel, *Doña Perfecta* (1876/1923), the idealist, liberal-minded protagonist, Pepe Rey, moves to an ultra-conservative town where he clashes with political leaders of the town's religious and political elite. Although he espouses a conscious, coherent ideology, he is nonetheless plagued by existential doubts, confusion, and questionable evaluations, and experiences a gamut of conflicting thoughts and emotions. A character's coherent ideology is no shield against other kinds of cognitive evaluations or against conflicting emotions or morals. Therefore, to say that a reader simply identifies with a character and thus adopts that character's perspective is simplistic.

Transportation

The term "transportation" is a metaphor intended to describe a reading experience in which a reader is immersed in the story world (Gerrig, 1993). Other terms, such as "engagement," "absorption," and "presence," are also used to refer to the ability of a reader to imaginatively experience the events of the story world, again metaphorically, from within it. Comparing children's and adults' role play, Harris (2000) claimed that once readers are absorbed in a narrative, they "begin to share the same spatial and temporal framework as the protagonist" (p. 49), although the research he cited was really only limited to physical perspective taking. As a metaphor, the term conjures up the stereotypical image, pictures of which abound on the internet, of a reader ensconced in a comfy chair, raptly engrossed in reading. This image captures some of the connotations of this prototypical experience: total attention to the story world, obliviousness to the surrounding circumstances, and rich visual imaging. For example, Green and Brock (2000) defined transportation "as an integrative melding of attention, imagery and feelings, focused on story events" (p. 701) in which readers lose their sense of time and place.

Green et al. (2004) posited that certain effects ensue from this intense engagement, such as the adoption of story-consistent beliefs, the positive evaluation of characters, and the evocation of feelings such as sympathy and empathy. Defined as this constellation of effects, transportation is typically associated with identification. However, the precise relationship between identification and transportation is unclear (Busselle & Bilandzic, 2009; Tal-Or & Cohen, 2010). Cohen (2001) saw absorption, or the "degree to which self-awareness is lost during exposure to the text," as one aspect of identification (p. 256), although later he was able to demonstrate that identification and story-world presence are separate experiences (Tal-Or & Cohen, 2010). Green and Brock (2000) argued that transportation also leads to a relative lack of "cognitive elaboration" in which readers might logically scrutinize the substance of claims as they might for a persuasive text (cf. Petty & Cacioppo, 1986). However, this process is different from the elaboration of the situation model that often happens during normal comprehension and which we argue (in the section "Second-Order Textual Features") is closely tied to perspective taking.

Both transportation and identification are assumed to produce psychological perspective taking (understood in the research in the imprecise, popular understanding of the term reviewed in the first chapter) and are assumed to naturally occur when readers are transported (Busselle & Bilandzic, 2009, p. 323). Presumably, it is by virtue of this imaginative transportation into, and absorption with, the fictional world that leads readers to identify with characters, see the world from the character's perspective, and feel empathy for that character (Bal & Veltkamp, 2013; Calarco et al., 2017). Mar and Oatley (2008) speculated that "we have to project ourselves into a story world in order to understand what the characters are thinking and feeling" (p. 178), and that through this projection "a reader essentially enters another mind" and "generally identifies with a protagonist" (p. 182). This view is reminiscent of the identity-merging theories reviewed earlier in this chapter. This ability to experience the story world from within has been said to constitute "cognitive perspective taking."

Elsewhere, we concluded that the transportation metaphor is "insufficiently precise to serve as a basis for theoretical advances" (Bortolussi &

Dixon, 2015, pp. 525–526). Instead, we argued that the critical feature of transportation is deep, elaborative processing of the text and that this processing produces the phenomenal sense of absorption. Consistent with this analysis, Tal-Or and Cohen (2010) maintained that involvement, which arguably is a form of transportation, "is the degree to which we invest emotional and mental efforts in decoding the text and making sense of the story" (p. 214). Schooler et al. (2004) also included the appreciation of language as one element of absorption. Busselle and Bilandzic (2009) argued that involvement is a function of the degree of effort invested in deciphering the sense of the story. Effort is also dependent on the individual variable of motivation, which in turn is related to interest. None of these inferential processes are captured by the metaphor of transportation. Busselle and Bilandzic acknowledged that readers apply general knowledge and experience in their reading; this accords with our description of perspective taking as the evocation of personal knowledge and experience in the service of understanding a character's evaluations. Along similar lines, Barnes (2018) argues that the assessment of transportation does not reduce to immersion per se, but rather "the extent to which a reader contributes imaginatively and creatively to a text by filling in gaps, puzzling over interpretations, fleshing out what is written, or otherwise imputing meaning onto the page that extends beyond what is written" (p. 127). On our view, this elaborative representation of the story world provides a basis of perspective taking based on analogical inferencing.

Our view is that this extensive processing is an essential ingredient in perspective taking since the elaboration is likely built upon the personal experience of the reader. (Indeed, the transportation metaphor suggests this type of personal connection to the story world.) In turn, this personal elaboration provides a fertile foundation for building a perspective-taking analogy: Building a representation of the story world using components of personal experience should make it straightforward to find analogical connections between that representation and the reader's personal experience. This implies that perspective taking and transportation could be closely related. In particular, the elaboration that is necessary for perspective taking could be demanding in the sense of involving extensive processing resources. The relationship could also be reciprocal: A successful perspective-taking analogy could lead to further inferences involving personal knowledge and experience, producing further elaboration and engagement.

An important empirical question not addressed in the transportation research is whether a reader who does not take a particular perspective can still feel transported and experience immersion or active engagement with the narrative. What happens, for example, when textual perspective is ambiguous, or transitory and dynamic, or inconsistent? We propose that the effort that readers make in following and parsing cues and upgrading their mental model of the story as new cues arise can be a sufficient basis for absorption, but that this absorption does not necessarily result in perspective taking. Evidence for this claim was obtained in a previous study (Bortolussi et al., 2018). The story used for that experiment was "Seventeen Syllables" (Yamamoto, 1994). Narrated in the third person by an external narrator, the story emphasizes the perspective of the focal character, a young girl who does not fully understand or appreciate her mother's dedication to writing haikus, and the story encourages the taking of the girl's perspective through its use of mental access. One of the manipulations of Bortolussi et al. was the use of interpolated evaluations, in which readers were periodically interrupted during reading and asked to evaluate aspects of the story world from the character's perspective. One might expect that these interpolated evaluations would enhance engagement with the story world because they would have to process the story world more deeply. In particular, the manipulation could foster perspective taking because it would require readers to identify and assess the character's perspective. However, the opposite result was found: Perspective taking was reduced with interpolated evaluations. Bortolussi et al. argued that this result was due to the use of ironic narratorial distance in the story. At the end of the story, the reader is made aware of the mother's perspective, leading to an increase in narratorial distance with respect to the girl and a decrease in distance with respect to the mother but without entirely abandoning the girl's point of view. It was argued that the enhanced immersive experience prompted by the interpolated evaluations made this perspectival shift more salient. The result of this ambiguous narratorial stance was to reduce readers' sense of how reasonable and understandable the main character was.

In sum, in our view, the process of elaboration provides a key to understanding the relationship between engagement and perspective taking. On the one hand, the more elaboration, the better and more personal a reader's understanding of the story world and the more likely the story is to be engaging. On the other hand, a greater degree of elaboration based on personal knowledge and experience makes it easier to construct a perspective-taking analogy (as we discuss in the section "Second-Order Textual Features").

First-Order Textual Features

We use the term "first-order" textual features to refer to identifiable aspects of the text directly related to perspectives and perspective taking. This includes textual attributes that allow the reader simply to identify evaluations and perspectives in the text as well as stylistic features that have traditionally been associated with perspective taking. After a discussion of these features, we turn to the relation between physical and psychological perspective.

Cues for Character Evaluations

There is a sense in which finding evaluations and perspectives in a text corresponds to the problem of mind reading in real life. In both cases, one uses objective information (either in the social environment or in the text) to make inferences about a target's state of mind. However, one can argue that because literature is an intentional object, reading the mind of a character may be easier than dealing with real people. Authors of fiction write to be read and understood and, presumably, craft their work to produce particular effects. Therefore, it would seem logical to expect that narrators provide the information and textual cues we need to "get the point" about their characters. Indeed, many literary theorists have maintained precisely that there is something about the way a fictional story is told that enables the reader to successfully identify and take a perspective in a way that is not typical in real life. For example, Chatman (1978) claimed that the author figure "instructs us silently through the design of the text" (p. 148). Riffaterre (1981) believed that literature commands the reader to take a perspective. More recently, Currie (2016) suggested that "the stimuli available in fictional cases, with direct access to the thoughts and feelings of the character is so much richer than ... in real-life cases" (p. 58). The stimuli in question take the form of "authorial input clarifying the character's situation and mental state, things much less easily available concerning real people" (p. 49). Langkau (2020) echoed this view by claiming that literature provides the information about mental states that is not readily available in real life. On this view, linguistic and stylistic characterization techniques are psychagogic; that is, they are "devices calculated to produce a particular response on the part of the reader" (Davie & Reinhardt, 2007, p. xxv).

However, authors may not always intend to provide such cues, and, even if they do, their attempts may not be clear to the reader. Further, as we discussed in Chapter 3, the accuracy of one's representation of a target's perspective is problematic as a criterion for perspective taking; this is even more true with respect to fictional characters. A critical disadvantage in this regard is characters' ontological status. As we noted at the beginning of this chapter, characters, unlike real people, do not have an existence independent of the text, and they cannot be interrogated in ambiguous cases about their beliefs and attitudes.

This concern notwithstanding, a variety of theorists have delineated a host of textual features that allow one to discern the psychological perspective of a character (Lubbock, 1921; Pouillon, 1946; Booth, 1961). Over several decades, linguists and literary scholars have developed elaborate typologies of textual perspective markers that presumably guide readers. For example, Uspensky (1973) proposed the categories of ideological/evaluative, perceptual/psychological, and spatial/temporal markers. A. Fowler (1982a) went a step further and produced a list of the specific linguistic devices that comprise each of Uspensky's categories. Here we are primarily interested in devices that signal evaluations (e.g., ideological, evaluative, and psychological). These include:

- modal auxiliaries, understood as words that communicate degrees of caution or confidence, such as *may*, *might*, *must*, and *should*;
- modal adverbs, such as *certainly*, *probably*, and *perhaps*;
- evaluative adjectives and adverbs, such as *luckily* or *regrettably*;
- verbs of knowledge, prediction, or evaluation, such as *believe*, *foresee*, or *dislike*;
- lexical and clause structures that communicate a system of beliefs, such as generic sentences, defined as "generalized propositions claiming universal truth and usually cast in a syntax reminiscent or proverbs or scientific laws" (A. Fowler, 1982a, pp. 216–217); and
- sociolect and lexical register that can link a character to a specific social group, leading to inferences about that group's beliefs or values.

Presumably, the reader can use these textual features to identify evaluations and a perspective (in the sense of an interpretation that unifies some set of the evaluations, as discussed in Chapter 2). In addition, these features are often part and parcel of mental access, the technique of providing information about a character's mental state, and this will be discussed later. We believe that what is typically most important in perspective taking is the reader's *attempt* to identify the perspective of a character. As well, identifying the perspective of the narrator can be important for some types of text, and this is discussed in the section "Perspective Taking and the Narrator."

Personal Pronouns and Narrative Mode

A text feature that intuitively seems closely related to perspective taking is the use of personal pronouns. In particular, it seems plausible to suppose that a reader will take the perspective of a first-person narrator. In fictional narratives, personal pronouns are markers of narrative mode – what traditionally has been known as first-, second-, or third-person narration. This classification of narrators and narration in terms of pronouns has been expanded to include more fine-grained delineation of types of narration (e.g., Prince, 1987): heterodiegetic (in which the narrator describes the story from outside of the story world) and intradiegetic (in which the narrator tells the story from within the story world). Intradiegetic narration can consist of either autodiegetic narration (in which a first-person narrator tells a story in which they are the protagonist) or homodiegetic narration (in which a narrator who is internal to the story world narrates some other character's story).

Although the relationship of narrative mode to perspective taking is intuitive, empirical investigations of its effects have not always produced clear results. For example, Dixon et al. (2020) found an effect of manipulating narrative mode in the story "Sin of Omission" (Matute, 1989a), but only for some types of items on their perspective-taking questionnaire. They referred to these as "experiential" items because they primarily concerned the feelings of the character. However, the effect was non-intuitive: Autodiegetic narration reduced the degree of perspective taking rather than enhancing it. A related result was obtained by van Lissa et al. (2016). They manipulated narrative mode in the first chapter of the novel *Hunger* (Hamsun, 2012). Overall, and contrary to the assumption that first-person narration makes readers feel closer to a character, the results indicated that "narrative perspective did not predict empathic concern for the character" (p. 51) but instead the third-person version elicited greater trust in the character. One type of explanation for both of these results is that autodiegetic narration is seen as the subjective impressions of the character, and, because in these particular stories that character acted in a morally problematic manner, the reader is less likely to trust that information. In contrast, heterodiegetic mode seems more objective and may lead the reader to more readily incorporate textual information into their representation of the character.

In other research, modest positive effects of narrative mode on perspective taking have been found under some conditions. Kaufman and Libby (2012) measured "experience taking" when reading short fictional passages; experience taking is likely related to perspective taking as we have conceived of it. They found that first-person narration produced somewhat more experience taking than third-person narration when the character was a student at the same university as the reader but not when the character was from a different university. Similarly, de Graaf et al. (2012) found an effect of narrative mode on identification when it was combined with a manipulation of physical vantage point, mental access, and discourse focus. Related results were obtained by Hoeken and Fikkers (2014). They wrote a story with an autodiegetic narrator from the perspective of either of two students, one who was in favor of a tuition hike and one who was against such a hike. In both cases, reasons were provided for the views. They found that participants identified more with the protagonist, but to a lesser extent if protagonist expressed views dissimilar to their own. In all of these results, narrative mode had an effect when it was combined with other variables that likely affect perspective taking, such as superficial similarity or homophily.

Other research, however, has failed to find clear differences based on manipulations of narrative mode. For example, Wimmer et al. (2021) found that narrative mode and physical vantage point did not affect readers' transportation and identification with characters as much as empathetic disposition and familiarity with the subject matter. Similarly, Salem et al. (2017) found no effects of a manipulation of narrative mode on identification in literary and nonliterary texts.

In contrast to these inconsistent effects, narrative technique seems to have a more straightforward effect on physical perspective or vantage point. For example, Brunyé et al. (2009) assessed whether pronouns produce representations of a physical perspective. Participants read sentences such as "I am slicing the tomato," "you are slicing the tomato," or "he is slicing the tomato," and then decided whether a picture matched or did not match the description. Response times were faster for the first and second person with pictures depicting an internal visual perspective and for the third person with pictures depicting an external visual perspective.

Inspired by this result, Sato et al. (2012) investigated whether third-person narration always produced an external visual perspective. They constructed short narratives of four lines for their experiment. All narratives were written in the third person but with either an omniscient narrator who provided mental access to the character or an objective narrator who only provided information about observable actions. To determine if participants took the physical perspective of the protagonist, they were asked to verify whether pictures with either an internal or external visual depiction was part of the story. They found that the internal visual perspective was faster with the omniscient narration and the external perspective was faster with the objective narration. In other words, the tendency to "take" the physical perspective of a character depended on the presence of mental access in the narration and was not a simple function of pronoun use.

In related research, Salem et al. (2017) produced different versions of an excerpt of a novel to determine if different modes of narration lead readers to follow the physical perspective of the protagonist. They measured the adoption of physical perspective by having participants mark on a diagram the perspective from which they imagined the scene. Their results showed that first-person narration produced greater adoption of the protagonist's (physical) perspective than third-person narration. However, they pointed out the "low percentage of cases in which a complete shift to the spatial location of the protagonist took place" (p. 15), and they concluded that narrative mode affects perspective taking "in a more gradient fashion" (p. 16).

Other research has examined the effect of second-person pronouns in single sentences based on the action-compatibility effect. This effect refers to more rapid manual responses toward or away from the body when those actions are compatible with the semantics of the sentence. For example, Glenberg and Kaschak (2002) asked participants to make sense/nonsense judgments of sentences such as "Courtney handed you the notebook." In different blocks, the "sense" response was made by moving either toward or away from the body. The response was faster when the direction was consistent with the movement implied by the sentence. Such results suggest that readers spontaneously imagine the scenario described in the sentence from the vantage point implied by the pronoun. As we discuss later, physical perspective can be related to psychological perspective under some circumstances.

Mental Access

A common assumption in literary studies is that the portrayal of a character's inner world can increase readers' empathy (Stanzel, 1981) and can promote "sympathetic identification" (Leech & Short, 1981, p. 181). Such mental access can be provided in a number of ways: The text may describe a character's mental state or evaluations through third-person narration; a quoted transcript of the character's thoughts can be provided as direct (inner) speech; or thoughts can be described using free-indirect discourse. (The effects of using free-indirect speech, rather than describing covert thoughts in other ways, are discussed more fully in the next section.) From our theoretical perspective, it is easy to understand why information about the character's internal thoughts would promote perspective taking. Mental access often provides relatively direct information about a character's evaluations (which might otherwise have to be inferred from their behavior). However, as with narrative mode, evidence for the effects of mental access on perspective taking is not overwhelming.

Van Peer and Maat (2001) investigated the effects of mental access in first- and third-person narrators. They selected a story featuring an argument between husband and wife. In one version, they changed the husband's spoken speech to internal thoughts; the other version did the same for the wife's. The results did show an increase in readers' sympathy for the character whose inner thoughts were represented, but the effect was small. They also found that readers who sympathized with one of the characters interpreted that character's behavior in situational, as opposed to dispositional, terms. Similarly, Wimmer et al. (2022) found somewhat greater identification with a passage that included mental access compared to a passage that was focused on action; however, mental access was not experimentally manipulated and the two passages described different story-world events. These results suggest mental access might make it easier to generate a perspective-taking analogy that connects those evaluations to related ones of the reader.

Despite this effect in some studies, the additional facility in identifying evaluations provided by mental access has not always translated into greater perspective taking. For example, null effects of mental access were reported by Wimmer et al. (2021); they found that, contrary to their hypothesized outcome, an external narrator's access to a character's mind did not affect readers' responses on transportation and identification scales or on measures of social cognition. (Social cognition was measured with the Reading the Mind in the Eyes Test; see our discussion of this instrument in Chapter 8.) Similarly, Eekhof et al. (2023) found minimal effects of mental access (manipulated in conjunction with physical perspective) on a variety of dimensions of character engagement.

In some cases, mental access may even decrease perspective taking. For example, Dixon et al. (2020) manipulated mental access by adding information, consistent with the story-world context, that the character might have been thinking. This manipulation reduced readers' tendency to see the character's behavior as reasonable, understandable, and appropriate. In that paper, we argued that this negative impact on perspective taking was because, in that story, the added story information reduced readers' elaborative processing of the text. As we discuss later, such elaborative processing might be more important than the ease of identifying a character's perspective. A similar result was obtained by Kotovych et al. (2011). In that case, an extensive description of the character's mental state reduced identification (and presumably perspective taking). Our argument was that without the mental state description, readers would need to infer the character's evaluations. Such reader inferences would promote perspective taking to a greater degree than simply finding the information in the text. We are left with the conclusion that what is important for perspective taking is what readers represent about a character's mental state and that this is not always obvious from the information explicitly provided in the text.

Free-Indirect Speech

As noted in the previous section, the free-indirect discourse style is often used to provide mental access by depicting the thoughts of the character. However, free-indirect discourse can also be used to convey overt speech rather than a character's internal thoughts. In this section, we consider the evidence that such free-indirect speech has an effect on perspective taking. Free-indirect speech poses interesting interpretational challenges because of its combination of narrator and character voices. For example, a free-indirect statement may include vocabulary and register appropriate for the character but tense and grammar appropriate for a third-person narrator. Some have argued that this technique can lead to perspective taking even if it is not used to convey mental access. For example, Dixon and Bortolussi (1996) found clear effects of free-indirect discourse, independent of the content. The story they manipulated, "Rope" (Porter, 1928/1975), consists predominantly of dialogue between a married couple conveyed entirely in free-indirect discourse. In the experiment, different versions of the original story were created that independently varied the speech style for husband and wife. The results showed a strong effect of free-indirect speech on transparency, that is, the extent to which the character seemed reasonable and rational. Critically, the same information was provided in all versions; only the style of speech attributed to characters was changed. One of the issues that arises in the assessment of effects of stylistic features such as this is the extent to which the features interact with the content. Dixon and Bortolussi (1996) also reported a follow-up study on the "Rope" experiment. In this case, the story was rewritten so that the roles and actions of the husband and wife were reversed. Readers' assessment of the characters changed with the role they played in the story, but the effects of speech style remained the same: Relating a character's speech using free-indirect style still increased the tendency to see that character as reasonable and rational. One interpretation of this effect is that the reader may be inclined to take the perspective of the narrator in this story. (The role of the narrator in perspective taking is discussed later.) Thus, when the narrator's voice is intertwined with that of a character using free-indirect speech, perspective taking may occur for that character as well.

On the other hand, Hakemulder and Koopman (2010) manipulated free-indirect speech in a Dutch translation of "Het Record" ("The Record") (Borowski, 1980) and found few substantial effects. In some cases, the technique led to a greater visibility of the character's thoughts and feelings. However, there was little impact on the reader's sympathy or understanding of the character. The content of the story, though, may make this result atypical: The protagonist is a Second World War officer who is determined to set a record for sleeping with a German prisoner who collects lampshades made of human skin. The researchers conjectured that perhaps their manipulation was "hardly strong enough to balance readers' objections against the immorality of the main character" (p. 51). On balance, our conclusion is that the use of free-indirect speech per se only has an effect on perspective taking in some contexts. For example, the texts used in these studies may vary in the extent to which they lead the reader to take the inferred perspective of the narrator.

Physical and Psychological Perspective

The problem we have set for ourselves in this book is an understanding of how readers adopt a psychological perspective based on some set of evaluations of the story world. A related phenomenon, though, is physical perspective, that is, the vantage point from which aspects of the story world are represented. Physical perspective is based on the deictic center, typically defined as "the speaker's location and time" (Yule, 1996, p. 129). Here, we use the term in a somewhat idiosyncratic sense to refer to the reader's *mental representation* of the vantage point from which the story is described. This representation is based on textual features such as deixis, or references that provide personal, spatial, or temporal information about a situation (Prince, 1987) or specific context (Yule, 1996). Generally, the text does not provide an unambiguous indication of the deictic center. Instead, the text merely provides various degrees of constraint using features such as deictic verbs, narrative mode (as discussed earlier), and simply descriptive passages in the text. Another type of constraint is perceptual access, that is, the ascription of information that might be perceived to the character. Such perceptual information typically constrains the locus in the story world from which the percepts might occur and thus provides information about the deictic center.

A wide range of research has established that readers maintain, as a mental representation, a deictic center based on this information under at least some circumstances. For example, Black et al. (1979) found elevated reading times for sentences with deictic verbs that conflicted with the main character's position. Rinck and Bower (1995) provided evidence that anaphor resolution times increased with the spatial distance between the character and the antecedent, suggesting that readers follow the narrative from the physical standpoint of the characters. When readers first memorize a map of a building in which a narrative takes place, Morrow et al. (1987) found that they track the room in which the protagonist is currently located. However, there is also evidence that the representation of the deictic center is not always precise. For example, Salem et al. (2017) found that the percentage of cases in which readers fully adopted the physical perspective of the protagonist was low. Similarly, Schneider and Dixon (2009) argued, based on reading times following interruptions, that tracking detailed spatial representations was only helpful for a portion of their participants that they referred to as "careful readers."

For our purposes, the critical question is the relationship between physical perspective (and the representation of the deictic center) and psychological perspective. At times, researchers have failed to make a distinction between the two. For example, "focalization" has been used to refer to both by Bal (1983) and Rimmon-Kenan (1983); van Krieken et al. (2017) grouped psychological and physical perspective together as one component of identification; and Lanser (1981) argued that physical perspective provides metaphorical information about psychological perspective (see also Uspensky, 1973). However, as we noted in Chapter 2, these are not necessarily the same, and it is easy to find narratives in which the deictic center is unrelated to the evaluations of the character or the narrator. For example, in *The Custom of the Country* (Wharton, 1913/2012), events are related from a character's perspective even though the narrator holds negative evaluations for that character and her actions.

In general, we argue that physical perspective provides information about evaluations and psychological perspective only under limited circumstances. Dixon and Bortolussi (2019) argued that when readers represent a character as the deictic center consistently throughout a text, they may simultaneously assume that the character is "reliable" and can serve as a source of valid evaluations concerning the story world. Presumably, such evaluations aid the reader in identifying and taking psychological perspectives. For example, Dixon and Bortolussi (2019) found that such reliable characters were seen as more reasonable and rational, suggesting that readers were more likely to have taken the characters' perspective.

Effects of First-Order Textual Features

Understanding how perspective taking varies as a function of textual features is central to an account of how literary texts have their effects on readers. It is clear from the features reviewed in the previous sections that authors have at their disposal a wide range of tools for directly and indirectly indicating the origin and nature of perspectives in their fictional texts. However, the available empirical evidence suggests that the effect of these features on readers' responses is tenuous at best. (See also Sanford & Emmott [2012] on the misalignment of features and effects.) These inconclusive results indicate that individual features may be insufficient on their own to evoke readers' perspective taking and that their effects on perspective taking depend on the context. Readers become interested in characters' thoughts, behavior, speech, and actions; they care about what characters think and why. However, merely understanding what a character is thinking at any given point in the narrative is unlikely to lead a reader to "take" that character's perspective. If there are obvious individual features of a narrative (such as narrative mode or mental access) that do *not* seem to have large and consistent effects on perspective taking, as the empirical evidence suggests, then clearly there is something else in the text that triggers the necessary reader–character connection. Thus, we conclude that readers' processing is more complex than has typically been acknowledged and that perspective taking is not linked in a simple way to textual features. As we discuss in the next section, we argue that the critical link between features and perspective taking is the process of elaboration based on personal knowledge and experience. Thus, the first-order textual features reviewed here may promote perspective taking only in contexts in which such elaboration takes place.

Second-Order Textual Features

We use the term "second-order textual features" to refer to aspects of the text that are not necessarily tied directly to perspective taking but that instead engender the type of mental processing that we regard as prerequisite: elaboration. In general terms, elaboration is a mechanism that allows readers to retrieve relevant knowledge and experience that helps them understand the text. To form a perspective-taking analogy, the reader typically adds information to their representation of the story world that derives from their own personal knowledge and experience. Thus, elaboration has the potential to contribute to a perspective-taking analogy by providing the information used in such an analogy, and when it does so, perspective taking is promoted. (It is also worth noting that elaboration may be a critical part of perspective taking in real life, in which a deeper, more extensive understanding of a target's situation could aid in taking the target's perspective. However, at present we do not have an account of what circumstances might lead to such elaboration.)

In research on discourse processing, elaboration is regarded as a type of inference (e.g., Graesser et al., 1994). Graesser et al. argued that elaboration (and other inferences) is controlled by a "search after meaning" in which a representation of the situation model was constructed that was consistent with reader goals. However, this general principle does not provide any clear predictions for precisely those circumstances in which elaboration will occur. Indeed, critiques of this position hold that few such elaborations are generated by default (McKoon & Ratcliff, 1992). Instead, the representation may include only that information that is readily activated in the course of processing the text (Gerrig, 2005). However, this so-called minimalist hypothesis can also be criticized as insufficiently precise about the circumstances in which information will be "readily activated" and incorporated into the representation of the text. Information from memory could be activated based on unspecified features of the context, as well as on mental representations that were activated from memory based on processing of the previous text. Thus, both a "search-after-meaning" and "minimalist" view of narrative processing suggest that elaboration is sometimes critical and will occur under some circumstances. What is important for us are situations in which such elaborative processing is based on the reader's personal knowledge and experience.

Barnes (2018) discussed how "imaginary engagement" is central to the effects of literature. This term refers to "the extent to which a reader contributes imaginatively and creatively to a text by filling in gaps, puzzling over interpretations, fleshing out what is written, or otherwise imputing meaning onto the page that extends beyond what is written" (p. 127). This process appears to be close to what we describe as elaboration based on personal knowledge and experience. Barnes notes that imaginary engagement (or elaboration, in our terms) is central to transportation (as we described earlier) and may depend on either literary texts or a reading style in which the reader is deeply involved with the story world. Similarly, Cohen (2006) conjectured that the amount of detail provided in the text about character thoughts, emotions, and goals can influence the reader's ability and willingness to identify. This may be because the details serve as a cue for elaboration.

As an example of how this process can work, consider the story "The Mask of the Bear" (Laurence, 1997) mentioned in Chapter 2. The story provides cues that mark a shift in the adult narrator's evaluation of her grandfather. As the narrator recalls the grandfather's apparently hostile behavior, readers may share her evaluation of the grandfather. When she relates an epiphanic experience that suggests there was more to her grandfather than she and the other women in her life had understood, readers may then empathize with the grandfather. At the same time, they may also empathize with the mature narrator's realization of her wrongful conclusions. Which perspective they endorse would likely depend on their own past experience. If the story cues memories of unjust evaluations of others and subsequent regret, the reader may endorse both the narrator's youth and adult evaluations, although contradictory. If the story cues memories of a hostile male relative, a reader may not empathize at all with the grandfather, and only with the younger narrator who judged him harshly. Readers who recall being misjudged by others may empathize instead with the grandfather and condemn the female characters' evaluations. Thus, the contents of autobiographical memory are crucial to the elaborative processing required to form an analogical connection with characters. However, in order to understand this process, research must focus not on direct causal links between specific features and predicted effects but rather on the properties of texts that give rise to elaborative, analogical processing.

In our view, the central question for understanding elaboration in discourse processing is identifying when it occurs and when it is likely to involve the reader's personal knowledge and experience. Importantly, not all elaborations involve the reader's personal knowledge and experience, and even when they do, perspective taking does not necessarily follow. However, in our view, such elaboration is crucial because it lays the foundation for perspective-taking analogies. We argue that elaboration can occur during comprehension because of individual differences in reading style, situational differences in the need to form elaborations, and features of the text that signal that elaboration. Individual and situational differences in elaborative processing are discussed in Chapter 6; here, we describe textual features that can prompt elaboration. We suggest there are at least five classes of textual features related to elaboration: showing versus telling styles, textual gaps, embodied descriptions, foregrounding, and narratorial implicatures. To a great extent, these properties are characterized more by what is not stated but rather suggested, so that the absence of explicit statements may prompt inferencing activity. We discuss each of these in turn.

Showing versus Telling Styles

The showing and telling styles of story-world depiction are an important aspect of literary narrative (Lubbock, 1921; Forster, 1927; Booth, 1961). However, they have received little to no attention in empirical studies of literature. Because each style fosters a different type of processing, creating more or fewer gaps, and prompting more or less elaboration on the part of the reader, it is important to revisit them. In outline, the "telling" style refers to a manner of conveying a story that employs an authoritative narrator whose judgment of characters is made obvious through evaluative descriptions. In effect, the narrative tells us what to think about characters' attributes, motivations, desires, intentions, and so on, as in many *romans à thèse*. In contrast, the "showing" style is more suggestive but more detailed; it employs an unobtrusive narrator who creates scenes in which characters' dialogues and actions are conveyed more precisely, but without explicit evaluative descriptors. Showing can also include the rendering of mental states through techniques such as free-indirect speech and stream of consciousness. Prince (1987) described both styles as "kinds of distance regulating narrative information" (p. 87). Narratorial distance is greater in the showing style, as the narrator's evaluations need to be inferred. In particular, such inferences may require the use of personal knowledge and experience applied to potentially analogous situations.

Although a total distinction between the two styles is not always maintained in any given work, we conjecture that the showing manner of narrating invites greater elaborative processing based on personal knowledge and experience. As a consequence, it should promote perspective taking. An excellent example of a showing style and its potential relation to perspective taking is "The Legend of El Cadejo" (Asturias, 1930/1997). A young novice in a convent sits at a window, contemplating life shortly before taking her vows and shutting herself off from the world. Rich, evocative, and meticulously detailed descriptions of the sights she views (summer fruit and leaves rotting on the ground) and sounds she hears (children's laughter) are provided to convey her state of mind. Such descriptions invite elaborative inferences on the part of the reader. For example, readers may recall seeing rotting fruit and leaves, along with how they reacted to the sight. In this way, the character's melancholic, doleful mood is evoked without the omniscient narrator ever offering any ascriptions of her thoughts or feelings. Further, because the elaborative processing is based on readers' own experiences, it can be straightforward to construct the remaining connections in a perspective-taking analogy.

Textual Gaps

Given that all fiction is schematic, fictional texts necessarily contain gaps. However, such gaps are of different types. For example, Iser (1976/1978) called the "suspension of connectability between textual segments ... blanks" (p. 195); readers attempt to supply the missing links to form "an integrated gestalt" (p. 186). These may correspond to what discourse-processing researchers have termed "coherence inferences" that require readers to draw connections by supplying information not stated in a text. Coherence inferences include low-level connections meant to solve, for example, problems of co-reference across sentences (e.g., Singer, 1980). A classic example is the pair of sentences, "The millionaire died in the night. The killer got away." In order for these sentences to be coherent, readers must infer that the millionaire was murdered by the killer. Such inferences would not typically require readers to recruit their personal knowledge and experience. In contrast to blanks, Iser (1976/1978) understood "gaps" as "arising out of the dialogue," leaving readers to infer "what is meant by what is not said" (p. 168). This may be related to the character's evaluations of aspects of the story world, and making such inferences would involve elements of perspective taking as we have conceived of it.

To make our interpretation of these ideas clear, we will use the term "evaluative" gaps. These are situations in which a character's evaluation of, reaction to, or interpretation of circumstances in the story world are left unexplained. We argue that such gaps invite the reader to generate inferences, often based on their own personal knowledge and experience, that would explain the character's evaluation. Similarly, de Mulder et al. (2017) suggested that texts that leave unexplained character relationships may lead readers to "contemplate characters' thoughts and social relationships in order to be able to make sense of the narrative" (p. 134). Such contemplation would generally entail inferences to fill the evaluative gaps. While such processing is typically not required for low-level coherence, it would be needed in order to understand the behavior of the character as plausible and consistent. When the inferences are based on the reader's experience, they provide the connection between the reader and the text needed for perspective taking and lay the foundation for a perspective-taking analogy.

What motivates readers to fill in particular gaps, and the mechanisms and associations used to create a more rounded representation of the characters, remain unaccounted for in Iser's (1976/1978) theory. Perhaps Ingarden (1931/1973a), whom Iser followed and critiqued, had the right idea. Ingarden maintained that "the reader must grasp [the characters] through empathy" (p. 172). The unacknowledged insight here seems to be that a more personal connection to characters is required, and this, in our view involves drawing on autobiographical personal knowledge and experience. However, what kinds of gaps invite readers to draw on their personal repertoire of knowledge? It seems unlikely that readers will inevitably attempt to fill all evaluative gaps they encounter in the text; such a strategy could lead to unconstrained elaboration that McKoon and Ratcliff (1992) and others have argued does not occur. One answer is that readers are more inclined to fill evaluative gaps when they are critical for narrative comprehension because they provide crucial links in the causal chain of events.

An example will illustrate how readers' elaborations based on their personal knowledge and experience can be central to comprehension. In *The Beginning Place* (Le Guin, 1980), the protagonist has an extreme reaction to superficially mundane events:

> He could feel his mouth hanging open, because he could not seem to get air into his lungs. His throat was closed off by something in it trying to get out. He stood there beside the armchair, his body trembling in a jerky way, and the thing in his throat came out in words. "I can't, I can't," it said loudly.
>
> Very frightened, in panic, he made for the front door, wrenched it open before the thing could go on talking. The hot, late sunlight glared on white rocks, carports, cars, walls, swings, television aerials. He stood there trembling, his jaw working: the thing was trying to force his jaw open and speak again. He broke and ran. (pp. 4–5)

In order to understand the behavior of the character and how it contributes to the plot events, the reader would need to ascribe some basis or justification for his panic reaction. Hints in the prior discourse suggest that it may be related to stifling circumstances of this life from which there is apparently no escape, and the reader may be able to recruit prior experiences that are analogous. While it is not obvious what kinds of perspective-taking processes may occur in the mind of the reader at this point in the narrative, reaching some hypothesis about the character's behavior is critical for understanding the plot events.

What we are terming evaluative gaps is related to hermeneutic, or "information," gaps in the analysis of Rimmon-Kenan (1983). Information gaps can be trivial or crucial, temporary (filled in later) or permanent (open even after the whole text has been read), and local or global (affecting smaller or larger portions of the text). Temporary gaps involve "a discrepancy between story-time and text-time" (p. 128) and can be future or past oriented. Both establish enigmas and create suspense regarding either what is to happen or what has already happened. Although Rimmon-Kenan did not address the question of how these gaps affect readers' understanding of characters specifically, we believe that information gaps are important in perspective taking when the missing information provides bases or motivations for the evaluations and actions of a character. One can easily find novels that illustrate the inferencing activity required of the reader to fill in information gaps. For example, *Forty Thousand in Gehenna* (Cherryh, 1984) consists of a sequence of related stories, typically separated by many years, and the reader must infer how the common characters have developed and dealt with the story-world circumstances during the intervening time. In many cases, such inferences would be central to identifying character evaluations and thus important for perspective taking.

Embodied Descriptions

One feature of texts that we argue produces elaboration (and potentially greater perspective taking) is embodied description. Embodied descriptions would typically generate embodied meanings: representations of the text that depend on or include sensorimotor content (cf. Barsalou, 2008). For example, the representation of the word "ball" may include information about what a ball looks like, what it feels like to catch or throw, or typical situations in which one might interact with a ball. Pexman et al. (2019) noted how word meanings differ in the extent to which they include such information and how this variation affects performance in word recognition tasks. More generally, Zwaan (2004), Caracciolo (2014), Gibbs (2006b), and others have described how embodied representations of this sort are often constructed during comprehension.

Embodied textual descriptions might cue readers to use their personal experience in their representation of the text (Tsunemi & Kusumi, 2011). Consider, for example, a passage such as the following (from *The Night Manager*):

> They crossed a high bridge and saw the lights of the town below them, and the black Dutch waterways cutting through the lights. They descended a steep ramp. The old houses gave way to shanties. Suddenly the dark felt dangerous. They were driving on a flat road, water to their right, floodlit containers piled four high to their left, marked with names like Sealand, Nedlloyd and Tiphook. (Le Carré, 1993/2008, p. 352)

This passage is much more evocative than an abstract description such as "we drove down to the wharf," presumably because of the plethora of specific, concrete words, each of which may elicit an embodied representation tied to personal experience. For example, the "steep ramp" might recall hiking down a sharp descent in the mountains; the "shanties" might bring to mind the memory of driving past the "favelas" (slums) of Río. What enables these recollections to provide a basis of perspective taking is the connection to prior evaluations that may be similar or analogous to those found in the text. As described in Chapter 2 (and in more detail in Chapter 5), the perspective-taking analogy would be constructed by finding evaluations justified by these prior experiences and connecting those to comparable evaluations in the text. In fact, the above passage contains an explicit evaluation: "Suddenly the dark felt dangerous." This evaluation may guide the reader in searching for those prior experiences that justified an analogous evaluation. For example, hiking down a sharp descent might have evoked a fear of slipping or falling. In this way, an elaborative, embodied meaning representation ties evaluations in memory to those in the text and thus forms the basis of broader perspective taking.

A literary example of how embodied descriptions can trigger autobiographical memory retrieval is Proust's (1922/2009) famous madeleine episode (from *Swann's Way*). It describes how the narrator's dipping of the madeleine cookie in tea plunges him into the sensual recollection of a part of his past. Readers, of course, might not have this precise experience with madeleines dipped in tea, but words in textual descriptions might evoke similar multimodal experiences. For example, descriptions of fragrant lilac bushes blooming in spring could evoke not just the smell of lilacs but also past memories associated with lilacs – the parental home, a city-dweller's trip to the country, and so on – and these memories could activate associated feelings and evaluations. In this way, descriptions of lilac bushes blooming would be different for each reader because of the subjective component of the evoked sense, but they could equally provide a basis for perspective taking.

Psychological research provides an explanation of how words come to have self-relevant meanings. For example, Klein and Loftus (1988) offer some evidence in support of an elaboration theory. With respect to a list-learning paradigm, they explained that "elaborating a word entails the formation of multiple associations between it and extralist material in memory" (p. 6). Thus, a word such as "dance" can evoke different experiences for different people: ballet lessons for some, high school dances for others. Extending this insight to descriptions in fictional texts, we can conclude that different readers might be struck by a specific word or words that trigger the recall of specific experiences. These recalled experiences are embodied to the extent that they are associated with feelings, sensations, or emotional undertones, that is, to the extent that they do not simply tap on abstract, semantic knowledge. More generally, retrieving the embodied meaning of a word may pull in associated, surrounding experiences from the reader's life, thereby creating the elaboration.

To conclude, our general argument is that embodied descriptions generate (generally perceptual-motor) elaboration and that these elaborations may connect situations in the story world to aspects of related experiences of the reader. As we discuss in Chapter 5, building an elaborated representation that includes these perceptual details is likely to involve episodic reconstruction in which prior experience is recombined and repurposed to match the story-world context. This connection and the elaboration may provide the basis for a perspective-taking analogy. This is consistent with several previous lines of argument. For example, it has been shown that more detailed recollections have an effect on empathy: Vollberg et al. (2021) reported that empathic accuracy increased as a function of a person's ability to imagine the scene surrounding a suffering person; greater detail generation led to increased empathy with that person. Kuzmičová (2012) argued that embodied descriptions were instrumental in creating "presence." Similar to our analysis of transportation earlier, our interpretation is that Kuzmičová's understanding of presence is related to elaboration based on personal knowledge and experience. Chow et al. (2015) found that previous experience with described actions modulated activation in the corresponding brain motor areas, suggesting that the representation of embodied descriptions is related to personal experience. Johnson (2012) found that transportation into the story world (which could be related to elaboration) was related to affective empathy. Mar and Oatley (2008) suggested that features such as figurative language demand greater cognitive effort, and this leads to mental representations of the story world that have a greater reference to personal experience. Johnson (2013) found that asking readers to generate multimodal imagery led to greater pro-social behavior. Our present hypothesis is that these elaborated perceptual representations provide the personal connection to the story world that underlies perspective taking.

Foregrounding

A textual property that is often discussed in connection with literary texts is foregrounding. In a very general sense, foregrounding consists of the use of stylistic features that are unusual or discrepant in some way. Based on the ideas of Mukařovský (1932/2014), Miall and Kuiken (1994) distinguished three categories of foregrounding features: phonetic, grammatical, or semantic. Phonetic foregrounding might include alliteration or rhyme; grammatical might include inversion or ellipsis; and semantic might include metaphor or irony. For Mukařovský, foregrounding produces "defamiliarization," or the sense of perceiving some aspect of reality anew. For Miall and Kuiken, defamiliarization leads readers to engage in a more complex, richer processing than would otherwise occur. In the current context, what is important is that foregrounding may produce elaborative processing and, if this elaboration is based on personal knowledge and experience, may foster perspective-taking analogies. (It is useful to note that metaphor, often cited as a source of foregrounding, may elicit embodied representations; Gibbs [2006a]. As we suggested in the previous section, embodied representations may be based on personal knowledge and experience.)

There is some evidence that this effect occurs under at least some circumstances. For example, Koopman (2016) found that removing foregrounding from a text reduced "empathic understanding," that is, the extent to which the reader showed "a felt understanding of what people in a similar situation as the character go through" (p. 88). In contrast, though, Kuzmičová et al. (2017) found, in a qualitative study, that removing the foregrounded features actually increased empathy. Kuzmičová et al. suggested that this unexpected result was because the foregrounding elicited "aesthetically distanced emotional memories" that were inconsistent with an empathic response (cf. Cupchik et al., 1998). Although not the same as empathy, van Peer et al. (2007) manipulated foregrounding in a poem and found little effect on evoked affect. Scapin et al. (2023) analyzed responses to open-ended questions concerning foregrounding that readers noticed. Based on these responses, and using a scheme developed by Harash (2021), they distinguished failed processing of foregrounding from full, partial, or shallow processing. Their empathy measure was lower with failed processing. Again, this suggests that readers' varying reaction to the foregrounded features may be critical in whether empathic responses occur. In particular, Scapin et al. argued that empathic responses depended on the depth of processing of the foregrounded features. In general terms, this is consistent with our view that perspective taking would be enhanced when the foregrounding leads to greater elaboration in terms of personal knowledge and experience.

Narratorial Implicatures

Elaborations may also be invited by communicative cues in the text. As hypothesized by Bortolussi and Dixon (2003), the reader may treat the narrator as a conversational participant who provides necessary and sufficient information (in the sense of Grice, 1975) for comprehension. Such a treatment leads to certain kinds of inferences about the character and the story world. For example, extensive descriptive details would typically not be necessary for understanding the plot events; consequently, the reader, under these assumptions, would be licensed to draw additional elaborative inferences to help understand why those details were provided. In effect, the reader may try to understand the point the narrator is trying to make with such detailed descriptions. Kotovych et al. (2011) termed such inferences "narratorial implicatures," analogous to Grice's conversational implicatures.

As an example, in *Spy Hook* (Deighton, 1989), a meal is described in some detail:

> Through the front window we could see the ankles of the people walking past the house, and they could see what we were eating. Which is perhaps why we had the sort of meal that women's magazines photograph from above. Three paper-thin slices of avocado arranged alongside a tiny puddle of tomato sauce and a slice of kiwi fruit. The second course was three thin slices of duck breast with a segment of mango and a lettuce leaf. We ended with a thin slice of Cindy's delicious home-made chocolate roulade. (p. 101)

These details invite inferences about the narrator's opinion of the meal and the context. The ingredients of the meal and the evaluation, "the sort of meal that women's magazines photograph," suggest that the dinner was stylish, but the repetition of "thin slices" is unnecessary. Thus, this phrasing suggests that the narrator has a point to make about the meal, namely that he regarded it as inadequate. In turn, such an evaluation suggests that the narrator preferred a more robust dinner and that he may have held the dinner and his host in some disdain. These kinds of inferences are licensed by the assumption that the narrator would not have provided this kind of description for no reason. Further, such elaborative inferences may be related to analogous prior experiences such as services that are inadequate in some way. If the reader succeeds in making such a connection, then they may be able to develop a perspective-taking analogy in which corresponding evaluations in the reader and the character are justified by corresponding experiences.

The concept of narratorial implicature also provides useful insight into ellipses in narrative. In any story, there are many events in the story world that are not described in the text, and their lack is not noticed because those events are not crucial for a subsequent understanding of the story. In this sense, the narrator is conforming to the convention of only providing necessary information. The reader's reliance on this convention is illustrated in *The Murder of Roger Ackroyd* (Christie, 1926/1997) in which the narrator uses such implicatures to deceive the reader. In this story, the narrator outlines his own actions on the night of the murder (but without detailing his precise location at every minute). Later, after the detective Poirot has solved the crime and identified the narrator as the murderer, it becomes clear that the previously undescribed actions were incriminating. For example, a ten-minute gap in the narrator's description of going from the house to the lodge is later revealed to include the murder of the title character. Such gaps in the original accounting of the narrator's actions are normally unnoticed because some version of the elided events is inferred by the reader in order to maintain coherence. In this particular instance, the reader would simply infer that the narrator walked from the house to the lodge without taking the time to commit a murder. Such an inference is licensed by the assumption (incorrect, in this instance) that if something important happened during that interval, the narrator would have described it.

Kotovych et al. (2011) provided evidence that narratorial implicatures can promote perspective taking. In one of the stories that they used, "The Office" (Munro, 1996), the narrator is a writer who expresses her concern that her vocation is not valued by others. This concern is described extensively even though one might suspect a priori that being a writer is a perfectly acceptable occupation. Thus, Kotovych et al. argued that the extensive apology for being an author constitutes a narratorial implicature that invites readers to infer a justification for this attitude. If readers find analogous experiences from their own lives, they may succeed in taking the narrator's perspective by analogy. Indeed, Kotovych et al. found that the original story produced more perspective taking ("transparency," in their terms) than a version in which the implicature material was replaced or preceded by an explanation that rendered the apology moot.

In our discussion of second-order features, we have attempted to identify some of the properties of texts that lead readers to elaborate based on personal knowledge and experience. Clearly, our list of characteristics is neither exhaustive nor detailed. Instead, our goal is merely to point to the types of stylistic devices that can cue readers to do the requisite elaborative processing, and such processing is undoubtedly determined by the reading situation and substantive content of the text.

Perspective Taking and the Narrator

Literature is a mediated product (Margolin, 2009), told by a narrator created by the author; therefore, an understanding of perspective taking in literature depends on a suitable analysis of the role of the narrator. Zeman (2016) noted that "it is the narrator that constitutes a major category of perspective," since, recalling the words of Schmid (2003), it is the narrator who "refracts narrated reality like a prism" (p. 8). In fact, this is not so different from real-life communicative situations. Individuals are narrators of their own stories in the selection and organization of their story content (cf. Bluck & Habermas, 2000). Further, we may hear versions of their story from other, at times conflicting, sources. Therefore, in both real life and literature, on hearing a verbal narrative, we must assess the reliability, motives, and intentions of the teller(s) of the story and the plausibility of what is conveyed in order to understand what might really have happened and why. In this way, the existence of this mediating agent adds another level of complexity to the reader's processing of text. As Jumpertz and Tary (2020) acknowledged, "the amount of information the reader receives about the narrator, how much we can infer from the contexts, means of characterization and the representation of the story world will affect the ability to create a representation of the narrator" (p. 111).

A. Fowler (1982) provided a list of features that help the reader distinguish between the voice of the narrator and that of the character. Notable among them is the mode of presentation: whether a character is presented externally or internally by an omniscient narrator. External narration privileges the discourse of the narrator, presenting only the character's physical appearance, words, and acts. Internal narration mimics the subjective discourse of a character, conveying the character's thoughts and feelings. Where a character's perspective is presented externally by an omniscient narrator, deictics are transferred to that agent, modalities of evaluation are replaced by words attributing thought, feeling, and perception, and clause structures and lexical choices serve to highlight the primacy of the narrator's evaluation. Narration of a character's perspective can range from greater to lesser objectivity on the part of the teller: The greater the degree of objectivity, the lesser the use of personal deixis and modal forms conveying the narrator's judgments. Presentation of a character's perspective by a more personalized, overt narrator will include personal deixis and explicit judgments (e.g., by means of evaluative adjectives). A hybrid combination of the internal and external modes is also possible through techniques such as free-indirect discourse, which interweaves both narratorial and character discourses. To varying degrees, such a hybrid-character presentation foregrounds properties of either the character or the narrator.

Other linguistic and stylistic features in Fowler's list also enable us to infer voice, that is, the origin of an utterance. Linguistic cues include sociolect and lexical register, which can suggest whether we are hearing the narrator telling us what characters think or the character's words directly. Stylistic features include stream of consciousness and interior monologue (which are markers of internal perspective). Also important are modes of speech and thought representation such as psychonarration, or narratorial discourse about a character's thoughts (Cohn, 1978), and figural narration, or the presentation of events through the eyes of character.

As decades of research in narratology have made abundantly clear, the relationship between narrators and characters can be very complex. There can be considerable ironic distance between them, and specifying that distance can pose a substantial interpretational challenge. Defining the narrator as "the highest-level speech position from which the current narrative discourse originates," Margolin (2014, p. 646) stressed that readers try to infer the communicative role of that narrative entity. Margolin provided a list of cues that guide the image that readers construct of the narrator, including features such as personal pronouns, verb tenses, and deictics of place and time. Other aspects of a narrator's discourse can include textual aspects such as summaries, analyses, comments, generalizations, interpretations, judgments, and reliability or unreliability. More broadly, readers may consider style: If a text's style is abstract, rational, and so on, readers may transfer those properties to the narrator.

Given these complexities, identifying the perspective of the narrator may be more or less difficult. In some cases, textual signs associated with a narrator may work in harmony to create a clear, consistent, discernible whole. This may be the case with literary stereotypes, such as a Don Juan, modest maid, chatty servant, court buffoon, or simpleton. With such characters, the position of the narrator toward these types is clear. However, most literary works portray characters who cannot be reduced to a simple psychology or moral stance, so that the narrator's stance toward them can be ambiguous. Further, there are a variety of narrative techniques that may make identifying the perspective of the narrator problematic. In some cases, the narrator may be unreliable (cf. Margolin, 2014), there can be perspectival shifts, and the perspective of the narrator and the character can be intertwined (Igl, 2016).

Whether it is possible for the reader to adopt the perspective of the narrator varies with the type of narrator. For autodiegetic narration, where the narrator is in fact the protagonist, one may take that perspective just as one would take the perspective of the character. For example, one is likely to take the perspective of the first-person narrator in *Frankenstein* (Shelley, 1818/1993). However, in this novel, as in many others, the autodiegetic narration is retrospective, occurring at some temporal and spatial distance from the experienced events. In such cases, there is a doubling of the narrative perspective, consisting of the narrator's present and past selves. This is illustrated in the following segment in which the narrator is introduced to a scientific laboratory:

> He then took me into his laboratory and explained to me the uses of his various machines, instructing me as to what I ought to procure and promising me the use of his own when I should have advanced far enough in the science not to derange their mechanism. He also gave me the list of books which I had requested, and I took my leave.
> Thus ended a day memorable to me; it decided my future destiny.

In this instance, the narrator expresses an evaluation of the events (that they were memorable and would decide his destiny) that would only be apparent later in his life. Taking the perspective of the narrator/character in this context could be subtly different than taking the perspective of simply a character (in, for example, a heterodiegetic narrative) because the present and future evaluations of the narrator/character could differ.

It may also be possible to take the perspective of other types of narrators who are in the story world and for whom there is adequate information concerning their background. One might, for example, take the perspective of Watson, the narrator in the Sherlock Holmes stories. Such a perspective might include the awe of Holmes's powers of deduction. To complicate matters, a large portion of literary fiction explores more innovative forms of narration; homodiegetic and heterodiegetic narrators can vary considerably. They can be more or less intrusive (e.g., dramatic modes of presentation consisting of pure dialogue that erase the detectable presence of narrator); they can function as protagonists or witnesses who are more or less involved; their narration can be more or less omniscient (e.g., some narrators purport not to have complete information); and their perspectives can be fixed, variable, or multiple (e.g., multiple selective omniscience involves a third person presenting several character points of view) (Niederhoff, 2014). Thus, taking the narrator's perspective would be more difficult for these other types of narrators.

According to our analysis, forming a perspective-taking analogy for the narrator requires that a correspondence be identified between the reader's experiences that justify evaluations and the narrator's experiences. This would be problematic when that kind of information is not available. For example, in "The Refusal" (Kafka, 1995), the homodiegetic narrator relates how the townspeople in his autocratically ruled village cowered in fear of the tax collector-colonel. Intermittently, the narrator expresses opinions, such as "now it is remarkable and I am continually being surprised by the way we in our town humbly submit to all orders issued in the capital" (p. 263). However, there is no background in the text about the narrator and his relationship to the townspeople or if he is any braver. As a result, we do not have the information that might justify that evaluation. Although the reader may agree with the narrator's evaluation under such circumstances, such agreement by itself, as we outlined in Chapter 2, would not constitute perspective taking. In order to take the narrator's perspective, the reader would have to infer a great deal of the narrator's background in order to construct an analogy with their own experiences. For example, the reader may have entertained similar evaluations of segments of their own society, such as fiercely devoted followers of authoritarian or religious figures.

An example of how this may work in conjunction with narratorial implicatures comes from the brief short story, "El Eclipse" ("The

Eclipse") (Monterroso, 2013). In the story, a Spanish missionary attempts to escape from a group of Indigenous natives preparing to sacrifice him. He believes that his knowledge of a pending solar eclipse can save him and threatens the natives with blocking the sun if they do not immediately desist. However, the natives possess a sophisticated cosmological knowledge, already know of the eclipse, and proceed to sacrifice him anyway. In the text, the narrator's use of temporal techniques invites readers to make inferences regarding the attitude of the narrator toward the main character. First, the missionary's entire stay among the natives is compressed into a single sentence informing the reader that he had been among the natives for three years. Second, an analepsis captures the missionary's last thoughts – a recollection that one day King Charles V deigned to visit his monastery in Spain. The treatment of these temporal intervals suggests an inference in which the protagonist unflinchingly believes in his cultural superiority and has failed to learn anything of the natives in the New World during his three-year stay. This suggests an unflattering evaluation of the character by the narrator, and the reader may agree with this evaluation. However, for this interpretation of the text to constitute perspective taking, elaboration by the reader using personal knowledge and experience would be required. For example, the reader may have experience with or detailed knowledge of being the victim of a condescending or superior attitude, and such experiences could be construed as analogous to the situation in the story. Alternatively, the reader may draw on general knowledge (e.g., of Indigenous peoples, colonization, and evangelization) that may function as experience by proxy. (This hypothesized mechanism is discussed in Chapter 5.) In this case, the target of such perspective taking would likely be the narrator.

A more complex situation occurs when a heterodiegetic narrator is closely associated with a character. Such an association can occur with consistent mental access, focalization, or free-indirect speech or thought with respect to a character (cf. Dixon & Bortolussi, 2019). Such a narrator may express sympathy with many of the evaluations of the character. In a sense, the associated narrator may then be inferred to be the character in the reader's mind. If this is the case, perspective taking may proceed as we discuss with respect to autodiegetic narration: Taking the perspective of the narrator would be the same as taking the perspective of the character.

However, this imputed narrator-character may also be somewhat distant from the character in important respects. This alignment/distance combination is typical in stories where an older, more mature narrator relates an experience that occurred in the distant past. For example, in "Seventeen

Syllables" (Yamamoto, 1994), the narrator describes the young protagonist's thoughts and evaluations consistently throughout the story. Thus, by virtue of being closely aligned with the protagonist, in a sense the narrator is that character, and taking the perspective of the narrator would amount to taking the perspective of the character. In this case, it might be straightforward for readers to infer analogous life experiences that would allow them to form a perspective-taking analogy with the narrator in the guise of the protagonist. However, the narrator's apparent evaluations also suggest some distance from the character. For example, at the end of the story, the narrator sympathetically portrays the protagonist's mother's fearful reaction to her daughter's burgeoning romantic relationship. Perspective taking in this story ends up being complex and ambiguous: The reader could end up taking the perspective of the daughter, the mother, or the narrator at some time in the future.

Complicating the situation is the even higher level of the implied author. (By "implied author," we mean the author that could be inferred from the text, rather than the actual, historical author.) Readers may assume that the characters who sustain their interest are part of a larger design, but trying to figure out that design is really an attempt to figure out the point of the narrative, and this requires drawing conclusions, consciously or unconsciously, about the relationship of the (implied) author, narrator, and characters. Such conclusions may not be clear even at the end of the reading. Although there may be explicit information about characters' mindsets, information about how those characters fit into the author's overarching thematic, ideological, or philosophical meaning can be indeterminate or ambiguous. For example, the story of the necrophile mentioned in the second chapter, in which an autodiegetic narrator matter-of-factly relates the shocking details of her deviant behavior, leaves us wondering why an author would create such a morally abject narrator-character. The answer is not obvious. Perhaps the point is simply to show us the workings of an aberrant mind or perhaps just to shock? Such inferences concerning the intention of the implied author can affect how the perspective of the character should be interpreted. For example, when the work is understood as satire, the evaluations of the character may not be taken seriously, and the reader's motivation to take the character's perspective may be minimal. For example, in *A Hitchhiker's Guide to the Galaxy* (Adams, 1995), the protagonist expresses a variety of evaluations of his circumstances, such as a resentment of administrative red tape and the failure of higher powers to take his concerns seriously. Although the reader may agree with these evaluations, the broadly humorous and satirical nature of the narrative would likely undermine serious efforts to construct a perspective-taking analogy.

Presumably, the likelihood of a reader taking or not taking any given perspective is related to these complications. Therefore, a crucial question is how readers respond not only to the presence or absence of perceptible perspective markers in the text but also to less tangible relations of narrative distance. When that distance is ambiguous, incomplete, indeterminate, or paradoxical, perspective taking may be challenged or inhibited.

The Reader and the Character

Independent of the features found in the text, a critical ingredient in perspective taking is the relation between the reader and the character. In this section, we examine how readers construct a relationship to the character not on a straightforward representation of the words in the text but rather from a presumed understanding of who the character is and what the text is about. We first consider character homophily, the extent to which the character is seen as similar to the reader; then, we turn to affinity, the extent to which the reader likes the character, perhaps because of the character's moral stature. In both cases, we conjecture that these relationships will foster elaborative processing of the text and hence lay the groundwork for perspective taking.

Character Homophily

Homophily, as summarized in Chapter 2, is the superficial similarity between the reader and the character. Aspects of homophily include objective features (such as age, gender, and demographics) and subjective traits (such as beliefs, opinions, and attitudes). In research on real-life perspective taking, as we saw in Chapter 3, there is evidence that perceived homophily has positive benefits, such as improved communication and cultural tolerance and understanding (Wang et al., 2014). Homophily has often been central to analyses of identification; in such discussions, it is assumed that a reader will identify with a character (and presumably adopt their perspective) to the extent to which the character is perceived to be similar (e.g., Slater & Rouner, 2002; Cohen, 2006).

There is some evidence for this claim. For example, Beyard-Tyler and Sullivan (1980) provided some support for the role of gender: Adolescents were more likely to prefer stories if the character gender matched that of the reader. Although in their research participants only read a synopsis rather than the story itself, the results suggested that readers have an expectation about the kinds of characters that they will appreciate. One study by Hoeken et al. (2016) examined educational homophily and found that law students identified more strongly with the lawyer character of a story than did humanities students. In media studies, Eyal and Rubin (2003) asked subjects to rate television characters and found a moderate relationship between homophily and identification. Similarly, Green (2004) found that readers who had homosexual friends or family were more likely to report transportation when reading a story with a homosexual protagonist. (As we argued earlier, the phenomenon of transportation is likely to be related to the construction of a perspective-taking analogy.) Thus, there is a range of evidence consistent with the intuition that taking a character's perspective depends on some form of similarity between the reader and the character.

On the other hand, there is reason to suspect that there is more to taking the psychological perspective of a character than superficial perceived similarity. Harding (1961) argued that not all similarity results in identification. For example, readers of fiction might recognize in a character aspects of themselves that cause them shame or embarrassment and that they therefore want to ignore; such similarity thus could lead to dissociation from the character. Another possibility mentioned by Harding is that a reader may envy the character. In such a scenario, the perceived similarity is between a character's quality and readers' ideal: Readers see in the character traits they would like to attribute to themselves.

Recent empirical work lends further support to Harding's (1961) insight that similarity perception does not necessarily entail identification. De Graaf (2014) conducted an experiment in which the living circumstances of the protagonist of a story were manipulated: In one condition the character was living with parents; in another, in student housing. The results showed that although participants perceived themselves as more similar to the protagonist whose living conditions matched theirs, this similarity did not affect identification. The results might be explained by Cohen's (2006) argument that psychological similarity is more important than demographics such as gender and age. It is easy to imagine, for example, a scenario in which a reader recognizes in a character a similarity of education and social status, but a radical difference in personality or ideology. This could plausibly make it difficult to take the character's perspective in spite of the superficial similarities. Cohen (2001) similarly argued that homophily is not equivalent to identification (and presumably perspective taking). In his view, finding similarity depends on "attitudes or judgments that people make about characters," which requires "drawing on one's own psychological schemas" (pp. 253–254); we would argue that this is the basis of the analogical inferencing required to take a perspective.

Rather than homophily, Sanford and Emmott (2012) considered the assumption that empathy (emotional perspective taking, in our terms) is driven by autobiographical alignment, or shared reader-character traits. They concluded that while shared similarity might enhance relatability and role taking, it cannot account for readers' experience of empathy for characters whose fundamental traits are different. In such cases, empathy might be fostered by a "much looser type of connection, where a situation in a narrative is seen to echo a similar experience in the reader's real life, by stripping away surface features of both and matching essential characteristics" (p. 212).

On our analysis, this "looser connection" really amounts to a form of analogy between the life of the reader and that of the character. Thus, perspective taking is related not to simple homophily but rather to the *constructed similarity* that arises from the development of an analogy between the character and the reader. Finding an analogy between the character and the reader allows the reader to see the character as similar. However, this means that what matters for perspective taking is the outcome or product of the analogy, not the initial perception of similarity. As described in Chapter 2 (and in more detail in Chapter 5), such an analogy allows readers to identify those evaluations of the character that are related to evaluations that they themselves make. Of course, simple homophily can aid the process of finding an analogy. It may be easier, for example, to find corresponding, analogous experiences when the reader and the character have demographic similarities. Thus, homophily could be a variable in promoting or easing the process of constructing a perspective-taking analogy even if it is not essential.

Character Affinity

Another potentially important variable in perspective taking is readers' affinity for the character. In our terms, affinity describes the reader's positive attitude toward a character. This can be a function of the character's moral stature, intellectual standing, or some other cause of likability. In many treatments of identification, it is assumed that the reader comes to like the character (e.g., Liebes & Katz, 1990) or that positive attributes are a necessary precondition to identification (e.g., Cohen, 1999; Tal-Or & Cohen, 2010). Zillmann (1991, 1994) argued that a character must be seen in a positive light in order for empathy to occur. Similarly, Tan (1994) suggested that in film, positive attributes of a character (such as pursuing a just cause or physical attractiveness) lead to feelings of sympathy for that character. Along similar lines, Wimmer et al.'s (2021) concept of "imaginative resistance" captures the idea that readers do not engage with immoral characters. For example, Heinlein's (1961) *Stranger in a Strange Land* strikes contemporary readers as disturbingly sexist, as social attitudes and expectations have significantly changed since the novel's initial publication. Therefore, readers' social and cultural sensitivities are important mediating variables.

Affinity may be more important than some of the textual features we have discussed so far. For example, affinity for a character may provide the motivation to think more deeply about the character and do the elaborative processing prerequisite for perspective taking. Tal-Or and Cohen (2010) argued that affinity or liking functions much as similarity does in leading the reader to activate personal knowledge. Indeed, the same textual features – personal pronouns or use of a focal character, for example – can be used to depict characters of differing moral standards and intellectual abilities, and it seems unlikely that such minor stylistic variations would override a tendency to take or not take the perspective of such a character. A deeper question, though, is the extent to which affinity varies with the contextual information provided in the text. For example, a murderer might be judged more or less harshly depending on the details provided. "Sin of Omission" (Matute, 1989a) is a perfect example. Most of the story provides detailed information about the orphaned protagonist's horrendous past in which he is cruelly exploited since childhood by a stone-hearted, rich uncle under whose protection he has been put. This accumulated information helps us understand his state of mind and his psychological anguish when, at the end of the story, he hurls a rock that kills the uncle. Although the character is objectively a murderer at the end, his innocence and humility to that point make it easy to understand how readers could like him.

As Sanford and Emmott (2012) concluded, literature often presents moral dilemmas, and these "may reflect the moral problems that readers encounter in their real lives" (p. 212). On our view, although the depicted dilemma might be very different from anything in the reader's history, such narratives can evoke analogically related experiences. Similarly, we conjecture that elaboration in one form or another can promote affinity for even apparently unlikable characters. Dostoyevsky's novellas provide an intriguing example. The author created characters who, on the surface, appear to be irredeemable outcasts we can spurn. The underground man's cruel humiliation of Liza in *Notes from Underground* (Dostoyevsky, 1864/1996) and Velchaninov's spiteful treatment of the old man and the widow in *The Eternal Husband* (Dostoevsky, 1870/2012) can easily lead one to a harsh and critical evaluation of those characters. However, in reading these works, readers face the enigma of what drives people to such irrational and ruthless behavior. As information accumulates in the stories about the institutional and social injustices and humiliations that the protagonists had suffered, readers might draw causal inferences that explain the protagonists' mental anguish, and such inferences might then mitigate their original assessment of the cruel characters. Of course, doing so requires an extensive elaboration of the circumstances of characters in their worlds and may allow them to identify analogical relationships to their own lives. Our suggestion is that these elaborative inferences may be prompted by some of the second-order features we discussed earlier. For example, *Notes* begins with what in effect is a form of narratorial implicature: "I am a sick man ... I am a spiteful man. I am an unattractive man." Because these are odd and perhaps unreasonable assertions to make about oneself, it invites the reader to infer a suitable justification.

What is critical in texts such as these is the extent to which readers draw on personal knowledge and experience during elaboration. Readers who have experienced some form of humiliation, perhaps through unmerited or overly harsh criticism, or bullying, body shaming, or hostile rejection of one's ideas, may understand what causes a person to lash out. They can therefore form a connection with Dostoyevsky's characters, and in that sense take their perspective. Both of Dostoyevsky's protagonists are filled with self-loathing. Readers who have at some point in their lives assessed themselves harshly will also be able to draw that personal connection. That, too, enables a more direct, personal experience with the characters that is the basis of perspective taking. Thus, in our view, character affinity is often likely to be a product of perspective taking rather than a prerequisite. When readers succeed in building a perspective-taking analogy, they will have ready justifications for the character's behavior, allowing the character to be seen as just and reasonable. Further, the personal connection to the character will make the character more self-like and appealing. Of course, objectively moral behavior and appealing personal characteristics should make this process easier, but it is not always necessary.

Summary and Conclusions

The goal of this chapter was to examine how perspective taking in literature is related to properties of the text. We first examined two processes often invoked in the context of perspective taking: identification and transportation. Our analysis was that both are based on the elaborative processing that we argue is also the key to perspective taking: Identification refers to the sense of similarity that occurs when that elaboration succeeds in making a personal connection to the experiences of the character, and transportation refers to the extensive mental processing that may be involved in such elaboration. We then summarized evidence on what we termed "first-order" textual features: identifiable stylistic devices believed to trigger perspective taking. These include cues for character evaluations, the use of first-person personal pronouns, mental access to a character, and the technique of free-indirect speech style. Our review of the evidence on the effects of these features suggested that the assumed causal effect on readers' responses is tenuous at best. We proposed that instead of being tied to relatively superficial aspects of narrative style, perspective taking is more fundamentally based on elaboration that makes use of personal knowledge and experience. Thus, we discussed "second-order" features that may foster this kind of elaboration. These included "showing" narrative styles, evaluative gaps, embodied descriptions, and narratorial implicatures. In the last part of the chapter, we examined two other issues: the complexities deriving from the role of the narrator in perspective taking and the relationship of the reader to the character.

Across the topics we covered here, there is a central thesis: Perspective taking is possible when readers elaborate the story world based on their own personal knowledge and experience. This elaborated representation can then be used to build a perspective-taking analogy that justifies the evaluations of characters. We do not have a simple account of how aspects of the text determine any particular analogical relation identified by a given reader. Rather, what we have attempted to do here is to stress how elaboration while reading is a critical first step in this process and how such elaboration can be linked to the text in various ways. In Chapter 5, we turn to a more detailed analysis of the cognitive processes that we assume are involved.

CHAPTER 5

Processing Components of Perspective Taking

In this chapter, we develop in more detail the processing components of perspective taking as a form of analogical inferencing. As we argued in Chapter 2, readers construct analogies between the story world and their own personal knowledge and experience. Such analogies serve to explain evaluations that characters form of people and events in the reader's eyes. Based on this analysis, problems and issues in perspective taking can be understood as aspects of three processes: memory retrieval, which allows personal knowledge and experience to be available; similarity construction, which connects that knowledge and experience with the story world; and analogical inferencing, which builds the relationships between evaluations of the character and the reader. Here, we first discuss these three processes and then describe several different ways in which such analogies can be formed during comprehension, elaborating on the types of perspective-taking dynamics that can unfold while reading narrative. For simplicity, we focus on perspective taking in reading literature. However, as we noted in Chapters 1 and 3, much of this analysis also applies to perspective taking in real life.

Conceptually, autobiographical memory retrieval, construction of similarity, and analogical inferencing have a functional relationship. First, during narrative comprehension, elaboration may entail or invite the retrieval of related personal knowledge and experience by the reader. As we have discussed previously, this retrieval is essential for perspective taking because it involves the reader with the character's world. Second, the reader needs to identify how the retrieved experiences are similar to the corresponding events and evaluations that characters make of other characters, situations, and events in the story world. Although sometimes such similarity relations are obvious, we argue that it is more common that similarity needs to be constructed because the relevant similarities are often more abstract than superficial homophily. And third, having constructed those similarity relations, the reader is in a position to find the parallel analogy structure discussed in Chapter 2 (and as shown in Figure 2.1), that is, similar evaluations of the reader and the character that are justified by similar experiences. One of our goals in the present theoretical treatment is to base an account of perspective taking on mental processes that are well understood and studied in other contexts. Some of the ideas and empirical work that apply to these processes are reviewed in what follows.

Retrieval of Personal Knowledge and Experience

As described in Chapter 4, an often-critical part of comprehension is elaboration in which the mental representation of the story world is extended beyond the denotative meaning of the text. In many cases, the relevant information for elaboration can be found in autobiographical memory. (New evidence on the role of autobiographical memory in perspective taking is presented in Chapter 7.) In this section, we first discuss the use of cues to retrieve information from memory. Critically, episodes in memory are not stored as verbatim recordings but must be reconstructed, and we describe the implications of reconstruction for perspective taking. Closely related to reconstruction is the idea that what might be retrieved is not actually something that was experienced, but rather a representation of a new situation (but based on related experiences). We then turn to the problem of experience by proxy: the retrieval of events and experiences that are known vividly but only experienced second hand through education, media, or interpersonal descriptions. We also discuss the mechanics of autobiographical memory retrieval and the distinction between direct retrieval and search. Finally, we describe self-referencing: the process of relating information to oneself.

Memory Cues

Episodic retrieval depends on available cues and retrieval criteria. In very general terms, the human memory system produces information from prior experience when it is presented with a memory retrieval cue. The cue matches some aspect of the information in memory, and the strength of the retrieval will vary with the overlap between the cue and the retrieved information. Theorists such as Franklin and Mewhort (2015), Murdock (1982), and Shiffrin and Steyvers (1997) have offered detailed accounts of the mechanics of this type of system. In these accounts, retrieval will be faster and more accurate when the prior event is distinctive, when it has occurred several times in the past, when the memory cue has a close match to that event, and when the event is recent. In the present context, important cues for the retrieval of autobiographical experience would be story-world events and circumstances, characters and their traits, and characters' evaluations of those in the story world. Generally, these will prompt the retrieval of related events, situations, people, and evaluations from the reader's personal knowledge and experience, and we assume that the efficiency of such retrieval will vary according to these variables. For example, in *Harry Potter and the Philosopher's Stone* (Rowling, 1997), Harry's experience of going away to boarding school might cue similar experiences of the reader. Presumably, if the reader had also gone to boarding school, there could be a relatively close match between the events described in the text and the reader's experience. Under such circumstances, retrieval would be efficient. Other readers might retrieve related but more dissimilar events, such as going away to camp or going off to college. Such experiences are more likely to be retrieved if they had been repeated, if they are recent, and if they are distinctive (i.e., dissimilar to other events in one's life).

Episodic Reconstruction

A core assumption in research on human memory is that episodic retrieval is reconstructive: Our memory of past events is reconstructed based on partial or fragmentary memory traces (e.g., Bartlett, 1932; Schacter & Addis, 2007). Thus, memory retrieval does not involve replaying a recorded memory "tape" but rather building a representation of a prior experience out of cues and memory fragments. This reconstruction leads to a variety of well-known memory errors and biases. For example, (reconstructed) memory is subject to suggestion (Loftus et al., 1978), bias from pre-existing knowledge and beliefs (Alba & Hasher, 1983), and effects of emotion (Bower, 1992). More generally, under the appropriate circumstances, people can reconstruct events that never actually occurred (e.g., Lindsay et al., 2004).

Our interpretation of the way episodic memory reconstruction operates in the context of narrative comprehension is as follows: First, a memory cue, typically from the text, serves to activate fragments of sensory and mental experience. These consist of sensory features encoded with the original experience and mental activity associated with that experience (Schacter & Addis, 2007). Second, a coherent interpretation is identified that ties these fragments together. That interpretation could be suggested by the memory fragments themselves or determined by the intended memory retrieval. For example, in the final episode of *A Christmas Carol*, Scrooge is delighted as he witnesses people engaging in Christmas activities; the evaluation "delight" could be used as an interpretation by the reader to unify experiential fragments that are activated by "Christmas." Third, in order to form a consistent and coherent representation of the event, the retrieved information is used recursively as a memory cue itself to retrieve further details about the episode (cf. Mewhort & Johns, 2005). Thus, delightful Christmas experiences might be used to retrieve related aspects of a particular Christmas event. This can be repeated to generate a sufficiently coherent representation of the situation. The ease with which such a coherent representation of the event is constructed in this iterative fashion provides an indication that the representation is veridical (cf. Johnson et al., 1993).

In this description of episodic retrieval, memory errors and distortions occur for two reasons. First, the retrieval cue may not be sufficiently specific and fragments from other events may be retrieved. For example, a cue such as "camping" might, for some people, elicit memory fragments from many different trips that occurred at different times and under different circumstances, and these may not readily cohere into a veridical representation of a single prior event. Second, the interpretation that provides coherence for these fragments may not be suitable and is subject to a variety of contextual influences. For example, the interpretation that camping is uncomfortable may bias the retrieval of sensory information from previous camping experiences and in fact distort the episodes that might be retrieved, such as aspects of camping experiences that were satisfying.

This view of reconstruction can also be used as a new, memory-based interpretation of the process that some have referred to as simulation (e.g., Carroll, 2001). In this case, the goal is not to construct a veridical description of a previously experienced event but rather to represent some potentially new situation. Nevertheless, fragments of experience that fill out this reconstruction derive from previous episodic memories. The difference is that a novel interpretation tailors how these fragments are used to "reconstruct" a new event. For example, in *Life during Wartime* (Shepard, 1987), the protagonist, while on leave from his army duties, gets a lift into town aboard a military helicopter. While this is not an experience that most readers will have had, they may be able to simulate a representation of this event from related experiences such as catching a ride with friends in a car, traveling by small plane, or going on a vacation. Combining elements from such prior experiences in an appropriate manner may lead to a "simulation" of the episode described in the text. Schacter and Addis (2007) use the term "episodic reconstruction" to refer to a similar idea.

The difference between such a simulated representation and a representation of an event that was actually experienced is that the latter is likely to be more detailed and coherent. This is because the memory fragments derived from the same, experienced episode will of necessity be consistent with one another, while fragments from disparate episodes used to synthesize a novel situation may not be. For example, in service of understanding Harry Potter's experience in going away to wizarding school, one may retrieve the experience of going away to boarding school if the reader had actually done so. As described earlier, the representation of this retrieved event could acquire details and nuance by the iterative creation of memory cues. However, one could also construct a simulated representation of such an experience from a variety of different but related events (as described in the previous paragraph). However, these different reader experiences have distinct contexts and qualities and thus the simulation of the story-world event typically would not be as coherent and compelling as an actual memory of attending boarding school.

These considerations are critical for understanding how memory retrieval is used in the service of building a perspective-taking analogy (as described in Chapter 2 and in Figure 2.1). We propose that, generally, information in the text provides cues for the retrieval of episodic fragments, as discussed earlier. However, in this case, the hypothesized analogical structure provides the interpretation that is used to reconstruct the episode from the retrieved fragments. In particular, the reader will search for events that justify a particular evaluation or evaluations that follow from a particular event, and fragments that fit with that schema will cohere together, allowing the analogy representation to be assembled. When readers use episodic reconstruction also to simulate (in the sense just described) the story-world situation, the parallel between the story world and the corresponding episodic representation can be close because the same memory fragments are used for both. For example, the reader may simulate Harry Potter's reaction to going away to wizarding school based on their own experience of going away to camp. Having done so, it would be easier to represent a broader analogy between that experience and Harry's.

A further example may make this clear. In *Smiley's People* (Carré, 1969/2006), George Smiley, after retiring from the intelligence service, has occasion to meet with two former colleagues, Strickland and Lacon. In this conversation, Smiley expresses disdain for bureaucratic restrictions and procedures:

> "The groups have been dustbinned, George," Strickland said. "The lot of them. Orders from on high. No contact, not even arm's length. The Vladimir's death-and-glory artists included. Special two-key archive for 'em on the fifth floor. No officer access without consent in writing from the Chief. Copy to the weekly float for the Wise Men's inspection. Troubled times, George, I tell you true, troubled times."
>
> "George, now steady," Lacon warned uneasily, catching something the others had not heard.
>
> "What utter nonsense," Smiley repeated deliberately. (p. 61)

While readers are unlikely to have experience with specific, similar administrative procedures, they could easily have in memory situations in which they thought some administrative powers behaved officiously to add unneeded complexity. An academic reader, for example, may have analogous feelings of annoyance and resentment toward an institutional review board. This evaluation could then provide an interpretation that allows the reader to retrieve event details that support the reader's evaluation of annoyance and resentment. This, in turn, could then be construed as analogous to Smiley's experience with his agency's administration.

Generalized and Constructed Experience

Critically for our analysis, personal knowledge and experience may be retrieved and used at different levels of generality. Retrieval can thus vary from a particular episode to more general information about types of experiences the reader may have had. At the extreme end of this continuum would be what the reader believes to be facts about the world, divorced from particular experience. Specificity can vary with the nature of the cues, so that specific cues are more likely to generate specific episodes. For example, in the concluding section of *A Christmas Carol*, Scrooge eats dinner at the home of his nephew. This event provides a general cue, eating dinner, that may lead to the retrieval of general facts, learned through experience, about the eating of a meal. It also provides a fairly specific cue: eating dinner at Christmas with extended family members in a relatively formal setting. This more specific cue may lead to the retrieval of a particular experience of the reader.

Some theories of memory provide precise descriptions of mechanisms for automatic generalization of this sort. For example, McClelland and

Rumelhart (1985) outlined a memory model in which individual experiences are stored in some detail (see also Anderson & Milson, 1989). In this model, memory retains many specific experiences or instances rather than general facts or abstractions (cf. Hintzman, 1986). Over time, a variety of experiences will be stored and these will have a range of similarity to one another. When a cue is presented that matches only one particular experience, information from that experience will be retrieved. It is more likely, though, that a cue will match several previous experiences to some extent. In that case, what will be retrieved will be what all of those experiences have in common. For example, one may have several different Christmas dining experiences. A cue that included specific information about one of those may successfully retrieve information from that episode: "That year the oven quit working while trying to cook the turkey" might retrieve information about who precisely was at that dinner. On the other hand, a more general cue, such as "Christmas dinner," would retrieve information that is common to many such experiences, such as turkey being prepared, typical Christmas dinner attendees, and so on. McClelland and Rumelhart describe the mathematics of how a general cue elicits automatically a generalization of the prior experiences.

As an example of the use of generalized experience in perspective taking, consider Mellet's short story, "Good Night Air" (Mellet, 1997). This story describes a male protagonist who feels trapped in a living situation with an unappreciative wife and an ailing, bullying mother; it culminates in the protagonist making a subtle, passive-aggressive action of leaving a window open, knowing that the mother wanted it shut. Although most readers will not have experienced situations particularly close to the situation described in the narrative, the story may cue the retrieval of a host of situations in which the reader felt trapped by unwelcome obligations. Each of those retrieved situations would have their own antecedents and specific circumstances, but they may share some common emotional evaluation such as resentment, a sense of unfairness, and resignation, and they might be linked to a desire to remonstrate in some fashion. These common emotions and desires provide a basis for understanding the story, for linking the reader's experiences to those of the story character, and ultimately for perspective taking.

Search and Direct Retrieval

Following Uzer et al. (2012), we envision that two kinds of episodic memory retrieval operations are important. *Search* entails a deliberate attempt to retrieve knowledge and experience that are relevant to the reader's goals. Search involves the strategic construction of retrieval cues to access prior experience. For example, to retrieve details about going away to camp, one might build a memory cue based on details that are already available or can be readily inferred, such as the camp location, peers, and activities. Using such representations as cues to memory may lead to the retrieval of other information in memory about the experience. This retrieved information can then form the basis for building further memory cues. This process continues until suitable information is found or the reader decides that nothing relevant is available. Critically, this process is iterative, intentional, and planful, and it can take some time. Readers may or may not make the effort.

A second type of operation is *direct retrieval*. We assume that direct retrieval occurs when textual information provides a strong cue for prior experiences. O'Brien and colleagues (e.g., O'Brien & Cook, 2016) have used the term "memory resonance" to describe the automatic retrieval of information (typically) encountered previously in the text, but we believe such a memory resonance process is also relevant for understanding more distant information available in episodic memory. In studies of autobiographical memory, direct retrieval can be distinguished from search on the basis of response time (Uzer et al., 2012): Direct retrieval can occur with little discernible delay, while search can last several seconds.

During reading, we assume that direct retrieval would be generated automatically by comprehension processes and would be characterized by relatively superficial matches between features of the text and the retrieved memories. For example, encountering the word "camping" in the text may quickly call to mind previous experiences with camping and camping trips. In contrast, search would be slower and, since it is effortful, would require some motivation by the reader to find relevant information. As discussed under "Routes to Analogy Formation" later in this chapter, search is more likely to be used in filling out an analogy under construction. For example, although camping experiences might be directly retrieved by textual cues, in order to construct an analogy like that shown in Figure 2.1, one may have to search for evaluations related to camping and their justification: For example, was the retrieved experience pleasant and why? This more deliberate search would be slower and more effortful.

Experience by Proxy

Our understanding of "personal knowledge and experience" includes experience by proxy. This might include direct observation of others' experiences, others' experiences that are related through conversation, and information about experiences acquired through media. For example, Wondra and Ellsworth (2015) noted that empathic emotional experience is not limited to observation in real life but may also occur with indirect observation through film or media. Their account has some connection to our analysis of perspective taking, as described in Chapter 3. What is critical for the present discussion is that these observed experiences are retained in memory and could subsequently be used as a basis for perspective taking in new situations. For example, at the end of *Tehanu* (Le Guin, 1990), the title character speaks to a dragon in the course of freeing her adopted parents from a magical spell. Clearly, readers will not have any direct experience with dragons. However, they are very likely to have experienced dragons of one form or another in media such as fairy tales, film, and television, and this could form the basis of understanding the character's perceptions and reactions.

An interesting feature of this conception is that literary reading could itself provide a source of experience by proxy. Thus, even if one does not take the perspective of a character in a given work, recollection of that character's experience could later provide the basis of analogies for taking the perspective of other characters in other stories. Perspective taking can, in effect, become recursive. For example, after reading and understanding the perspective of Harry in *To Have and Have Not* (Hemingway, 1937/2002), one presumably would have representations of Harry's experiences as he felt forced by economic circumstances into engaging in illegal smuggling. Such representations could then subsequently form the basis for interpreting the behavior of other characters engaged in actions outside the law. For example, in the space opera *The Pride of Chanur* (Cherryh, 1982), the protagonist Pyanfar resorts to illegal measures to transport an alien between worlds. In this case, she might be seen as trapped by political exigencies in an analogous way to Harry in *To Have and Have Not*. Similarly, a reader of *Madame Bovary* (Flaubert, 1857/1972) might attribute the protagonist's downfall to her character and thus be unable to find justification for her behavior. However, if a reader had previously encountered other stories of female protagonists caught in restrictive societies – for example, Gothic novels – such stories might more readily allow a contextual explanation for the behavior of the newly encountered protagonist.

When an extensive amount of experience by proxy has been acquired, the retrieval of that information appears to follow the same rules as the retrieval of direct experience (Yang et al., 2022). For example, Brown and

Shi (2019) found that fans of the Harry Potter novels and films made use of search and direct retrieval for Harry Potter events much as they would autobiographical events. Similarly, both autobiographical memories and Harry Potter episodes conformed to a typical narrative structure: For example, successive events in both Harry Potter episodes and autobiographical episodes are often linked causally, or they may share a common theme or goal. Both Brown and Shi and Yang et al. argued that both kinds of memories share the same memory substrate and retrieval processes.

Self-Referencing and Relevance

Cognitive scientists have framed self-referencing as the process that facilitates the understanding, learning, and recall of new information. More specifically, it has been defined as "the cognitive processes individuals use to understand incoming information that pertains to them by comparing it to self-relevant information stored in memory" (Escalas, 2007, p. 421). Self-referencing has been found to produce certain benefits. For example, Bower and Gilligan (1979) and Klein and Loftus (1988) claimed that self-referencing improves attention and recollection of the text. Tsunemi and Kusumi (2011) found that when subjects were asked to recall personal memories relevant to a perceptual description, a relevant target word was read more slowly. They proposed that the personal recollections led to greater elaboration during reading.

Presumably, self-referencing makes the text self-relevant so that the reader feels personally connected or specifically tied to the material in a text. Kuzmičová and Bálint (2019) argued that self-relevance can be expected to produce greater elaborative processing (cf. Bálint & Tan, 2019) and, we assume, greater facility in perspective taking. Critically, Kuzmičová and Bálint claimed that self-relevance occurs when the text has "special importance with respect to the individual reader's self, knowledge, or past experiences" (p. 430); thus, it must be a factor in the retrieval of personal knowledge and experience as we have discussed here. Although it is plausible to suppose that self-relevance is related to homophily between the reader and the character, this variable does not seem to be determinative. For example, Bortolussi et al. (2010) found that both male and female readers evaluated stories more highly when they had a male protagonist, independent of gender match.

More generally, a number of researchers have explored the idea that readers of fiction draw on personal memories (Seilman & Larsen, 1989; László & Larsen, 1991; Cupchik et al., 1998). However, the elaborative processing of the story world that self-referencing entails has not been rigorously examined in this context. In some consumer research, elaboration occurs when something specific in an advertisement triggers the retrieval of self-referencing autobiographical memories (Escalas, 2007), and these memories are believed to be structured as narratives (Fiske, 1993). Escalas found that advertisement texts that cued narrative self-referencing produced more positive evaluations of the product, presumably because self-referential narrative thoughts produce absorption or transportation and "the transfer of affect from memory to the brand" (p. 422). It is plausible to assume that something similar occurs during the reading of fictional texts: Some textual information or property prompts cognitive elaboration via the evocation of autobiographical memories. (We provide several hypothesized mechanisms as second-order features in Chapter 4.) Interestingly, consumer research has also provided evidence that a greater focus on autobiographical memories interferes with the processing of information, so that too many personal memories overpower textual features (Sujan et al., 1993).

Construction of Similarity

An essential component of the present account of perspective taking is the ability of the reader to find similarity between the elements of the story world and the personal knowledge and experience that they retrieve during elaboration. As outlined in Chapter 2, similarity underlies the relation between reader evaluations and character evaluations, as well as between story-world events and the reader's real-life experiences. However, similarity is a complex concept and its nature varies with context, knowledge, and goals. For example, as noted in previous chapters, simple trait or demographic overlap between the reader and the character may be neither necessary nor sufficient for perspective taking. Thus, a more powerful and nuanced understanding of similarity is critical. In the present section, we outline some of the issues and theoretical problems in such an approach to similarity.

Similarity Space

At its heart, the nature of similarity depends on the nature of mental representation. In many theories of representation, objects are described in terms of features, where a feature is some atomic representational element that distinguishes objects in the environment. For visual object identification, for example, color and oriented line segments are often listed as likely features (e.g., Treisman & Gelade, 1980). The features that are used to delineate semantic interpretations have been described as "semantic primitives" or "primes" by Wierzbicka (1996). In a feature-representation scheme, the similarity between two objects has a simple interpretation as shared features: Objects are similar to the extent that they have overlapping feature representations. However, the objects in a perspective-taking analogy require a much more complex representational scheme. Characters, story-world situations, and plot events cannot be easily reduced to a relatively small number of semantic primitives. In particular, the representations would require a description of characters, their mental states, and their attitudes and relations to other characters and situations. This makes it difficult to identify a system of semantic features that would suffice for identifying similarity.

An alternative account of how similarity might be conceptualized, without recourse to semantic features, can be found by considering recent research on how lexical semantic representations can be derived from word usage. In this work, similarity spaces are constructed mechanically from the co-occurrence statistics of words in large corpora (e.g., Landauer & Dumais, 1997; Mikolov et al., 2013; Aujla et al., 2019). In these models, similarity is based on the similar contexts in which a word appears. In such schemes, there is no need to specify semantic primitives a priori; the similarity dimensions emerge naturally as a function of how words are used in language. For example, "cat" and "dog" are similar not because they share features such as <fur>, <four legs>, and <domestic>, but because in the language corpus they both appear in a variety of similar sentences, such as, "I need to go home to feed my cat/dog" or "I'm very sad today because my cat/dog died." The statistics of co-occurrence are used to construct a similarity space with a very large number of dimensions, and the semantics of each word corresponds to a point in that space. Although a semantic representation in such a space has a conceptual relationship to a feature-based representation, similarity does not map in any simple way to particular features. Instead, similarity can be calculated directly based on the geometric relationship in the similarity space.

The critical insight from this conceptualization is that any two objects can be seen as similar under the right framing. The key is to find a subset of the space (technically, a hyperplane) in which the two objects differ minimally and then to ignore the balance of the space in which the objects are more disparate. This is always possible when there are very large numbers of dimensions of comparisons. In many situations, this effectively amounts to finding a common description of the two objects (and that often ignores obvious feature-based comparisons). Consider two characters from literature: Ahab from *Moby Dick* (Melville, 1851/1991) and Frodo from *The Lord of the Rings* (Tolkien, 1937/2008). These characters would seem to have little in the way of overlapping features: They live in different worlds, have radically different statures and dispositions, and Frodo is not even human. However, both can be described as focused on a single-minded quest that is all-consuming: in Ahab's case, the search for Moby Dick, and in Frodo's case, the destruction of the ring. In both cases, this quest determines many of the characters' actions and at times leads them to behave irrationally. In a sense, the two characters can be seen as similar by limiting the consideration to a single piece of the similarity space; namely, the character's relationship to an overarching goal. We refer to the common description that fits both characters as a similarity plane; this is the portion of the high-dimensional similarity space in which the two elements differ minimally.

The process of finding a similarity plane is intuitive in many contexts. For example, in *A Christmas Carol* (Dickens, 1843/1992), Scrooge comes to regret past actions; readers may also be able to find actions from their past that they regret. Thus, despite the many differences between the reader and Scrooge, they may be seen as similar in this particular respect. As another example, Harry Potter (Rowling, 1997) is put upon by his adoptive parents and cousin; in order to find similarity to the character, readers may be able to retrieve memories in which they were put upon by their parents (or other authority figures), even if their childhoods were generally happy. Such a description of reader life circumstances that matches Harry's amounts to finding the similarity plane. Because there are a very large number of possible descriptions that could be considered, it is almost always possible to find some form of similarity between two such elements. For this reason, we argue that similarity is not a fixed, immutable property of the story-world elements and the reader; rather, we suggest that similarity is *constructed* by a search for a suitable common description that constitutes the similarity plane.

Finding a common description is related to the concept of ad hoc categories as discussed by Barsalou (1983). In his analysis, an ad hoc category is a description of objects that could be used to satisfy a particular goal, such as "activities to perform on a camping trip." Presumably, this category is not stored in memory but must be constructed (at least the first time) based on an understanding of a particular scenario or situation. Barsalou emphasizes the importance of a goal to be achieved in a particular scenario; our conception of a similarity plane would seem to be more general. However, both his view of ad hoc categories and our concept of a similarity plane depend on a description that would apply in some imagined situation.

Similarity is central to the construction of analogies. In some approaches to analogy in simple domains, similarity has been conceptualized in terms of feature overlap. For example, it has been found that in laboratory settings "people focus on superficial features when using analogy" (Dunbar, 2001, p. 314). However, Dunbar also found that in real-world contexts, people such as politicians and scientists use structural features with some frequency. Yet even in the most obvious cases, there is still the problem of deciding how much similarity is needed and which similarities are the most relevant. One possibility is to limit attention to some subset of possible features. This amounts to a type of similarity plane because it defines a subset of the similarity space in which the objects are most similar. Others have argued that feature overlap is not always relevant (Tversky, 1977). Gentner (1983) explained that trait or attribute overlap is relevant for literal similarity comparisons, but that the strength of an analogy depends not on the "overall degree of featural overlap" (p. 156) but rather on higher-order functions or relations. This is comparable to our view that similarity can be determined by a common description. Her example of the analogy between an electrical battery and a water reservoir makes this point: Batteries and reservoirs have little overlap in terms of features such as size, shape, color, or substance. However, both have a common functional description: They store resources for later use.

In sum, it may not be possible to identify any objective criteria for what counts as "similar" in the mind of the reader. Instead, there are many different ways in which entities might be represented by the reader as similar, limited only by the effort and ingenuity in constructing a suitable common description. Of course, when the reader and the character in fact do share a variety of obvious features (as would be the case for simple homophily), the process of finding a similarity plane is straightforward; it would consist of precisely the features shared by the reader and the character. However, we argue that this is merely a limiting case and that identifying similarity is a more flexible process that can apply even when there are few obvious commonalities.

Salience

A further issue in constructing similarity relations is whether possible correspondences are noticed by the reader. We refer to this general variable as salience. Information in the text could be salient if it is highlighted by the narrator (e.g., Mullins & Dixon, 2007). Information that is inferred by the reader in the course of comprehension may also be more salient than other textual information. Stylistic techniques such as figurative language – tropes and metaphors, flashbacks, or foreshadowing – may serve to highlight information or interpretations of the story world to the reader, and thus contribute to salience. Similarly, aspects of the plot will lead some features of characters or situations to become more salient and available. For example, in *Smiley's People* (Carré, 2006), many plot developments hinge on loyalty: Villem's loyalty to Vladimir, Ostrakova's loyalty to her daughter, Connie's loyalty to Hilary, and so on. One might surmise that loyalty (and actions motivated by loyalty) would more likely be used as a basis for similarity between the reader and the character.

More generally, though, what is likely to matter in identifying similarity is the way in which aspects of the story world are described by the reader, that is, the similarity plane. As we discussed earlier, overlap in obvious features is generally not essential for a common description of disparate elements. Thus, the function of salience is to make that common description easy to find. In this sense, variations in salience distort the similarity space in ways that might make some descriptions more obvious than others.

Inhibition

Similarity can be construed in a wide range of ways depending on the reader's goals, the information provided in the text, and the reader's efforts. In many circumstances, a similarity relation might be entertained even if the elements being compared are superficially quite different, with few common features. This means that in order to process such a (potentially nonobvious) similarity relationship, other aspects of the representation that do not support that similarity need to be inhibited so that they do not interfere with the construction of a perspective-taking analogy. In particular, finding a similarity plane may require actively inhibiting superficial mismatching features in order to develop an analogy based on a constructed, common description. For example, in taking the perspective of Harry in *Harry Potter and the Philosopher's Stone* (Rowling, 1997), readers would need to ignore the fact that they do not have magical powers and do not attend wizarding school and instead focus on features that have a more universal commonality, such as loyalty to friends, perseverance in the face of adversity, and so on.

This issue is often important when the reader must find similar evaluations to construct a perspective-taking analogy. In Chapter 3, we reviewed the psychological research on mind reading and perspective taking that stressed the importance of inhibiting one's egocentric default (e.g., Apperly, 2012; Carlson & Moses, 2001; Converse et al., 2008). This entails adopting the target's evaluation rather than a (potentially conflicting) evaluation of one's own. For example, in the initial part of *Moby Dick* (Melville, 1851/1991), the main character Ishmael expresses a need to go to sea: "Whenever I find myself growing grim about the mouth … I account it high time to get to sea as soon as I can." Many readers will find this attitude unusual, and some may even be strongly averse to traveling by sea. Such a reader might easily find experiences of their own that play an analogous role in their lives, and a similarity plane might be identified by describing both as, say, "experiences that dispel ennui." However, in order to use this similarity, readers would need to inhibit their a priori, personal reaction to the idea of going to sea as found in the story world. A general characterization of inhibition in this context is that the reader must focus on the similar aspects of the reader and character evaluations and not process those aspects that are dissimilar.

In situations such as this, we refer to the reader's reaction to the story-world situation as their "direct" evaluation; this direct evaluation would need to be inhibited in order to find an analogical evaluation that matches that of the character. In some cases, though, the reader may find it difficult to inhibit this direct evaluation if it is too strong or compelling. If this occurs, it would be difficult to take the character's perspective. An interesting third possibility is that the tension between the direct and analogical evaluation may lead the reader to reconsider the direct evaluation. In the *Moby Dick* example, for instance, readers may decide that the sea may be more interesting than they had initially thought. Salience and inhibition together can be used to index the strength of the similarity relation between two elements. A similarity relation is strong if the similarity plane is salient (i.e., obvious and easy to identify) and if it requires little inhibition of other disparate features that might interfere with a judgment based on the similarity plane.

Todd et al. (2011) provided what we regard as a demonstration of the importance of inhibition. In their research, participants were primed to look for either commonalities or differences in presented pictures. After this priming task, they performed different types of perspective-taking tasks, including the processing of perceptual perspective, communicative intent, and false belief. Somewhat paradoxically, perspective taking was superior following a prime task focusing on differences rather than commonalities. Our interpretation of this result is that highlighting the differences makes participants more sensitive to differences that need to be inhibited in order to take a perspective.

Analogical Inferencing

The last component of our account of perspective taking is analogical inferencing. Discussions of analogy have a long history in logic and philosophy, dating back to Plato and Aristotle. However, the early conceptions of analogy were relatively unstructured, consisting of shared abstractions based on attributes or features, but also ideas, regular patterns, effects, or functions (Shelley, 2003). Since that time, analogy has been related to facilitating the understanding of abstractions; explaining, reasoning, and strengthening arguments; and problem solving and decision making. Based on the range of mental processes related to analogy, some have argued that the analogy formation is a key element in human cognition and cognitive development (Hofstadter, 2001; Holyoak et al., 2001). Research on the use of analogies has documented, for example, its use in problem solving (e.g., Ross & Kilbane, 1997), how difficult it is to spontaneously identify analogies across dissimilar domains (Gick & Holyoak, 1983), and how analogical examples function in written directions (LeFevre & Dixon, 1986).

Current theories of analogy agree that an analogy is a mapping between two domains, referred to as the source and target domains. The source domain (also called the "base" by some researchers) serves as the source of knowledge that can help understand the lesser-known or target domain. In our analysis of perspective taking, the source domain is the reader's knowledge and experience and the target domain is the story world. Following Gentner et al. (2001), an analogy consists of two or more corresponding elements in the source and target domain. The elements are related to one another in their respective domains, and those relationships are similar across domains. For example, a water reservoir can be thought of as analogous to an electrical battery. The elements consist of a resource in each domain (water, electrical energy) and a receptacle for the resource (the reservoir, the battery). The essential ingredient in such an analogy is the relation among the elements in each domain: The reservoir stores water for later use and the battery stores electrical charge for later use. Thus, the relation between elements is the same in the two domains. The similarity between the elements (such as water and electrical charge) is more abstract.

When analogies are described in this way, they can entail the mapping not just of individual elements but also of the relations among those elements (Gentner, 1983; Holyoak & Thagard, 1989). In Gentner's (1983) words, analogies are "characterized by structural parallelism (consistent, one-to-one correspondences between mapped elements) and systematicity – an implicit preference for deep, inter-connected systems of relations governed by higher-order relations such as causal, mathematical, or functional relations" (p. 8). As noted by Richland and Morrison (2010), identifying the analogical connections may require one to inhibit superficial similarities in favor of deeper abstractions. A suitable analogy allows one to draw inferences that may not be obvious in one domain or the other. For example, one may surmise that both batteries and reservoirs have a limited capacity, that they both might be replenished, and that resources might be lost even when not in use.

Analogies have been previously discussed in literature, independent of their use in perspective taking. Literature can present readers with unfamiliar situations, relations, and behaviors that challenge readers' assumptions about reality. Aspects of the fictional world, then, are something to be understood, enigmas to be deciphered, problems to be solved. Analogy plays an important part in such interpretive processing. For example, Holyoak (1982) used analogy theory to explain the comprehension of metaphors and allegories. Gentner et al. (2001) proposed that readers of poetry can connect "the relational patterns of a novel experience with that of a familiar, emotion-laden one" (p. 5). In other words, the psychologists conceive of the source domain as the reader's knowledge and experience and the target domain as the world of the poem. Moreover, this insight is comparable to our view of perspective taking as depending on an analogy between the story world and the reader's personal knowledge and experience. Kolodner (1993) maintained that analogies form an important part of reasoning in the sense that when individuals are faced with new problems, they retrieve and adapt analogs. This point is crucial to our theory: Readers connect relational patterns in the depiction of characters (the target domain) to something in their own past experience that is stored in memory (the source domain). Holyoak et al. (2001) explained that mapping allows one to make analogical inferences about a target and thus to fill gaps in understanding. Indeed, as we discuss later under "Perspective-Taking Dynamics," the use of analogies to make inferences about the story world is a critical part of taking a character's perspective.

We argue that when perspective taking is conceived of as analogical inference, one needs to map relations in the reader's personal knowledge and experience to relations in the story world. The core relation is between evaluations and their justification. To elaborate, the character has some evaluation of an element of the story world; this evaluation is presumably justified by events of the story world (even if such events are not explicitly described). Readers also have evaluations in their personal experience that are justified by events in their life. This justification relation is the same across the two domains. Thus, to construct a perspective-taking analogy, the evaluations of the reader and the character must be construed as similar in some way, and the justifying events in the reader's life and the characters must also be construed as similar. This provides the parallel structure of an analogy. Readers take the character's perspective to the extent that this structure can be developed in a coherent fashion across evaluations and events in the text.

With this account of analogy in hand, we can now elaborate more precisely on the inferences involved in perspective taking that we summarized in the discussion of Figure 2.1. In processing perspective, an evaluation on the part of the reader is matched to an evaluation on the part of the character. These evaluations are similar in some form. As we described earlier in our discussion of similarity, the elements need not be identical but simply share some common description. To cite an example, in the story "Very Happy" (Matute, 1989b), a newly engaged young man experiences resentful, critical, hostile evaluations of the people in his life. As the story unfolds, he reflects on how all his life he was controlled by others, such as his parents, societal expectations, and now his fiancée. Readers may be able to find comparable evaluations in their own life in which they felt manipulated, constrained, or resentful. If readers succeed in making this connection, they will also be aware of the justification for those feelings. To complete the parallel analogy structure, readers would assume that the feelings of the character are similarly justified by events in his life, even though they are not detailed in the story. Instead, readers would be able to infer that those justifying events were similar to those in their own lives. In our view of this perspective-taking analogy, the corresponding elements (evaluations of resentment; justifying events for that evaluation) are connected by (abstract) similarity relations, and in both the source and target domain, evaluations and events are linked by the "justified by" relation.

Analogy Quality

Once an analogy has been constructed, the implications of that analogy for further processing (and for perspective taking) will vary with the quality of the analogy. An important question is thus how to assess the appropriateness and strength of readers' analogies. We hypothesize that the stronger the analogies, the greater the degree of perspective taking. Here we discuss two aspects of analogy quality: the match of evaluations and their justifications and the scope or breadth of the analogy.

First of these is the analogical match. In the context of the perspective-taking analogy, analogical match refers to how compelling the similarity relation between the story world and the reader's life is. A nearly isomorphic analogy would be one in which, say, the events described in the story world are nearly identical to events that occurred to the reader, and those events lead to the same evaluation by the reader and the character. Take, for example, the beginning of *Shades of Twilight* (Howard, 2019), in which a young orphan hears adults talking about the prospect of adopting her. It might happen that both the reader and the character were orphans. In this case, the analogy could be quite close, with very similar evaluations by the reader and the character. However, we presume that this degree of match is rare. Instead, for a reader to take the perspective of the young orphan, other kinds of analogies would need to be generated based on more abstract similarities. For example, recollections of feelings of isolation caused by being excluded from some group during recess in elementary school might be a sufficiently close analog for taking the character's emotional perspective. Some story-world situations might present greater mapping challenges. Coming back to the story "Very Happy," the protagonist seeks his liberation from others' control by burning his father's cheese factory and getting himself imprisoned. In prison, he is then "very happy." Even if the reader is able to construct an analogy to such an extreme set of behaviors and evaluations, it is likely to be tenuous. More generally, we can index the strength of the analogical match in terms of how difficult it is to find some form of similarity between the corresponding analogy elements (cf. Holyoak & Thagard, 1989). As we discussed earlier, similarity would be strong if the similarity plane is salient and if there are relatively few dissimilar features that need to be ignored.

In addition to the match of the analogical elements, analogies can vary in terms of their breadth or scope. In general, analogy breadth would be indexed by the number of corresponding elements. With respect to perspective taking, analogy breadth can refer to the generality of the evaluations and to the extensiveness of the justifying events in the reader's experience that match those of the story world. Thus, a narrow analogy in perspective taking might involve the evaluation of a particular situation or event; a broad analogy might involve a character's attitude toward many events and situations. A broad analogy would support taking a very general perspective, as described in Chapter 2.

Perspective-Taking Dynamics

As we have emphasized at several points in this book, perspective taking is not a unified, monolithic event that results in a coherent, definitive state. Rather, it is an ongoing process that unfolds over time and to various degrees. Thus, in order to understand perspective taking, we need to identify the incremental processes that contribute to or hinder its development. We first turn to the dynamics of constructing the perspective-taking analogy in terms of the possible routes to analogy formation and then consider the implications of having such an analogy available. In Chapter 6, we will consider some of the problems that may occur during such an incremental development of perspective taking.

Routes to Analogy Formation

With reference to Figure 2.1, there are many possible routes to the construction of an analogy that would produce matching evaluations justified by personal knowledge and experience. These routes differ in terms of how they are initiated and in terms of the interplay of inference and memory retrieval. Here, we describe two broad classes of such dynamics, event-driven analogies and evaluation-driven analogies, based on where in Figure 2.1 the process begins.

Event-Driven Analogies
The first class of dynamics is what we refer to as *event-driven* analogies. In this case, the comprehension of the text generates remindings of events from the reader's personal knowledge and experience that are related to events in the story world. This is depicted in Figure 5.1. We assume that such remindings are typically automatic and unintentional and based on direct retrieval (as discussed previously under "Search and Direct Retrieval"). In any event, these remindings produce the event similarity relationship at the bottom of the figure. As an example from *A Christmas Carol* (Dickens, 1843/1992), consider when Scrooge, with the Ghost of

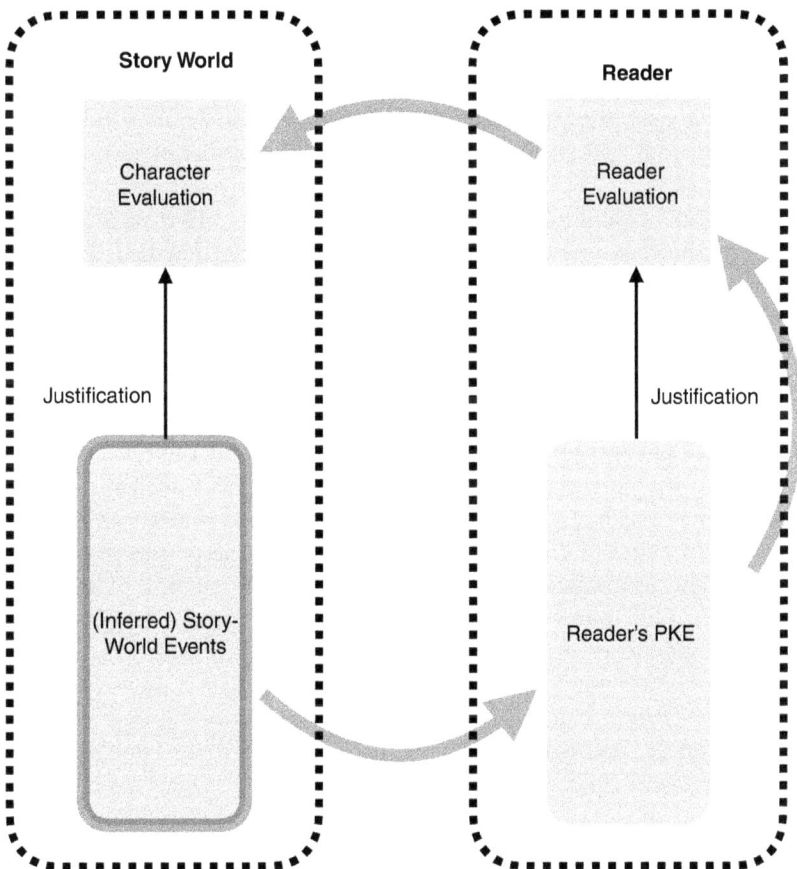

Figure 5.1 Event-driven analogies. PKE = personal knowledge and experience.

Christmas Present, visits his nephew's home and watches the family play a succession of parlor games. This might remind the reader of experiences of their own of playing games in a family group. Although the events are not identical and do not transpire in identical circumstances, there would be a common description that captures the similarity between the reader's experience and the story-world situation.

In order to produce an analogy, though, these events would have to be associated with matching evaluations. The first possibility is that events from the reader's memory justify evaluations in memory and that such evaluations lead the reader to search for or infer comparable evaluations on the part of the character. (This may be related to the phenomenon of projection as described by Carroll [2001].) For example, the experience of playing family games might be remembered warmly, and the reader would expect Scrooge to have a similar evaluation of the events in his nephew's house. Imputing that evaluation to Scrooge would produce the relevant analogy by completing the evaluation similarity link at the top of the figure.

A second possibility, not depicted in Figure 5.1, is that the reader reacts to the retrieved events with a new evaluation that had not been considered before. This evaluation might be guided in part by evaluations or circumstances in the story world. For example, in the beginning of *The Fellowship of the Ring* (Tolkien, 1937/2008), Bilbo bequeaths the ring to his nephew but parts with it only with great reluctance. Potentially, the passing of the ring may remind the reader of an occasion in which a personal item was gifted to a friend or relative, and Bilbo's emotional reaction to the potential loss of the ring may lead the reader to consider whether they also had some regrets about their gift. If readers can identify some similar kind of emotion, it would complete the perspective-taking analogy. The occurrence of such an effect would be an example of literature affecting real life, but it is by no means a predictable outcome guaranteed by any specific text feature.

Evaluation-Driven Analogies
In addition to event-driven analogical processes, there could also be *evaluation-driven* analogies as depicted in Figure 5.2. One type of evaluation-driven analogy could occur in the service of gap-filling during comprehension. In particular, if the reader encounters a seemingly unjustified evaluation in the text, they may be motivated to justify that evaluation based on their own personal knowledge and experience. Under some circumstances, the text might automatically bring to mind a related evaluation in analogous circumstances. In other cases, the reader would have to search their memory for an evaluation that has some similarity to the target evaluation in the text.

As an illustration, consider the behavior of Scrooge in the early part of *A Christmas Carol*: In one scene he dismisses two gentlemen seeking Christmas donations with, "It's enough for a man to understand his own business, and not to interfere with other people's. Mine occupies me constantly" (Dickens, 1843/1992). Scrooge's apparent negative evaluation of the gentlemen has no obvious justification – in fact, readers might believe that his behavior was rude or at least unnecessary. However, the retrieval of a similar evaluation would serve to explain and justify Scrooge's

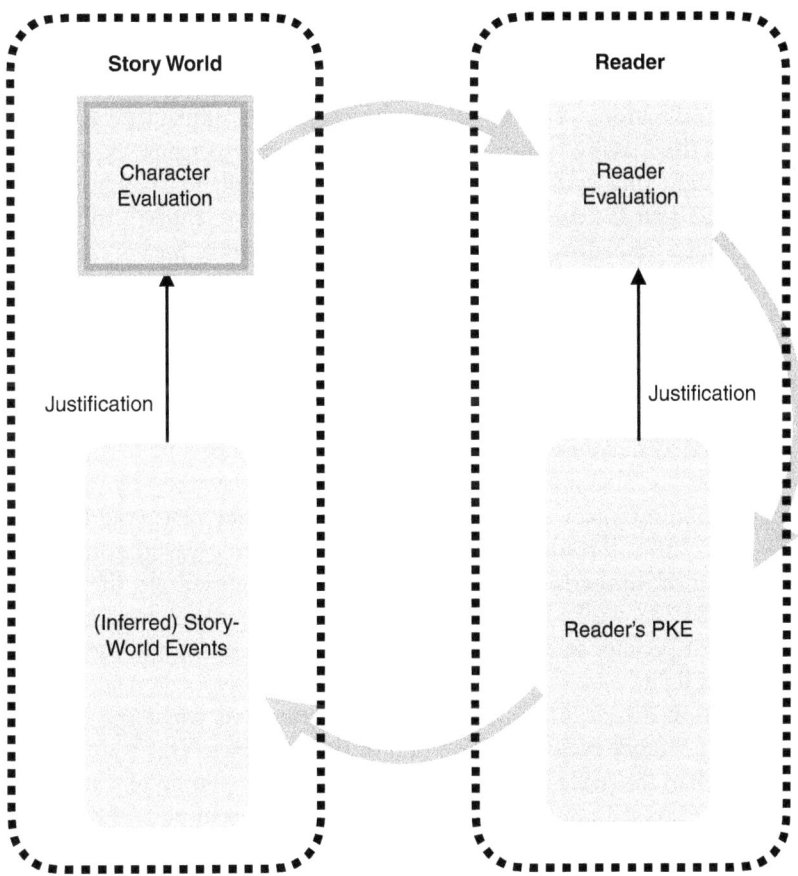

Figure 5.2 Evaluation-driven analogies. PKE = personal knowledge and experience.

story-world evaluation. For example, the reader might have memories of dealing with persistent telephone solicitors that they thought were annoying and worthy of an abrupt dismissal. Having retrieved this comparable evaluation, the reader would then presumably be able to retrieve the previous events and circumstances that were believed to justify that evaluation. To complete the analogy and justify Scrooge's evaluation, one might infer that there was a comparable history of requests for money in the story world that Scrooge similarly viewed as unreasonable. In this way, the initially baseless evaluation becomes justified by inferring analogous events involving the character in the story world. Even if such inferences about the story-world events are made, though, it still might not reflect well on Scrooge. For example, in the reader's experience, they may have refrained from acting rudely to the ostensible telephone solicitors or they might have felt a certain amount of guilt about the negative evaluations of those asking for charity. A subtle aspect of this analysis is that having formed this analogy with their personal experience, readers might thus attribute a certain amount of guilt to Scrooge on the assumption that his evaluation is similar to their own. Indeed, this inference would foreshadow Scrooge's expression of remorse for his comment later in the story.

As another example, in *Beowulf*, the hero boasts of his feats in the Danish King Hrothgar's great hall of Heorot (Anonymous, 800 BCE/2006). Potentially, this could remind readers of situations from their own lives where they felt compelled to produce glowing self-evaluations, such as in a job interview or resumé. Presumably, readers would be able to justify the protagonist's evaluations based on their experience and, by analogy, imagine circumstances and events in the story world that would justify Beowulf's claims. If readers construct the analogy in this way, they may also be aware of the limitations of the self-evaluations. For example, they might imagine that Beowulf's boasts, as well as their own resumé, were basically truthful but perhaps selective and designed to put Beowulf and themselves in the best light.

Evaluation-driven analogies can also be prompted when the reader's evaluation of story events matches that of the character. This is somewhat different than the reader searching for a matching evaluation of something in their personal knowledge and experience. For example, while being escorted by the Ghost of Christmas Past, Scrooge witnesses the encounter with Belle when she breaks off their romance. Scrooge finds this event painful, and asks the Ghost, "Why do you delight to torture me?" In this case, both the reader and the character may understand that the event was terrible for Scrooge and represented an important missed opportunity to change his life. However, on our analysis, these matching evaluations would not produce perspective taking as we have defined it. What is needed in addition is the involvement of personal knowledge and experience in justifying a similar evaluation in the reader's life. In particular, in order to form a perspective-taking analogy, the similar evaluation would have to cue the retrieval of justifying events from the readers' own lives. For example, Scrooge's regrets may remind the reader of an important decision that was later regretted. Perhaps the reader did not pursue a romantic engagement, did not take a promising job offer, or did not go on an exciting adventure. The perspective-taking analogy would be constructed if the justifying events for that evaluation of regret are then related to the story world, as in Figure 5.2.

This dichotomy between event-driven and evaluation-driven analogies is merely intended to illustrate components of the perspective-taking process. We imagine that in many cases, the construction of an analogy will normally work both ways at once or at different times. For example, the mechanisms described by Holyoak and Thagard (1989) might allow matching of both evaluations and events simultaneously using a constraint satisfaction approach (in which adjustments are made incrementally to achieve the best match). In particular, there are no limits on when inferential connections are made or how the identification of similarity proceeds. Although some analogies may be mostly event driven and others mostly evaluation driven, there may be others that derive from a mixture of inferences over time.

Resonance and Dissonance

The process of forming analogies unfolds gradually over the course of a narrative because the process of identifying or inferring the character evaluations and then searching for analogically matching evaluations must occur in a piecemeal fashion. Further, as we described in Chapter 2, a "perspective" should be thought of as a consistent interpretation of some set of those character evaluations. Therefore, taking a character's perspective also involves finding some coherence among the character evaluations. This outcome may occur to a greater or lesser extent or may not occur at all. Thus, a variety of dynamics may unfold as the reader continues to process the narrative. We describe two such dynamics in this section: perspectival resonance and perspectival dissonance.

Perspectival resonance between the reader and the character occurs to the extent that perspective-taking analogies can incorporate many evaluations of the character and to the extent that these evaluations have a coherent interpretation. (Note that perspectival resonance – the identification of a set of consistent, matching evaluations – is different from memory resonance [e.g., O'Brien & Cook, 2016], referring to the automatic and direct retrieval of relevant information during comprehension.) Under many circumstances, this resonance would increase as the reader progresses through the text and forms an increasing number of matching evaluations. Resonance would be stronger when there are a relatively large number of matching evaluations that are generated by a relatively small number of analogies, and it would also be stronger when the interpretation of these evaluations is more general and more coherent. It may take time and effort to find a suitable global interpretation for those matching evaluations. Further, this process could easily be slowed (or even thwarted entirely) if too few of the evaluations found in the text can be matched to similar ones on the part of the reader.

As an example of how this resonance can unfold, consider the novel *Neverwhere* (Gaiman, 2009) about a character who becomes involved in a fantastic "London Below." Early in the novel, the character Richard befriends a homeless woman by giving her an umbrella during a rainstorm. The reader may be able to find a comparable act of charity in their personal experience. Presumably, the reader could justify their own behavior based on prior experiences that dictate that one should help those in need. To complete the analogical structure, the reader could infer that Richard had comparable experiences that led to his actions (even though such experiences are not described in the text). Later, in what is a pivotal plot event, he cares for an injured girl he encounters lying on the sidewalk despite it being inconvenient (and likely ending his relationship with his fiancée). The reader may again be able to identify an analogous humane act of their own, perhaps using a related analogy. Subsequently, he befriends an orphaned girl with interest and support and is shocked when she apparently dies while helping him cross the treacherous "Knightsbridge." Again, the reader may be able to retrieve analogous feelings of caring about vulnerable strangers. All of these evaluations have the common theme of being bighearted, and as they are encountered in the text, finding analogous evaluations would strengthen the personal connection to this perspective.

An interesting question is whether the interpretation of the character's evaluations (i.e., the character's perspective) needs to correspond to a general interpretation of the reader's own, analogous evaluations. We believe it is not necessary; however, when it does, it would strengthen the resonance between the reader and the character. Indeed, finding an interpretation of the character evaluations may allow the reader to impute such an interpretation to their own corresponding evaluations, even when that interpretation was not obvious previously. In the *Neverwhere* example, readers may decide that the analogous actions and evaluations from their experience have a similar interpretation of being charitable and big-hearted even if this is not a salient self-description. Conversely, the inference may proceed in the opposite direction: When the reader has a global interpretation of their own evaluations, it may suggest one for the character evaluations. At different moments of this online process a reader can, through critical assessment of a character and deliberate self-introspection, engage in reflection that helps the reader understand and embrace aspects of that character's plight, feelings, and decisions.

There is also the opposite possibility: perspectival dissonance. This would occur when the reader cannot readily form analogies incorporating matching evaluations or when the matching evaluations are diverse and do not form a consistent, coherent whole. This might occur either because of difficulties in finding matching evaluations or because the reader's evaluations of the story world conflict with those of the character and cannot be inhibited. This would impede the process of completing the analogy structure with matching justifications. We consider some of these difficulties in more detail in Chapter 6. Because both resonance and dissonance refer to piecemeal processes that evolve over time, there is the potential for variation over time: The reader may initially feel that they have taken a character's perspective but then subsequent dissonance undermines perspective taking at that point.

Instances of unreliable narration can follow this arc. For example, in the initial portion of "The Yellow Wallpaper" (Gilman, 1892/1997), the text invites the reader to take the perspective of the character and sympathetic reactions may occur. However, perspective taking becomes more difficult as the narration becomes increasingly bizarre and incoherent. Of course, the reverse is also true: Perspective taking may be difficult initially but resonance may increase over the course of the text. *A Christmas Carol* may function in this way for many readers: Readers may find Scrooge's initial behavior objectionable, and this makes it difficult to construct perspective-taking analogies. However, the range of situations and character evaluations encountered over the course of Christmas Eve become gradually more approachable, leading the reader to take Scrooge's perspective.

Once some degree of perspectival resonance is achieved, subsequent inferential work by the reader may be easier. A successful analogy might serve as the model for analogies with other evaluations. Evaluations or justifying events that are consistent with the evolving resonant perspective might be inferred in the story world. More generally, the perspective-taking analogies that support perspectival resonance provide a powerful mental structure for understanding and interpreting the actions of the character because they provide strong links between the character and the reader's own knowledge and experience. For example, if a reader of *Harry Potter and the Philosopher's Stone* (Rowling, 1997) forms a perspective-taking analogy with Harry's boarding school experiences, they might attribute emotions of their own to Harry, such as timidity at making new friends, that are not explicitly described in the book. This provides the basis of phenomena such as identification and empathy. Consistent with the real-life mentalizing research reviewed in Chapter 3, this essentially makes the target (in this case, the character) more self-like.

Summary and Conclusions

In this chapter, we have laid out the theoretical underpinnings for an account of perspective taking. The core idea is that taking a character's perspective entails constructing an analogy between the story-world evaluations and experiences of the character and the real-life evaluations and experiences of the reader. In this way, the character's perspective becomes analogous to the reader's perspective. The perspective-taking analogy depends on elaboration of the text, the retrieval of relevant personal knowledge and experience, identifying similarity relations between those memories and the story world, and an inferential process that builds an analogical structure based on the parallel justification relations in the reader's life and the story world.

This theoretical analysis provides a basis for a description of the possible dynamics of perspective taking. In some cases, perspective taking may begin by noticing a correspondence between a character evaluation and a reader evaluation; in other cases, there may be a parallel between the events of the story world and the experiences of the reader. These parallels are then filled out with further memory retrieval and inferences about the character's experiences and, possibly, the reader's. Further, perspective taking is an incremental process in which these analogical structures are identified again and again, so that a consistent interpretation of the evaluations of the character can be matched to one of the reader. Many things can go wrong with this process, but when it succeeds, a strong personal connection is developed between the reader and the character.

CHAPTER 6

Challenges to Perspective Taking

As should be clear from the ideas developed in this book thus far, perspective taking and related processes are far from simple. Rather, perspective taking relies on a range of information, cognitive processes, and skills and capacities. Here, we more fully examine some of the variables and challenges that may arise in these processing components. First, we consider potential issues with the information that might be used to construct a perspective-taking analogy. Second, we discuss the effect of variations in perspectival resonance, that is, the extent to which matching evaluations and a consistent interpretation of the perspective can be found. Third, we consider the complexity of the character and how variations in the perspectives available in the text may affect perspective taking. Finally, we consider individual differences that relate to perspective taking, including cognitive skills, age, empathic and other emotional disposition, and motivation.

Available Information

As outlined in previous chapters, our view of perspective taking involves drawing analogical connections between the character (or perspective-taking target) and the reader. These connections are, of necessity, based on information about the reader and the target. Thus, the nature and amount of information available to the reader is crucial for constructing the perspective-taking analogy. In this section, we describe a few more specific issues in acquiring the requisite information. We consider information available about the character (or perspective-taking target in real life); variables that affect the information the reader has available by virtue of their knowledge, experience, and culture; and how information might be inferred by the reader through elaborative representation of the story world and through attribution.

Information about the Character

Social or literary categories can be used to describe the information a reader has about a character. For example, Brewer (1988) identified social categories that might exist at various levels of specificity, such as "older men," "businessmen," and "uptight authoritarian boss who is a tightwad and a stickler for details." Gerrig and Allbritton (1990) suggested that at a high level of abstraction in fiction, a character might be categorized as a "good guy" or a "bad guy." Schneider (2001) argued that categorization depends on the quality and quantity of information provided about a character. For example, categorization can occur with ease when textual information is consistent with a known category. However, in the face of inconsistent or contradictory information, or when a reader focuses on information external to the category, "de-categorization" can occur. "Individuation" occurs when new information is added that changes some aspect of the category without invalidating it. "Decontextualization" occurs when new information contradicts the essential features of the category. "Personalization" may occur when readers do not apply categories but instead make use of detailed textual information to understand a character. However, we would expand on this view and suggest that readers may do more than simply attend to detailed information about a character; they may also bring something of themselves to their character representation. In particular, personalization may include an analogical connection between the reader and the character.

Related analyses of perspective-taking phenomena also imply that there should be important effects of the information about the target. For example, de Graaf et al. (2009) noted that a persuasive message in an engaging text might have little effect when there is insufficient information about the character. Similarly, in Wondra and Ellsworths's (2015) appraisal theory of empathy, a necessary requirement is that the information about the target's situation be adequate and sufficient to make the perceiver "feel confident in his appraisal" (p. 420). In their analysis, empathy occurs when the perceiver assesses the target's situation in the same way as the target does. Our theoretical approach is related. However, we would say that empathy occurs when the information is adequate to form an analogical connection to the perceiver's personal knowledge and experience.

Lamm et al. (2007) provided a demonstration that relatively subtle aspects of the information provided about a target can affect perspective taking. They asked participants to rate the imagined pain and unpleasantness when watching video clips of people listening to painful auditory stimuli. They were told that the people in the clips were undergoing a treatment for a neurological disease, *Tinnitus aurium*. An important result was that both the pain and unpleasantness ratings were less when participants were told that the treatment was effective (as opposed to ineffective). Presumably, the information about treatment effectiveness led to a cognitive and motivational process that influenced empathic perspective taking. For example, participants may evaluate a painful experience as more acceptable when it has a beneficial outcome.

It is straightforward to find instances in which the available information constrains perspective taking in reading literature. For example, early in *A Christmas Carol* (Dickens, 1843/1992), it would be difficult to empathize with Scrooge because the reader does not have adequate information about the circumstances and history that lead to his bitter appraisals of the world. However, as the story develops, more information becomes available that make empathy and perspective taking more likely. More generally, novels often have a variety of minor characters about whom little information is provided, making it difficult to take their perspective. For example, the narrator of *Madame Bovary* (Flaubert, 1857/1972) does not describe in any detail the protagonist's neglected and spurned offspring. Thus, it is difficult for the reader to construct a fulsome representation necessary for perspective taking.

Despite one's best efforts to access all necessary information, and in spite of one's success at obtaining relevant information, an appropriate assessment of a situation may be difficult. For example, situations may be morally ambiguous, rendering the meaning of a person's actions prone to misinterpretation (Cervone & Tripathi, 2009). Unfamiliar situations can also leave perceivers uncertain about how to assess the observed. In contrast, individuals are better at taking the perspective of people they know than that of strangers (Norton et al., 2003). We conjecture that this effect is attributable to the additional information that is available about the target. With respect to literature, the portrayal of moral ambiguity and unfamiliar circumstances is often the intended goal. For example, in the conclusion of *Oryx and Craik* (Atwood, 2010), the protagonist prepares to murder the last survivors of an apocalyptic plague. This action is potentially justified by the goal of replacing humankind with a new, artificial species without many human flaws, but the murder also seems reprehensible on an intuitive level. We might surmise that the creation of this unfamiliar situation with its novel moral choices was part of the author's goals. However, these ambiguities may also make perspective taking more difficult.

Reader Background

An important source of information in perspective taking is related to the reader's background. We argue that the richer and more diverse one's social, cultural, and historical knowledge, the better one's chances of taking the perspective of a target who appears to be different. This is because such diversity provides a broader basis for finding similarities to the target's circumstances. By the same token, the more restricted one's life experience, the lesser one's chances of understanding the target's mental and emotional states. There are two aspects of reader background: a reader's personal experience and more general cultural knowledge.

With respect to personal experience, Wondra and Ellsworth (2015) point out that our "past experiences help observers appraise targets' situations" (p. 420). In support of this view, Gerace et al. (2015) found that rated ease of taking a person's perspective in a problematic situation was related to their rated familiarity with that situation. Similarly, it has been demonstrated that individuals achieve higher empathic accuracy dealing with friends than with strangers (Buck, 1984), perhaps because one has more knowledge about the background and circumstances of one's friends. Relatedly, Galinsky and Moskowitz (2000) found that when participants wrote narratives about a pictured person, they used fewer stereotyped traits and more personal traits when they were asked to take the person's perspective. Although it thus appears that personal knowledge of a target's situation supports perspective taking, we would claim that such knowledge is not essential: With some effort, it should generally be possible to find more abstract levels of similarity description even when the target's situation is unfamiliar.

Cultural knowledge is another aspect of reader background that can affect perspective taking. Such knowledge can include the norms and general openness of the society in which one lives. For example, barring inevitable exceptions, Canada is generally perceived as a country open to immigrants, tolerant, and less racist and sexist than, say, Saudi Arabia; such cultural knowledge may lead to more effective perspective taking. Wu and Keysar (2007) provided evidence for this idea that perceptual perspective taking can be influenced by culture. In one experiment, Chinese and American participants were observed using eye-gaze technology while playing a communication game in pairs that required perspective taking. The results showed that "Chinese participants were more tuned into their partner's perspective than were the American participants" (p. 600). Although untested, we conjecture that the same effect might be found for psychological perspective taking. More generally, familiarity with the culture of the perspective-taking target can provide the knowledge and background for perspective taking and without that knowledge readers would have to adopt other comprehension strategies (Sommer, 2013). (This point is demonstrated by Experiment 1 reported in Chapter 7.) We assume that such effects occur because information about the cultural context can make it easier to construct suitable analogies to the reader's own experience.

Determinants of Elaboration

As we noted in Chapter 4, we believe a critical ingredient in literary perspective taking is elaborative processing in which the reader uses their own personal knowledge and experience to fill out information in the story world. In that chapter, we described several characteristics of the text that are likely to promote elaboration, such as showing (as opposed to telling) style, textual gaps, and embodied descriptions. In addition to these textual determinants, Myers and Hodges (2008) argued that the ability to draw accurate inferences about another's thoughts and feelings depends on "the extent to which an observer can create a complex and fleshed-out representation of the other person" (p. 281). Here, we discuss other factors that may affect such elaboration, including individual differences and the reading context.

To begin with, elaboration can vary as a function of reader knowledge. For example, relevant knowledge that is easily activated in memory can make elaboration more likely. Gerrig (2005) suggested something along these lines with the idea that the reader's representation will include concepts that are readily available in memory. In particular, information that has the "greatest support" (p. 237) from long-term memory is likely to be incorporated. In general, a memory-based discourse-processing view suggests that anything that makes personal experience more accessible would make elaboration more likely. For example, Kuiken et al. (2004a), in a study of poetry reading, found that readers who had experienced a significant (but temporally remote) loss were more inclined to report "feeling resonance"; feeling resonance likely involves elaborative processing and might be interpreted as related to personal, analogical connections to the situation described by the poem.

Expertise in a particular domain can also produce nearly routine elaborations as a function of the nuanced semantic interpretations that are available. For example, Spilich et al. (1979) found that readers who were knowledgeable about baseball developed more elaborated representations of an account of a baseball game than non-baseball experts. Similarly, we suspect that literary texts that are situated in a particular locale and era would be processed differently depending on whether the reader has relevant expert knowledge. Readers knowledgeable about London during the Second World War, for instance, would be able to build a more detailed representation of the circumstances in *Blackout* (Willis, 2010) in which future characters time travel back to that period.

Knowledge of a particular genre may also facilitate elaboration. For example, Chafe (1980) hypothesized that we store our experiences of style in memory. Thus, we may have mental schemas leading to a set of expectations that would provide the basis of elaborative processing. This was supported experimentally by Bortolussi and Dixon (1996): They found that formal training in a particular genre (magical realism) improved their sensitivity to unique aspects of the genre. In many cases, formal training may not be necessary. Indeed, Dixon et al. (2015b) found that genre-specific expectations can be generated in experienced readers simply by viewing a book's cover.

Another variable that may determine elaboration is individual reading style. For example, Schneider and Dixon (2009) referred to readers who tend to make extensive spatial elaborations as "careful" readers. Careful readers are characterized by relatively slow reading times but high comprehension accuracy (suggesting that they were not simply having reading difficulties). Although the Schneider and Dixon work pertained to elaborations regarding spatial aspects of the situation model, we suspect that careful readers are likely to produce more elaborations of other types as well. Thus, we suggest that the extent to which a reader is "careful" will predict a general tendency to form elaborations and, potentially, take a character's perspective.

Elaborations can also vary as a function of intentional reading strategies. For example, a reader may intend to develop a detailed, elaborated interpretation of a story under one set of circumstances and not in another. Such variation might arise because of external constraints (e.g., reading for a class assignment). Literature instructors might assume, for example, that asking students to think about or focus on certain aspects of the character or the story world will have an effect on how the story-world representation is elaborated. Periodically asking readers evaluative questions may also have such an effect, as demonstrated by Bortolussi et al. (2018). Further, we know from the work of Cupchik et al. (1998) that readers can take one character or another's perspective as a function of instruction, and this effect might be mediated in part by elaborative processing of the text.

Both individual and situational differences in elaboration may be related to what has been termed "standards of coherence" (van den Broek et al., 1995). The standard of coherence is the degree to which the reader constructs inferences to reconcile apparent gaps in the text. We can extend the concept of standard of coherence to also refer to the degree to which the representation of the text is augmented to include different possible connections among textual elements. For example, when reading a novel such as *The Orient Express* (Christie, 1934/2011), an individual with a high standard of coherence may speculate about the motivations that different characters may have for murdering the victim; an individual with a low standard of coherence may merely wait until the motivations are revealed at the denouement. Thus, we expect readers who have a high standard of coherence (or reading situations that encourage such standards) would generate more elaborations than other readers (or other reading situations).

The apparent relationship between the reader and the character likely also makes a difference. For example, readers may be more inclined to elaborate the representation of characters that they like or who appear to be similar to themselves on some dimension. As we discussed in Chapter 4, perceived similarity can be the result of successful perspective taking; here, we note that such similarity can foster elaboration as well. In particular, when the character is similar to the reader, it may make personal knowledge and experience more readily accessible and more likely to contribute to elaboration (cf. Cupchik et al., 1998). Thus, identification and elaboration can have a reciprocal relationship in which each reinforces the other. Similar effects are likely to occur because of interest in a topic (cf. Hidi & Baird, 1986; Renninger & Hidi, 2016). (The effects of interest are discussed more fully later.)

Attribution

Perspective taking can also depend on how individuals attribute causality to a target's behavior. Research on attribution theory has shown that individuals tend to make more situational or contextual attributions to explain their own behavior and more dispositional attributions to explain targets' behavior (Jones & Nisbett, 1971; Pronin et al., 2004); this is the so-called fundamental attribution error. In part, the difference can be due to the information available to actors and perceivers: Actors have greater information (e.g., of the specific circumstances of their own past actions), while perceivers have only the immediately available perceptual information. Consistent with this distinction, we hypothesize that when observers take a target's perspective, they should be more likely to make situational attributions about the target's behavior because it should match the situational attributions the observer makes about their own behavior. For example, by his actions, one might judge Holden Caulfield of *The Catcher in the Rye* (Salinger, 1951) as self-centered and insensitive; however, if one successfully takes the character's perspective, one might judge his actions as a product of what he perceives as his uniquely alienating and inauthentic circumstances.

Several researchers have found evidence that perspective taking affects the nature of behavioral attribution. In a study by Regan and Totten (1975), for example, half of the participants were instructed to empathize with one of two actors engaged in a conversation, while the other half were asked to simply observe her (cf. Storms, 1973). The results showed that participants given empathy instructions provided more situational and less dispositional attributions to the target. The researchers interpreted the results as evidence that "empathic orientation affects attribution not only by affecting *what* the individual attends to, but also by affecting *how* this information about the target was processed" (p. 855; italcs in the original). A related result was obtained by Galper (1976): When participants were asked to take the perspective of a character in a short passage, their subsequent description of the character's behavior was more likely to contain situational rather than dispositional causal attributions.

Although the link is not definitive, we suspect that when reading literature, the association between causal explanations and perspective taking may also run the other way: that is, readers may be more likely to take the perspective of characters when their behavior is described as situationally determined. This prediction follows from our account of perspective taking by analogy. Because readers typically have situational determinants of their own behavior in memory, it would be easier to see the connection to a character when that character's behavior is also determined by (analogous) situational factors. Some evidence relevant to this hypothesis was reported by van Peer and Maat (2001) and described in Chapter 4. In their study, an argument between a husband and wife was rewritten by adding mental access to either one character or the other. The authors argued that the mental access generated more sympathy for the character (and perhaps perspective taking) and that this sympathy led to the attribution of more situational determinants of the character's behavior. However, in many cases, the mental access that was added consisted of the character thinking about situational determinants of their behavior. For example, the sentence, "'Can't she ever leave me alone?' he thinks," was added, suggesting that chronically not leaving him alone could be a determinant of the character's behavior. Consequently, an alternative interpretation of the results is that these added attributions in the experimental texts supported perspective taking, leading to the increment in sympathy that was measured in the study.

Variations in Perspectival Resonance

Even when there is sufficient information about the character, a range of connections between the character and the reader need to be made in order to take a perspective (as we outlined in Chapter 5). When these connections are less than perfectly consistent and coherent, the reader needs to resolve and synthesize the conflicts in order for perspective taking to be successful. Here, we describe two classes of problems that may arise in building a perspective-taking analogy: difficulties in building analogies based on matching evaluations and difficulties in constructing a coherent interpretation of the character's evaluations.

Challenges in Building Analogies

In the analysis described in Chapter 5, the process of building an analogy begins when the reader identifies some form of similarity between the story world and the reader's experience. That similarity relation can be easy or difficult to discern. (Of course, if no similarity is detected, analogies cannot be formed and no perspective taking would occur.) Difficulty in finding similarity can occur for several reasons. One possibility is that the reader is uninterested in the character and the story and thus lacks the motivation. In part, this may be because the text has not generated this interest, or it may be that the content is inherently uninteresting to the reader. Another type of impediment to identifying analogical connections can arise when readers are distracted by superficial differences between the character and themselves and are thus unable to detect more abstract similarities. For example, a reader may decide that the protagonist, Marlowe, in *Heart of Darkness* (Conrad, 1899/2006) is a racist. Readers might believe that such attitudes are abhorrent and thus that they could have little in common with the character. If readers cannot overcome this level of description, it would be difficult to take the character's perspective. A related possibility is that readers might have similar attitudes to an objectionable character that they are unwilling to acknowledge. Thus, readers might reject characters to whom they feel similar in undesirable ways. More generally, what readers often must deal with is character evaluations that may differ from their own. As discussed in Chapter 5, this requires that the reader's direct evaluation be inhibited in favor of an analogical evaluation that matches that of the character.

Once some form of similarity is detected, perspective taking requires the construction of an analogy that matches evaluations and their justifications. As described in Chapter 5, we can, for heuristic purposes, delineate two routes to such analogy formation: event-driven analogies and evaluation-driven analogies. Different problems can arise in each case.

Problems with Building Event-Driven Analogies

In event-driven analogy construction, the reader starts with matching events and searches for an evaluation of that event that is similar in some way to the evaluation of the character. One issue that may arise at this juncture is that the evaluation inspired by the retrieved events does not obviously match that of the character or only matches it in some weak fashion. For example, when the main character, George Smiley, in *Tinker, Tailor, Soldier, Spy* (Le Carré, 1974/2001) arrives at his home street, he takes stock of the familiar cars and their locations. This could remind the reader of similar inventories they may have performed when arriving in a familiar locale. However, Smiley's motivation is one of fear "that one day, out of a past so complex that he himself could not remember all the enemies he might have made, one of them would find him and demand the reckoning" (p. 31). Presumably, the reader's comparable familiar inventory experiences do not involve fear, leading to mismatched evaluations.

When such mismatched evaluations occur, readers have four options: First, they may decide to abandon the prospective analogy, effectively deciding that although the events of the story remind them of events in their own lives, the reminding is not sufficiently potent to form a connection with the character. Second, they may attempt to find a different similarity plane for comparing evaluations; this amounts to looking for a different level or description of similarity. For example, an inventory of the familiar family home may lead readers to anticipate future distressing events, such as their parents dying, and such anticipation may be construed as analogous to Smiley's fear. Third, readers may decide to reinterpret what seems to be the character's evaluation so that it is more in line with their own. For example, in processing the previous episode of *Tinker Tailor*, the reader might decide that Smiley does not really experience fear but merely curiosity. This amounts to a novel reinterpretation of the text with uncertain ultimate effects on perspective taking. Finally, readers may be able to find a new evaluation of their own experiences that matches the evaluation of the character. For example, they might decide that a previous encounter of novelty in a familiar locale might have evoked some apprehension and that this was analogous to the fear mentioned in the text. In such a strategy, the text could provide new insights into readers' lives.

Problems with Building Evaluation-Driven Analogies
Related problems can occur with evaluation-driven analogies. In particular, readers may be able to find that, having encountered some analogical similarity between the character's evaluation and their own, there appears to be little correspondence between the justifying events. For example, in *The Lathe of Heaven* (Le Guin, 1971/2008), the protagonist, George, has a fear of dreaming, and the reader might readily find in their own experience an analogous fear of nightmares or other bad dreams. However, George's fear of dreaming (in the fantastic context of the novel) derives from the fact that some of his dreams change reality, and the reader might find it difficult to find anything analogous in their own experience.

As before, there are several strategies for coping with this difficulty. Besides simply abandoning the developing analogy, they may look for other justifying events that have a closer correspondence. This may include searching for other events in the reader's experience that might also serve to justify their evaluations but do so in a way that is more similar to the situation in the story world. For example, the reader may have experienced fear and bad dreams after sending an ill-considered email that might lead to the deterioration of some relationship. The reader might make an analogous connection between George's fear of changing reality and their own anxiety over the repercussions of their actions. Another possibility is to make an inference about the story that makes the corresponding justifications more comparable. For example, the reader of *Lathe* might decide that George's so-called effective dreams were also anxiety-or fear-inducing by their nature, so that George fears the content of his dreams (as a reader might fear nightmares) rather than simply their effects. Finally, as we discussed earlier, readers may be able to identify a looser or more abstract description of the similarity between justifying events, perhaps at the risk of making the analogy weaker. For example, the reader may conclude that George's effective dreams are a metaphor for action in the world that changes one's life. Thus, both the reader and George could share a fear to act.

Challenges in Integrating Analogies

As described in Chapter 2, we defined a "perspective" as an interpretation that integrates a set of evaluations. Following from this, perspective taking requires finding analogous matches to some proportion of those evaluations. Thus, even if there are good analogies that lead to matching evaluations, perspective taking would occur only if there is a coherent interpretation of those character evaluations. For example, early in the novel *A Wizard of Earthsea* (Le Guin, 1968/2012), a variety of evaluations of the main character, Ged, are mentioned for which the reader might be able to find analogies: Ged was full of temper, enjoyed roaming in the forest, resented his father, and so on. However, because these evaluations do not have a simple, global interpretation, finding analogous evaluations in the reader's personal knowledge and experience would not constitute perspective taking. Instead, only when other evaluations are found that have a common interpretation would perspective taking occur.

In contrast, Ged's hubris provides a consistent interpretation of a variety of evaluations: his joy in learning his first magic spells, his resentment of a fellow apprentice wizard's jibes, and his willingness to attempt a forbidden spell. Perspective taking would occur to the extent that the reader is able to find analogical matches to such evaluations. We argue that there is no problem, in general, in having multiple, unrelated analogies supporting each of these. For example, the reader might be able to form an analogy to the first based on an experience of learning a new skill and an analogy to the second based on memories of childhood taunting. Each of these analogies would be separate, each with its own justifications in the reader's experience. Perspective taking would occur to the extent that the character evaluations supported by these separate analogies have a common, global interpretation. More generally, the more coherent that interpretation is, the stronger the perspective taking would be.

These complexities mean that "taking a character's perspective" can mean many things. Perspective taking can be a matter of degree because evaluations are matched only to some extent. It can also vary in nature because of the different possible analogies that might be constructed. Perspective taking can also vary with the importance or centrality of the character's perspective, as well as the importance to the reader of their own matching evaluations.

Perspective and Character Complexity

Challenges to perspective taking occur even after a coherent perspective with matching evaluations has been identified. We describe three such challenges here: A character may have multiple perspectives that overlap or conflict; perspectives may change or develop over the course of a work; and a work may provide perspectives of different characters, which again may overlap or conflict.

Multiple Perspectives of a Character

A given character may have multiple perspectives that are partially overlapping and only partially consistent. This aspect of characterization can be related to genre and period styles. Denizens of literary story worlds are typically "round" characters: complex and in some ways enigmatic. In contrast, characters in formulaic fiction, while displaying some differentiating features, are often "flat" in that they conform to a known type. In general, we can assume that each type of fiction induces different kinds of processing, recognizing at the same time that there are variations within each. Perhaps the greatest difference is that more sophisticated literary works invite greater elaboration of the characters, story world, and manner of the story's telling. For example, in *Heart of Darkness* (Conrad, 1899/2006), the main character, Marlowe, seems to maintain a perspective of disdain for the European imperialism in Africa while also appearing to have a racist perspective that respects Europe's maintenance of "civilization" among the "savagery" of the surroundings. Readers might find these perspectives difficult to reconcile, and this may frustrate efforts to understand the protagonist.

Changing and Unreliable Perspectives

A general problem in a work of any length is that character perspectives are likely to change. This creates a difficulty for the reader because the analogies that produce matching evaluations early in a story may not be appropriate for a character's evolving perspective later. For example, the protagonist in *Doomsday Book* (Willis, 1993) begins the story with a perspective of naïve enthusiasm for her work in time traveling to the Middle Ages but ends up with a perspective of resigned loss for the loved ones she could not keep from dying in the plague. In order to fully appreciate the character and the story, the reader would need to find analogous evaluations for her reactions early in the story and late in the story and for her transition from one to the other.

A related example can be found in *The Prime of Miss Jean Brodie* (Spark, 1962/1999). Sandy is a central character in the story with significant mental access, but her perspective is potentially unreliable given her immaturity and apparent misconstrual of events. Moreover, her perceptions change as she grows into adolescence. For the reader, this kind of narration could create perspective-taking challenges. Some of Sandy's perceptions (e.g., that Brodie abused her authority over the girls) seem reliable, and this evaluation could spark the retrieval of analogous evaluations in the reader's experience. However, Sandy's possible unreliability might obstruct the motivation to find connections. On the other hand, readers may also recognize analogous confabulatory evaluations from their own youth as they attempted to understand an intriguing adult. Such a recognition could be the basis for an analogy: Sandy's flawed perception of Brodie would be analogous to the reader's own flawed perception of that intriguing adult.

Multiple Perspective-Taking Targets

In addition, there is the question of whose perspective in the story world the reader should take. This question arises when the text provides information about the perspective of several characters in the story world. For example, in *Anna Karenina* (Tolstoy, 1878/1998), information about the perspective of many characters is provided, including Karenina, Oblonsky, and Vronsky, and each perspective may include distinct evaluations of the same events in the story world. These different, potentially conflicting perspectives may allow the reader to ultimately acquire a deeper appreciation of the events of the story world, independent of the perspective taking that may occur for each character. Jabali (2015) referred to this as "data aggregation and statistical smoothing that result in stable and coherent representations" (p. 126). (See also Ackermann, 1996.)

Works such as *As I Lay Dying* (Faulkner, 1930/1990) pose a more complex perspective-taking problem. Each chapter focuses on one specific character's mind and provides a perspective regarding the dead man whose wake they are walking toward. Each character has different and, in some cases, contradictory views on the same person. Such novels highlight the relative value of individual points of view, but how readers process the characters is still not well understood. Do they attend to and take the perspective of mainly one character, and if so, why? Do they form analogical connections with more than one and take the perspective of characters with conflicting evaluations of the dead man? Perspective taking ultimately depends on how the perspectival cues are processed: Which ones readers perceive and retain and how they relate them are critical. Yet there is no guarantee that even if readers noticed, tracked, and remembered everything in the text, they would react alike. On the contrary, their emotional and cognitive response to the same cues that present some aspect of characters' perspectives could vary significantly; readers might or might not resonate with a character's evaluation, and they might process the same cues to construct different interpretations of that character's states of mind.

There is empirical evidence that if perceptual attribution is consistent, readers can apply a simple heuristic for understanding perspective in the metaphorical or psychological sense (Dixon & Bortolussi, 2019). However, many multiperspectival works obviate such a simple solution. For example, *Middlemarch* (Eliot, 1872/2000) has close to thirty principal characters and even more minor ones. Unlike the simple situation considered by Dixon and Bortolussi (2019), there is no consistent mapping of perceptual attribution to characters that would single out a perspective-taking target. Instead, readers may be led to side with one character at some times on some issues and with another at other times on other issues, rendering it difficult, if not impossible, to adopt a coherent, uniform perspective. In most fiction, characters interact with each other and with their surroundings, form inferences to produce assessments and judgments, including of themselves, and attribute motivations, desires, feelings, and causality. Such complexities place enormous cognitive demands on readers, who must not only track all shifting perspectives but also remember who said what to whom when and for what reason, a potentially overwhelming task of perspectival bookkeeping (cf. Graesser et al., 1999a, 1999b). How such complex fiction affects our elaboration of the story world requires further empirical attention.

Individual and Contextual Differences

Previous research has attempted to find individual difference variables related to perspective taking in literature and real life. Next, we discuss cognitive capacities, age, empathic and related dispositions, and motivation. (The role of exposure to text as an individual difference is covered in Chapter 8.) An unresolved issue, though, is what these differences mean for the components of perspective taking as we have developed in this book. For example, individuals who are better at taking a perspective might be better at retrieving relevant personal knowledge and experience, better at identifying similarities at an abstract level, or better at doing the analogical inferencing we hypothesize to be at the heart of perspective taking. We will suggest some possibilities in the discussion that follows.

Cognitive Skills and Capacities

The cognitive components of perspective taking as we have analyzed it can be very resource demanding. Indeed, the demands of perspective taking have been noted by many researchers. Far from a simple process, it is said to entail "a complex and critical set of cognitive abilities" (Barnes-Holmes et al., 2004, p. 18) and a set of differing cognitive capacities that we rely on in different situations (Ryskin et al., 2015). Oatley (1999) understood that in order to simulate (what we would understand as taking a perspective), a reader must first "get the whole thing to run – to imagine the story world with its people, and to become absorbed in it" (p. 441). However, running a simulation of the whole text presupposes an ideal text-processing ability that exceeds the cognitive capacity of normal human brains. Thus, we might infer that some approximation of this ideal would be cognitively demanding. Based on our theoretical approach, we suspect that successful perspective taking would vary with working memory capacity, reading comprehension, executive control, and inferencing ability.

Working memory capacity has been implicated in language comprehension and discourse processing in particular (e.g., Just & Carpenter, 1992; Just et al., 1996). As well, it seems reasonable to assume that tracking different perspectives and integrating evaluations and analogies would involve manipulating and maintaining large amounts of information; this would seem to imply that a large working memory capacity would be an asset in perspective taking. Baddeley (2000) developed the concept of an "episodic buffer" in his working memory model. According to Baddeley, the episodic buffer serves to integrate information from different sources and to model possible situations. Because the episodic buffer is used to access and manipulate (long-term) episodic memories, it seems likely to be critically involved in perspective taking as we understand it. Consistent with this analysis, Lin et al. (2010) and Ryskin et al. (2015) found effects of working memory span on a perceptual perspective-taking task, and Davis et al. (1996) found an effect of cognitive load in a role-taking task.

Another plausible correlate of perspective taking, at least in processing literature, is simply reading comprehension skill. As we noted at the beginning of this chapter, perspective taking depends on acquiring information and nuance from the text, and if the reader were to have difficulty in comprehending this information, perspective taking would be more difficult. In particular, comprehension deficits are likely to interfere with the other components of perspective taking, such as finding similarities to the reader in the story world and constructing analogies. The logic is that if all of the reader's attention were devoted to processing the text, little attention would be left to devote to these other concurrent processes. For example, although not specifically directed to perspective taking, research has demonstrated that weak comprehenders fail to develop high-level inferences about the story world (LaBerge & Samuels, 1974; Perfetti, 2007). We suspect that processing a wealth of textual information may distract readers from identifying more abstract analogical relationships in favor of processing more superficial aspects of the text.

The effects of reading skill presumably interact with the nature of the text. For example, a moderately difficult text might be demanding for some readers but not others. When a particular text is difficult for a particular reader, the poor assimilation of story-world information would likely make perspective taking more difficult for that individual. One might argue that avant-garde techniques, such as temporal and spatial fragmentation, stream of consciousness, multiperspectivism, and unreliable narrators, have this effect for some. Such techniques disrupt the traditional organization of information, thereby rendering the processing of the story world more difficult (Harker, 2010). Similarly, Richardson (2015) identified several "anti-mimetic" techniques, typical of some postmodern literature, that he argued thwart readers' ability to identify with characters: unconventional plot trajectories, metalepsis (i.e., the crossing of fictional boundaries from the fictional to the real world), the entering of the author in the fictional world, the use of metafiction and metadrama (i.e., fiction about the construction of fiction and drama), and the writing of another's "autobiography." In our view, the impact of these techniques, even when the text is comprehended at a superficial level, interferes with the use of resources for the analogical processing needed for perspective taking. For example, *La Muerte de Artemio Cruz* (*The Death of Artemio Cruz*) (Fuentes, 1962/1991) intermixes episodes from different points in time, so the reader must expend considerable effort to reconstruct the story's chronology. Readers who do not have the requisite capacity for such efforts may not be able to form a coherent representation of the protagonist.

However, it is also possible that although such techniques increase the effort needed for comprehension, that effort may also lead to the kind of elaborative processing that promotes perspective taking, particularly for readers who are familiar with those techniques (cf. Bortolussi & Dixon, 1996). Some evidence for such an effect was provided by Alber et al. (2020). He investigated the use of "unnatural" narrators, in this case a narrating parrot and a speaking coin. He found that although professional readers found the nonhuman narrators more estranging, they nonetheless regarded them as being personally relevant. In other words, readers found a connection between the story worlds and their own experiences. These results support the hypothesis that readers who accept the challenge of engaging attentively with challenging texts may, in spite of the processing difficulties, succeed in constructing the necessary analogical connections for perspective taking.

As we suggested in Chapter 3, there are many circumstances in which readers must inhibit their own evaluations and reactions to events of the story world in order to find an analogy to the evaluation of the character. This implies that executive control must be involved and that individual differences in executive control may be related to perspective taking. Indeed, as discussed in the next section, the development of executive control in childhood has been linked to performance on theory-of-mind tasks (e.g., Carlson & Moses, 2001). Surtees and Apperly (2012) claimed that adults, like children, still demonstrate egocentric interference when performing "perspective taking tasks that are more complex and that require judgments of certainty about what someone else will do or think" (p. 452). In support of this argument, they described research in which adults had to make quick judgments about the number of dots seen by a depicted avatar. Adult subjects were slower and made more errors when they themselves saw more dots than the avatar could see; this was interpreted as evidence of egocentric bias because "the participants' own discrepant perspective interfered with judgments of the avatar's perspective" (p. 453). Extrapolating from such results, it seems plausible to suppose that there are variations among adults in the ability to suppress direct, egocentric evaluations, and such variation is likely to be important for perspective taking in some situations.

Relatedly, Todd et al. (2018) examined the influence of anxiety on perspective taking. One of the hypotheses they tested was that anxiety diminishes the executive function necessary for inhibitory control. Their results showed that individuals experiencing anxiety, as opposed to other emotions such as anger or disgust, "were more likely to describe an object using their own spatial perspective [and to] mistakenly assume that an uninformed person would interpret an ambiguous message, or otherwise behave, in line with their own privileged knowledge" (p. 29). Thus, their results suggest the importance of executive function for perspective taking, albeit indirectly through the influence of mood.

Finally, it seems plausible in our theoretical analysis that perspective taking would be related to analogical reasoning ability. The ability to see abstract relationships in problem solving could aid in constructing perspective-taking analogies during reading. Indeed, such skills have been found to be related at least to some extent to working memory capacity (Alexander et al., 2016; Frischkorn et al., 2022). However, it is also possible that analogical inferencing, although important with respect to processing, is not a limiting factor in perspective taking. For example, perspective taking might fail because readers are unable to find matching evaluations, independent of their ability to build abstract analogies.

Age and Development

In Chapter 3, we reviewed research on the false-belief task suggesting that prior to the age of about four, children have difficulty reasoning about another's state of knowledge. This failure of mind reading indicates that they would have difficulty taking another's perspective. Other research demonstrates that this difference is not simply a matter of having or not having a "theory of mind" and that performance on more difficult versions of the false-belief task continues to improve into adulthood. Thus, it is reasonable to suppose that age is an important variable in success in perspective taking, both in real life and in reading literature.

One conjecture is that the effect of age on perspective taking is mediated by the development of inhibitory control (Carlson & Moses, 2001). It is well established that inhibitory control associated with executive function improves with age (e.g., Elke & Wiebe, 2017) and that this development is often associated with the maturation of the frontal lobes (Huttenlocher & Dabholkar, 1997). Inhibitory control has been defined as "the ability to inhibit responses to irrelevant stimuli while pursuing a cognitively represented goal" (Rothbart & Posner, 1985). This control is important in overcoming egocentric biases that can occur in perspective taking. For example, Epley, Morewedge, and Keysar (2004) studied perceptual perspective taking by asking participants to follow directions to manipulate objects in an array. However, the construction of the array was such that some of the objects were hidden from the experimenter (so that the instructions could not reasonably refer to the experimenter). Adults were less likely to reach for these hidden objects than children and were faster to look at the correct object. The authors' interpretation was that adults were better able to correct their initial egocentric perceptual interpretation of the instructions.

Surtees and Apperly (2012) compared children's and adults' response time on a task in which participants were asked to judge either what they or a depicted avatar could see. Responses were slower when the avatar had a view that was different from the participants, and this difference did not decrease with age. Thus, these results also suggest that even adults have an initial egocentric perceptual interpretation that must be inhibited. Surtees and Apperly conjectured that age-related improvement in inhibitory control may increase the efficiency of perspective taking even though the egocentric interpretation remains available.

Carlson and Moses (2001) examined the relation between theory of mind and inhibitory control to determine if a deficiency in one was also a deficiency in the other. In the experiment, three- and four-year-olds were given a battery of theory-of-mind and inhibitory-control tests. The results demonstrated that four-year-olds performed better than three-year-olds on both sets of tests and that performance on both was correlated. However, the researchers also suggested that inhibitory control alone may not be sufficient to explain the role of executive function in theory of mind and that other developing skills, like working memory, could be involved. Similarly, Nilsen and Graham (2009) found that children's performance on executive function tasks predicted their ability to consider a speaker's perspective in both language comprehension and production: "children's performance on the inhibitory control measures was [negatively] related to the children's egocentric interpretations of the communicative context" (p. 234).

In addition to the development of inhibitory control through early adulthood, there is also some evidence that perspective-taking ability declines in older adults. For example, Maylor et al. (2002) found that performance in theory-of-mind tasks declined with age, and Helson et al. (2002) reported a decline in empathy later in life. Similar results were reported by Fernandes et al. (2019). However, Zhang et al. (2013) attributed this decline to a decrease in motivation. In particular, they found no age-related decrease in the ability to recognize contextually inappropriate remarks when the target was a relative or friend.

The results of these studies lead us to the conclusion that the ability to inhibit egocentric biases – a crucial component of perspective taking – increases with age at least up to adulthood. Although the evidence for a decline in later life is equivocal, it is unreasonable to think that perspective taking is unchanged over a lifespan. In particular, we strongly suspect that increases in knowledge and experience over a lifetime should have positive quantitative and qualitative effects (cf. Li et al., 2004). However, at the moment, it is difficult to disentangle such effects from the potential decline in fundamental capacities.

Empathic Dispositions

It seems reasonable to assume that some individuals are more empathetic than others or more able to take another's perspective. Our analysis is that such differences should apply to both perspective taking in life and in reading literature. There is some evidence that measures of empathy are related to literary perspective taking. For example, Koopman (2015) found that trait empathy, measured with the Toronto Empathy Questionnaire (Spreng et al., 2009), predicted empathic understanding of depression and grief. Similarly, Eekhof et al. (2023) found that a measure of emotional empathy from the Multifaceted Empathy Test (Dziobek et al., 2008) predicted some aspects of character engagement. Using the Basic Empathy Scale (Jolliffe & Farrington, 2006), van Lissa et al. (2016) found greater perspective taking for a character among those who reported greater dispositional cognitive empathy. Relatedly, "need for affect" (Maio & Esses, 2001) has been shown to be related to transportation (Appel & Richter, 2010) and might be involved with perspective taking as well.

There seems to be less consistency in the relation between such measures and real-life perspective taking. In principle, self-report measures of empathic concern should show a correlation with one's empathic accuracy. However, several studies have shown that correlation to be weak (Ickes, 1993; Batson et al., 1997; Hodges et al., 2010). This evidence suggests that "empathic concern and empathic accuracy are separate constructs and that consequently empathic concern is not necessarily a good predictor of empathic accuracy" (Myers & Hodges, 2008, p. 285). One explanation for the discrepancy between empathic concern and empathic accuracy is that individuals who assess their own empathic disposition may lack sufficient awareness, or metacognition, of their own perspective-taking abilities. More generally, though (and as we argued in Chapter 3), successful perspective taking does not imply empathic accuracy but merely that the perspective taker identifies an analogous, not necessarily identical, emotion. Thus, in our analysis, we might not expect to find a strong relation between empathic concern and accuracy.

There seems to be little compelling evidence that good performance on empathy tests carries over into real-life behavior either. For example, one might conjecture that political polarization could be reduced by perspective-taking ability (as indexed by empathic concern). However, Simas et al. (2019) provided evidence that "individuals high in empathic concern show greater partisan bias in evaluating contentious political events," suggesting that "contrary to popular views, higher levels of dispositional empathy actually facilitate partisan polarization" (p. 258). However, even when empathy does not have undesirable consequences, it may not go very far in terms of converting emotion to altruistic action (Ellison, 2021). On balance, measures of empathic concern do not seem to be related to real-world behavior.

Empathy, like perspective taking more generally, is also affected by contextual factors. Konrath et al. (2011) found that students' empathy declined between 1979 and 2009, possibly due to new pressures such as the increased cost of higher education. Similar results were found by other researchers (Twenge et al., 2012). Potentially, these contextual effects might be due to variations in cultural knowledge or attitudes, as described earlier under "Reader Background." More generally, such results highlight the fact that if there are stable individual differences in perspective-taking ability, we do not know their ultimate cause: Variations in perspective taking could be due to innate mental makeup, the social context, differences in upbringing, and so on. Among this array of possible causal influences, cultural or environmental variables that vary over time are quite possible.

To the extent that empathic dispositions are related to perspective taking, we conjecture that those who are high in trait empathy are more likely to be successful in finding suitable similarity relations in constructing a perspective-taking analogy. Thus, empathic individuals are those who can identify similarity between themselves and others even in the face of superficial differences. If this is true, it suggests that there may be important interactions and tradeoffs among variables related to perspective taking. For example, it is possible that a more inexperienced but intelligent, sensitive, and open-minded young person can achieve greater empathic accuracy than an older, very experienced, but jaded and cynical person. In such a comparison, the older individual has the benefit of knowledge that would allow the identification of similarities but not the motivation to do so.

Motivation and Interest

A necessary requirement for effective perspective taking and empathy is the motivation to find the reader–character relations that underlie the analogy. For example, as we noted in Chapter 3, Myers and Hodges (2008) argued that a perceiver must be motivated to collect "a set of cues about the other person's thoughts and feelings" (p. 283). Epley and Caruso (2009) described a study showing that subjects assigned to experimental conditions in which they were instructed to take a perspective performed better than those in non-role-playing conditions, suggesting that motivation was lacking in the latter.

Motivation is often generated by interest. Renninger and Hidi (2016) pointed out that interest predicts both motivation and engagement, but that once engagement is triggered, it needs continual support to be maintained. Moreover, the relation between interest and engagement may be complex: Although interest can lead to motivation, motivation is not always a sign of interest. For example, experimental instructions to take a point of view might foster the motivation to do so, but that motivation is not a sign of interest in the experimental material. Renninger and Hidi argued that interest is both a psychological state and a motivational disposition. As a psychological state it involves attention, effort, concentration, and affect. As a motivational disposition it involves both situational and individual factors. Interest can be short term, limited to situational reactions, or long term, involving a predisposition for reengagement. In particular, interest is not static but can develop through interactions. For example, we argue that the active construction of character–reader relationships (such as perspective-taking analogies) can sustain interest.

Carpenter et al. (2018) developed a "Mind Reading Motivation" scale that was intended to measure the extent to which a person is interested in and concerned with the mental states of others. The scale predicted the tendency to take the perspective of the character, confirming that this measure of motivation was important for perspective taking. It also correlated with engagement with the narrative, suggesting that motivation was related to the tendency to elaborate the story-world representation. Of course, it also possible that these relationships are not causal but rather due to the effects of a third variable, such as interest in the story.

A variety of other variables can affect motivation as well. Converse et al. (2008) provided evidence that sadness "is associated with more systematic and deliberate processing" and happiness "diminishes the likelihood of engaging in deliberative processing" (p. 725). Happiness, then, would appear to diminish motivation. Galinsky and Ku (2004) found that self-esteem affects perspective taking. Notably, perspective takers "with high self-esteem evaluated an out group more positively than perspective takers with low self-esteem" (p. 594). Thus, low self-esteem also appears to be a motivation mitigating factor. Open-mindedness can also affect motivation. In their study of the effect of firmly held moral beliefs, Skitka and Morgan (2009) stated that "tolerance of differing points of view has little or no room at the table when moral connections are at stake: right is right and wrong is wrong" (p. 360). In other words, individuals can choose to be closed-minded, and this dispositional attitude quashes the motivation to acquire more relevant information that would allow for an unbiased assessment of the target.

The context in which perspective-taking research is carried out can influence motivation and effort. For example, in experimental situations, implicit instructions to take another's perspective have been shown to make a positive difference (Regan & Totten, 1975; Galinsky et al., 2008; Dore et al., 2017). This may be because in role-playing experiments, participants make a more concerted attempt to understand the perspective of a target individual. This leads them to explain the target's behavior in terms similar to those they use to explain their own behavior, that is, in terms of contextual, not dispositional, factors (Regan & Totten, 1975; Galper, 1976). In other situations, lack of motivation can be overcome with intentional goals or reading strategies, as might occur, for example, with class assignments or experimental instructions. Jabali (2015) noted that when people are motivated to learn from a text, they "will instinctively gravitate towards the adoption of an action perspective" (p. 128). Presumably, more perspective taking would occur under such circumstances. These results are encouraging in that they point to the possibility that perspective taking can be intentionally improved under at least some conditions. Although role-playing directions provide motivation to take a given individual's point of view, in everyday situations motivation depends on the individual and their circumstances; in many cases, motivation can be woefully in short supply. Because mind reading and perspective taking hinge on drawing inferences, an activity that is in itself subject to inaccuracies and misrepresentations of various sorts, a lack of sufficient effort to take the other's perspective can likely result in further misattributions.

Summary and Conclusions

In the present chapter, we have surveyed a collection of variables that affect the processes involved in perspective taking as we have defined it.

Heuristically, we have divided these problems into four areas: First, there is the available information that might be used to take a perspective, including information about the character provided in a text, information the reader has because of their background or experience, information that can be generated during elaboration, and information related to causal attribution. Second, there are process variables that have an impact on our hypothesized components of perspective taking. In particular, the nature of a story can provide challenges in building analogies and in integrating analogies into a coherent perspective. A third area has to do with aspects of literary characters that make perspective taking complex, including multiple and labile character perspectives and multiple targets for perspective taking in a work. Finally, we described individual differences in the reader or observer related to perspective taking. The ones we noted pertain to cognitive capacities, age, empathic dispositions, and motivation.

From our discussion of these variables, though, it should be clear that complex interactions can occur and that our organization of these issues is to some extent arbitrary. For example, motivation can compensate for a lack of cultural knowledge, character complexity can undermine even consistent and powerful analogical connections, and so on. Thus, the present chapter merely provides a catalog of the kinds of theoretical and empirical issues that remain unresolved in any account of perspective taking.

CHAPTER 7

Evidence for Analogy in Perspective Taking

In this chapter, we present evidence that perspective taking depends on the formation of analogies based on personal knowledge and experience. We describe three experiments: The first examines the effect of cultural knowledge and background in perspective taking; the second analyzes the relationship between perspective taking and personal remindings while reading; and the third explores the effect of priming relevant personal knowledge and experience. The experiments demonstrate that having the knowledge available to form analogies to the evaluations and experiences of the character fosters perspective taking. This research provides support for a central component of our approach, namely that prior knowledge and experience is critical to perspective taking. Of course, an exhaustive empirical foundation for our theory would involve a much broader range of investigations. For example, evidence on the construction of similarity, the effects of the second-order features of the text that induce elaboration, the analogical reasoning component in perspective taking, and the effect of textual cues for elaboration are just a few relevant topics. We discuss further ideas on future empirical directions in Chapter 8.

Measuring Perspective Taking

In general, readers' responses to texts can be measured either online, while reading, or offline, after a text has been completed. Online measures are designed to capture responses experienced during the course of reading a passage. One type of online measurement requires participants to respond to probes of one sort or another during reading. For example, Larsen and Seilman (1988) asked participants to stop reading and underline sections of the text that prompted remindings. Experiment 2 (described later) uses a related approach; like Kuiken et al. (2004b), we used an online technique but during a second reading of the text. A variety of unobtrusive, online measurement techniques have been used in empirical investigations of literary processing. These include galvanic skin response (e.g., Halasz, 1968), pupil dilation (e.g., Egan et al., 2020), heart rate (e.g., Eisenberg et al., 1994; Fuyama & Hidaka, 2016), electrical evoked potentials (e.g., Hoorn, 1996), and neural imaging (e.g., Angelotti et al., 1975; Citron et al., 2019). To our knowledge, these have not been used in connection with perspective taking per se. However, with some further assumptions about the relationship to components of perspective taking in a particular situation, they could be useful. For example, in some narrative contexts, one might hypothesize that a reader might experience fear or suspense if they take the perspective of a character. If such a hypothesis is warranted, then perspective taking could be indexed by physiological measures related to those emotions, such as heart rate or pupil dilation. More global aspects of reading, such as reading time and eye movements, could be used but would require even more extensive theoretical analysis to link the measures to aspects of perspective taking.

Offline measures, often in the form of questionnaires, sometimes rely on retrospective recollections of readers' reactions. However, reactions to a text can persist for some period of time, so measures that are obtained after reading can also be concurrent with readers' reactions under some circumstances. Empirical studies of perspective taking, identification, and related phenomena have typically relied on such post-reading questionnaires. In this case, readers indicate their response to a series of questions on, for example, a Likert scale.

A critical aspect of using such a questionnaire is its validity. Validity refers to whether the questionnaire or instrument as a whole measures what it is intended to measure. In some cases, a questionnaire can be assessed in terms of criterion validity: Does the questionnaire correlate with an independent assessment of the intended construct? For example, an instrument designed to measure extroversion could, in principle, be validated by comparing it to observational measurement of extroverted behaviors. It is not clear to us that this approach is practical with respect to the measurement of perspective taking.

A second, more approachable, index of validity is face validity: Do the items seem to tap the intended construct "on their face"? Even if the items seem suitable to the researcher, though, it is possible that participants taking the questionnaire understand the items differently. For example, a broadly worded item, such as "I could identify with the main character," could be understood by the participant as a question about understanding, similarity, agreement, or empathy. In our view, this is not necessarily a problem. Instead, broadly worded items allow the respondent to respond with respect to that component of the item that they feel is most important. Across a sample of individuals, then, the aggregate response represents the extent to which participants agree with some aspects of the item's meaning. This should provide at least approximate information about the construct as long as the item is not misinterpreted by most people. Moreover, when there is a range of such items on the questionnaire, the average response to those items indicates something about whatever those items have in common. Thus, having multiple, similar items on the questionnaire guards against idiosyncratic interpretations of any given item. A final consideration is that we are primarily interested in how participants' responses vary across individuals and conditions. Thus, what is important is whether the variation in responses is related to the variation in the construct.

A third aspect of validity is sometimes termed construct validity. Construct validity can be thought of as the degree to which there are sensible relationships between the hypothetical construct measured by an instrument and other measures in the same domain. For example, does empathy covary with identification or with imagery? De Graaf et al. (2012) provide an example of this type of effort when combined with factor analysis; Dixon et al. (2020) represents a related approach. To do this properly requires a commitment to a detailed theoretical analysis of the relevant concepts. Moreover, our suspicion is that the underlying factor structure of perspective taking, broadly considered, will vary with the nature of the material and the reading context. (De Graaf et al. [2009] also made this point.) In addition, our theoretical understanding of these concepts may be limited (the present book notwithstanding). Consequently, our approach with respect to construct validity is to cast as wide a net as possible in the hope that the aggregate result will correspond to major components of perspective taking.

In the present context, there are two different approaches to measuring perspective taking. In a theoretically driven approach, we would attempt to assess the components that we hypothesize underly perspective taking, that is, autobiographical memory retrieval, similarity detection, analogical reasoning, and so on. However, this approach is potentially circular in that we would simply find evidence that these processes are used rather than evidence that these are components of perspective taking. Instead, we have taken a more bottom-up approach and attempted to measure, in an aggregate manner, what other researchers have thought of as perspective taking, and then examine how such a measure covaries with manipulations related to our theoretical approach. We argue that when we have evidence for our hypothesized mechanisms contributing to this phenomenon, it would be strong support for our theory. However, doing so involves assessing phenomena that we have argued are not directly tied to our definition of perspective taking, such as identification, phenomenal similarity, empathy, and so on. As we have argued in previous chapters, these phenomena are often correlated with or dependent on the process of matching evaluations analogically that we believe is central to perspective taking.

A Perspective-Taking Questionnaire

Based on these considerations, we developed a questionnaire for the experiments reported here intended to assess the extent to which a reader takes the perspective of the main character. To create this instrument, we examined the items used in research that has investigated perspective taking and related phenomena. We drew on the materials used in several studies, including Busselle and Bilandzic (2008), de Graaf et al. (2009), Dixon et al. (2020), Kaufman and Libby (2012), Kotovych et al. (2011), and Tal-Or and Cohen (2010). Tal-Or and Cohen based many of their items on Cohen (2001); de Graaf et al. incorporated items from Green and Brock (2000) and Kim and Biocca (1997). In order to span the range of experiences that might be included in the phenomenon of perspective taking, we started by simply collating all of the items used in these studies. We then eliminated items that seemed redundant and attempted to phrase all of the items in a similar manner. Because these researchers had somewhat different theoretical goals in creating their items and to make the collating task manageable, we also attempted to omit items that seemed peripheral to our understanding of perspective taking. Perhaps the most significant pruning pertained to items that reflected immersion and attention to the story world (e.g., Green & Brock, 2000): Following from our interpretation of transportation in Chapter 4 (as well as in Bortolussi & Dixon, 2015), we deemed that such items could reflect effort and involvement with the process of reading without tapping perspective taking per se.

The final set of items is shown in Table 7.1. Nominally, these span four aspects of perspective taking and related phenomena: empathy and sympathy, justification, matching evaluations, and similarity and remindings. Although we did not construct the questionnaire with these goals in mind, each of these categories can be linked to aspects of perspective taking that we have discussed. Empathy was described as emotional perspective taking

Table 7.1 *Perspective-Taking Questionnaire items*

Empathy and Sympathy	
I felt sympathy and compassion for the main character.	E1
I felt concern for the character in his/her situation.	E2
At times I felt I knew exactly what the main character was going through emotionally.	E3
I shared some of the main character's emotions.	E4
I never really felt in tune emotionally with the characters.	E5 R
I really got involved with the feelings of the main character.	E6
Justification and Transparency	
The main character's actions were reasonable and justified under the circumstances.	J1
The main character's actions were irrational.	J2 R
The main character's feelings made sense to me.	J3
The main character's feelings in his or her circumstances were understandable.	J4
I could imagine doing what the main character did in that situation.	J5
I could imagine feeling the same way if the events of the story happened to me.	J6
Matching Evaluations	
It was difficult to understand why the main character reacted to situations as he or she did.	M1 R
I understood the reasons why the main character did what he or she did.	M2
I think I understand the main character well.	M3
Under the main character's circumstances, I would feel the same way.	M4
I shared the main character's reactions to the events and other characters in the story.	M5
I had the same impression of the events and characters as the main character did.	M6
Similarity and Remindings	
I think that in some ways, I am like the main character.	S1
As I was reading the story, I felt like I was in the character's shoes.	S2
The main character's situation reminded me of instances in my own life.	S3
Characters in this story remind me of people I actually know of.	S4
The story reminded me of emotions or reactions I have felt in the past.	S5
The character's actions reminded of things I've done in the past.	S6

in Chapter 3; justification is related to the analogical link between the justifications for the character's evaluations and those of the reader's past experience; matching evaluations, of course, is key to building a perspective-taking analogy; and finding similarity, as we argued in Chapter 5, is central to finding analogical connections. However, these categories are for organizational purposes only, and we have no evidence that these are psychometrically distinct. We refer to this instrument as the Perspective-Taking Questionnaire or PTQ.

As described earlier, our primary goal in collating these items was to assess what most people (and researchers) think reflects perspective taking. Thus, it provides an informal sort of construct validity in the sense that our items have substantial overlap with the items that have been used in other contexts. In future research, it might be valuable to assess perspective taking in a manner that is more closely associated with our theoretical perspective. For example, we might devise items that were more specifically focused on the activation of personal knowledge and experience, that were more obviously related to matching character evaluations, or that explicitly identified analogical relationships.

Experiment 1: Cultural Knowledge

In the first experiment, we assessed the most basic type of knowledge that might be used in building an analogical connection to the character, namely shared cultural background and social interaction schema. This factor was discussed in Chapter 6 as a form of knowledge relevant to the formation of perspective-taking analogies. The simple prediction is that when the reader shares the cultural background of the story world, perspective taking should be easier. In contrast, since, as we argue, perspective taking depends on making analogies to prior experience, having a different cultural background from the characters should make perspective taking difficult. (Experiments 2 and 3 examine the role of more personal, autobiographical knowledge and experience.)

Clearly, we are not arguing that perspective taking cannot occur given disparate cultural background. Indeed, a central point of our analysis is that one need not have similar experiences in order to take a character's perspective; as stated earlier, analogy consists of finding abstract descriptions of similarity despite apparent differences. As we outlined in Chapter 5, perspective taking depends on finding a similarity relation between the character and one's own life, and similarity relations can be quite diverse. Further, as we note in Chapter 4, good literature is often successful at fostering such similarity relations in spite of superficial differences. Nonetheless, if the reader's cultural background is comparable, it should be easier to identify analogous experiences, and, in contrast, the more distant and dissimilar the context, the more difficult it would be to find suitable analogies. We expect that the effect of comparable cultural background would make it easier to identify character motivations, stereotypic social interactions, evaluative judgments, and typical planning strategies.

In the present study, we had Canadian, British, and American participants read two stories: a Grimm fairy tale (Grimm & Grimm, 1819/1982) and a story from the oral tradition of the Alaskan Chandalar Kutchin (McKennan, 1965). In this case, we expected the Grimm story to make use of situations and conventions that were familiar to those of our participant population. In contrast, those of the Alaskan folktale were expected to be uncommon and perplexing to our participant population. In particular, our participants would generally be unfamiliar with the genre conventions and stereotypical interactions. Both stories had a superficially similar structure, in which a group of travelers have a series of largely unrelated encounters that culminate in a happy ending. The study is similar to that of Kintsch and Greene (1978) who also used Alaskan folktales from McKennan. However, Kintsch and Greene were interested in the effect of a clear story structure on comprehension and recall and providing a modern update on the classic work of Bartlett (1932). We were more specifically interested in readers' reactions to the character and in the extent to which the reader takes their perspective.

Method

Materials

Two short folktales were selected for materials: Grimm's "The Bremen Town Band" (Grimm & Grimm, 1819/1982) and the Alaskan Natsikutchin native story "Spider Woman and the Lost Two Sisters" (McKennan, 1965). (We will refer to these as "The Musicians" and "Spider Woman" in what follows.) Both include nonhuman characters and revolve around a form of quest; the four protagonists of "The Musicians" are farm animals and one of the characters that the two human sisters interact with in "Spider Woman" is a talking wolverine. There were 1,392 words divided into 8 paragraphs in "The Musicians" and 985 words divided into 15 paragraphs in "Spider Woman."

Participants

Participants were 111 volunteers who were paid for their services. Thirty-nine were recruited from Amazon Mechanical Turk (www.mturk.com) and seventy-two were recruited from Testable Minds (www.testable.org). Data from thirty-seven (mostly Mechanical Turk) participants were not used because the mean reading time per word for either story was less than 0.1 s (corresponding to more than 600 words/m), suggesting that they were not reading carefully. The results reported in what follows are based on the remaining seventy-four. (The large number of unusable participants in this study is presumably because participants had little extrinsic motivation for comprehending the story.)

Procedure
Each participant read both stories, with thirty-four reading "The Musicians" first and forty reading "Spider Woman" first. The stories were presented one paragraph at a time under the participant's control using the online platform Gorilla (http://gorilla.sc). After reading each story, the items from the PTQ were presented one at a time, and participants rated their agreement with the item by moving a slider from "strongly agree" to "strongly disagree"; "neither agree nor disagree" was below the center of the slider. The response was measured on a 0–100 scale. The measured perspective taking was the average of these responses after reversing the negative items (the "R" items in Table 7.1).

Analysis
We used a model comparison approach to quantify the evidence for different possible interpretations. Nested linear mixed-effects models were fit using the program lmer (Bates et al., 2015) running in the R statistical environment (R Core Team, 2022) and then compared using adjusted likelihood ratios (e.g., Glover & Dixon, 2004); this approach is tantamount to selecting models based on Akaike Information Criterion (AIC) values, a common approach to model selection (Akaike, 1973; Zucchini, 2000). In this case, the overall mean and the size of the story effect were assumed to vary over participants.

Results

The responses to the PTQ for the two stories are shown in Figure 7.1. The results are clear: There was substantially more perspective taking with the culturally familiar story. This was supported by model comparison: A model that incorporated an effect of story was better than a null model, $\lambda_{adj} > 1000$, indicating strong evidence for an effect of story. There was some evidence that perspective taking was higher for the first story read than for the second, $\lambda_{adj} = 6.34$. There was little evidence that there was any difference in reading speed between the two stories, $\lambda_{adj} = 2.05$. (The time for "The Musicians" was 0.324 s/word, SE = .013, and for "Spider Woman" 0.372 s/word, SE = .013.)

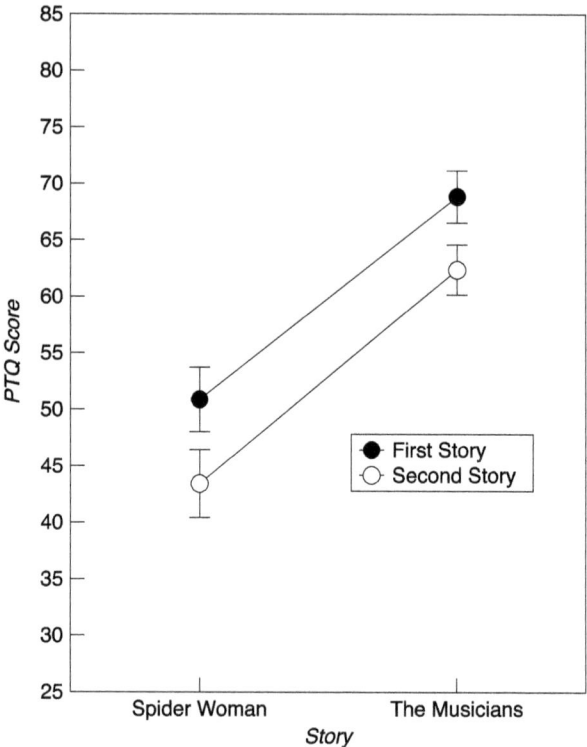

Figure 7.1 Mean PTQ score as a function of story.
Note. Error bars indicate the standard error of the mean as derived from a fit of a full model.

Discussion

Our interpretation of these results is that the culturally unfamiliar story included situations and conventional contexts that our readers had trouble understanding. Thus, they would have difficulty finding suitable evaluations and justifications. For example, after their brother dies falling from a swing they built, and in fear of their parents' reaction, the two sisters in "Spiderwoman" run away from home and wander through the woods "pleasantly all summer without meeting a single person." The "pleasant" evaluation here might be puzzling for our participants; instead, they might have expected the sisters to experience grief for their brother and wandering in the woods alone to provoke fear or foreboding. At another point, the sisters join a tribe of "well-dressed and handsome people" who turn out to be weasels. We suspect that arriving at an appropriate evaluation of this event depends on a knowledge of conventions for this genre. As a consequence, our participants may have had difficulty finding a suitable perspective-taking analogy. In contrast, in "The Musicians," there is a series of conflicts that have the clear, conventional goal of tricking a band of robbers. The stereotypic nature of the interactions presumably allows participants to find analogies, in spite of the fact that the main characters were animals and thus less superficially similar than the human characters in "Spider Woman."

There are alternative interpretations of the present results. Because our participants may have found some of the episodes in "Spider Woman" unusual, they may have simply formed an inadequate representation of the events of the story world. In a sense, though, this is not overwhelmingly different from our interpretation that readers could not find analogous experiences. In both cases, the relative lack of perspective taking results from not have a representation of the story world that makes contact with the reader's personal knowledge and experience. In one case, this is because of inadequate knowledge of cultural and genre conventions, and in the other case, it is due to more general comprehension difficulties. More generally, the unfamiliar content of the Alaskan folktale may have imposed a greater cognitive load that interfered with the processing necessary to form perspective-taking analogies. (Some further ideas along these lines are presented in Chapter 8.)

It is also possible that the difficulties in processing the Alaskan folktale may arise from the manner in which the text was obtained rather than a lack of familiarity with cultural schemas per se. For example, we have no certainty that there were not shortcomings in the oral elicitation of the folktales, their transcription, or their translation. Such issues do not necessarily undermine the overarching conclusion we draw from the results, though: The results support the view that the perspective-taking analogies are difficult to construct because the evaluations and justifications are not easily connected to the reader's experience. This difficulty could occur either because the evaluations and justifications derive from an unfamiliar cultural background or because they were presented in an inadequate manner for our readers.

This result is similar to that obtained by Kintsch and Greene (1978). Kintsch and Greene had participants read either stories from the same collection of Alaskan folktales in McKennan (1965) or from *The Decameron* (Boccacio, 1353/1972) and, after reading each story, write a summary. Other participants ranked those summaries on the extent to which they conveyed the main events. The *Decameron* summaries were ranked substantially higher than those for the Alaskan folktales. The authors concluded that "culture-specific schemata play an important role in story comprehension" (p. 6). The critical difference between their results and ours is that we were interested specifically in perspective taking rather than comprehension and memory more generally.

Wu and Keysar (2007) also examined the effect of culture on perspective taking but with a somewhat different goal. While we were interested in the effect of a cultural match between that of the reader and the story, Wu and Keysar asked whether perspective taking varied across cultural backgrounds. They hypothesized that participants from a Chinese background that emphasized interdependence would be better perspective takers than those from an American background that emphasized independence. The task involved moving objects in a grid sitting between the participants. Some of the cells in the grid were only visible to one participant and other cells were only visible to the other participant; effective communication thus required being able to assess how the grid appeared to the other participant. The results confirmed the hypothesis: The Chinese participants made fewer perspective errors and were less confused by potential distractors. While this study was limited to visual perspective, the results suggest that the Chinese participants might also be better at psychological perspective taking. This result is very broadly consistent with the present results in that both demonstrate that cultural background is important for perspective taking.

Experiment 2: Tracking Remindings during Reading

Having established that general cultural knowledge affects perspective taking, the next step was to investigate the effects of more personal knowledge and experience. In particular, we examined the effect of recollected autobiographical memories or remindings. This study was a modification of the paradigm developed by Larsen and Seilman (1988) and László and Larsen (1991). Larsen and Seilman asked participants to read either a short story or an expository text and to mark with a pencil any point that produced remindings. After completing the text, they responded to a series of rating scales for each reminding. The literary text produced more remindings in which the participant took an active part. László and Larsen used a similar method combined with a manipulation of perceptual access. They found that the remindings were somewhat more emotional when the story included mental access to the main character. Neither study measured perspective taking per se; however, some aspects of their results are suggestive. For example, the sensitivity of narrative remindings to personal involvement in Larsen and Seilman may be related to perspective taking. In Lázló and Larsen, the fact that mental access affected the emotionality of the remindings is consistent with the view that mental access promoted perspective taking and that this perspective taking involved emotional prior experiences.

Measuring remindings during reading is a form of online measurement in the sense that it is intended to capture ongoing processing during reading. In our case, we expect that processing to be related to perspective taking. In designing the experiment, though, we were concerned that a "true" online approach might interfere with the usual comprehension and perspective-taking processes. Indeed, Larsen and Seilman (1988) were also concerned about this issue and asked participants only to make a mark in the text when a reminding occurred; they saved more elaborate assessment of those remindings for a subsequent text reading. Our design involved a similar compromise: Participants were asked to read the story twice, once for comprehension and then a second time to assess remindings. Our assumption with this method was that if remindings occurred on first reading, they would also be available when participants read the text a second time and they would be able to report it without compromising the flow of comprehension processing that had occurred on first reading.

In more detail, our version of the task consisted of four phases: First, participants simply read the text for comprehension and answered a set of multiple-choice comprehension questions. Then, participants read the story again and marked each sentence on whether it reminded them of a memory, produced an image, generated an emotion, generated suspense, or none of these. Third, each of the sentences that generated imagery or remindings was rated on a series of scales designed to index how strong the image or memory was. Finally, participants completed the PTQ. Our prediction was that the number of remindings and the strength of those remindings should predict perspective taking. This is because remindings should be an indication of participants finding similarity relations between the story and their personal experience and finding such relations should provide a basis for perspective taking.

We also added a manipulation of reading orientation: In the memory condition, participants were asked to focus on remindings that occurred while reading, and in the imagery condition, they were asked to focus on imagery evoked by the text. Our hypothesis was that a focus on remindings would lead readers to think more deeply about related personal experiences and that such processing would provide greater support for perspective taking.

We suspect, based on the analysis in Chapter 4, that a focus on imagery might lead to greater elaboration of the story world but would not affect perspective taking as directly. Previously, Cupchik et al. (1998) found effects of reading orientation on the elicitation of emotional memories. Participants were asked to take either an "identification" set (in which they were asked to "imagine yourself to be the protagonist" [p. 366]) or a "spectator" set. With the identification set, readers experienced more specific, intense emotions when reading a descriptive passage (although these differences disappeared when the passage was already emotional). Although Cupchik et al. did not measure perspective taking, their results are broadly consistent with the view that reading orientation can affect emotional perspective taking.

Method

Materials

Two texts were used, both consisting of the first few pages of a romance novel. These were *Shades of Twilight* (Howard, 2019) and *One Summer* (Robards, 2011). The *Twilight* excerpt was 1,583 words and 84 sentences long; the *Summer* excerpt was 1,544 words and 104 sentences long. In *Twilight*, a young girl overhears a conversation about her imminent adoption by her aunts and uncles and ruminates about her relation with her relatives; in *Summer*, a woman picks up at a train station an ex-convict that she had previously befriended.

This study was conducted prior to the completion of the development of the scale shown in Table 7.1, and consequently the scale used was somewhat different. In particular, it did not include items E6, M3, M4, M6, S5, and S6. Items J3, J4, and J6 used a different phrasing. In addition, it included two items about reader emotions: "I found the story moving" and "The story left me with lingering emotions."

Design and Procedure

As discussed earlier, there were four phases in the study. In the first phase, participants read one of the two texts sentence by sentence, using the space bar to advance through the text. Sentence reading time was measured. After reading the text, participants answered three multiple-choice comprehension questions. In the second phase, participants read the text again but for each sentence they pressed a key to indicate one of five categories: remindings, imagery, emotion, suspense, or none of these. In the third phase, each sentence that was classified as producing a memory or an image was presented again, and participants rated the

Experiment 2: Tracking Remindings during Reading

memory or image on three agree/disagree scales. For memory sentences, these were: "The memory was exceptionally vivid"; "The memory was associated with strong emotions"; and "The memory was only familiar and not very specific." For imagery sentences, these were: "The image was exceptionally vivid"; "The image was associated with strong emotions"; and "The image was fuzzy and not very detailed or concrete." Participants responded to each scale by using the computer mouse to click somewhere along a gray-scale bar with the labels "definitely disagree," "disagree somewhat," "agree somewhat," and "definitely agree" arrayed underneath. We refer to these as "strength" scales because they were intended to index how strong the reminding or image was. An aggregate strength score was calculated by averaging the responses (after reversing the third item) and then scaling this value to the range 0–1. In the fourth phase, participants completed a paper-and-pencil version of the PTQ scale. For each item, participants selected one of: "definitely disagree," "mostly disagree," "disagree somewhat," "neither agree nor disagree," "agree somewhat," "mostly agree," or "definitely agree." The responses were assigned the numbers 1–7, and the PTQ score was the average of these after reversing the negative items.

There were two reading orientation conditions. In the memory condition, participants were told to "think of things from your life that the story reminds you of" while reading the story. In the imagery condition, participants were told to "think about images that the sentence evokes in your mind" while reading the story. A reminder of this orientation instruction remained on the screen while participants were reading.

The original design called for participants to come to the laboratory for two sessions one week apart, with one story and one orientation condition in each session. However, the study was interrupted by the onset of the Covid-19 pandemic, and the design was not completed. Data from forty-nine participants had been collected but not all of those completed both sessions. In the analysis presented here, each participant session (consisting of a combination of participant, text, and orienting condition) was treated as an independent observation. There were a total of eighty-four such participant sessions.

Participants
Participants were undergraduates in an introductory psychology course who served in exchange for course credit. Data from seven participant sessions were not used because the reading time per word was less than 0.1 s in either the first-pass reading or the categorization phase, suggesting that participants were not reading carefully. Data from an additional

Table 7.2 *Distribution of participant sessions across design in Experiment 2*

	Orientation Condition	
	Memory	Imagery
Summer, Session 1	12	13
Twilight, Session 1	10	11
Summer, Session 2	5	9
Twilight, Session 2	8	8

participant session were discarded because accuracy on the comprehension question was less than .67 (i.e., two or three of the questions were answered incorrectly). This left a total of seventy-six sessions distributed as shown in Table 7.2.

Results

The critical question for our purposes was whether task orientation or the number of remindings that participants reported was related to perspective taking. Participants' categorization responses were classified as including no remindings, one to five remindings, six to ten remindings, or more than ten remindings. The relationship to perspective taking is shown in Figure 7.2 for the two orientation conditions. As can be seen, the PTQ score increased with the number of remindings for the remindings orientation condition but not for the imagery orientation condition. Most of this effect consisted of the difference between those sessions in which no remindings were reported and those in which one or more were reported.

This interpretation was supported by the fit of nested models. A model that included a difference between 0 and more than 0 remindings in the memory condition was substantially better than a null model, λ_{adj} = 219.14. Adding a similar contrast for the imagery condition produced no improvement, λ_{adj} = .38. Adding the remaining degrees of freedom in the remindings × condition interaction was substantially worse, λ_{adj} = .02.

Among participant sessions in which at least some remindings were reported, there was a tendency for PTQ scores to increase with the remindings' mean strength score. This is shown on the left of Figure 7.3. There was some evidence for this relationship, λ_{adj} = 4.06, but it was

Experiment 2: Tracking Remindings during Reading

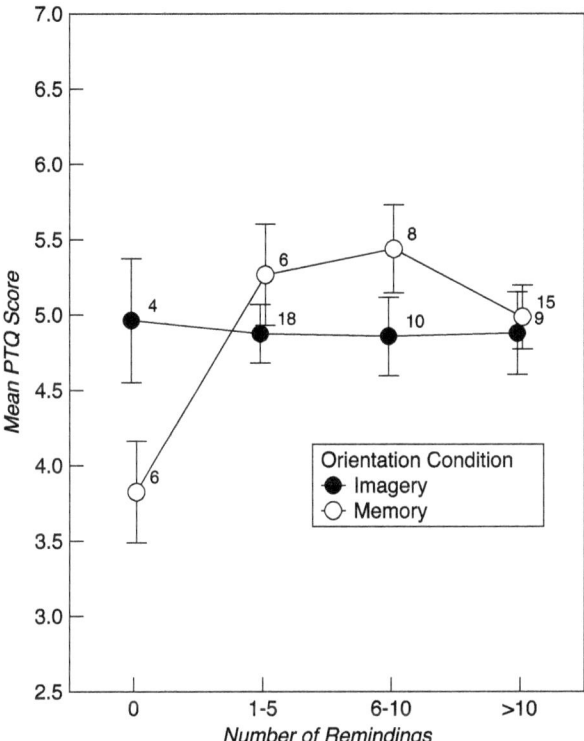

Figure 7.2 Mean PTQ score as a function of remindings and reading orientation condition.
Note. Numbers next to each data point indicate the number of participant sessions contributing to that data point. Error bars indicate the standard error of the mean.

not strong. As shown on the right of the figure, among participant sessions with at least some reported images, there was no evidence for a relationship between the strength of the reported images and perspective taking, $\lambda_{adj} = .46$.

Reading time was slightly slower in the memory condition ($M = .339$ s/word, $SE = .006$) than in the imagery condition ($M = .324$ s/word, $SE = .005$). However, the evidence for this difference was weak, $\lambda_{adj} = 2.75$.

Discussion

Our expectation was that reading orientation and remindings would be related to perspective taking: In particular, we hypothesized that focusing

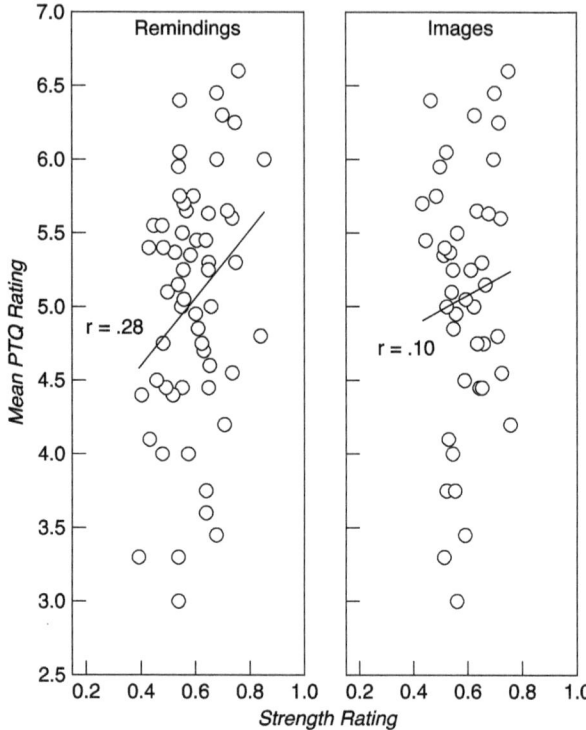

Figure 7.3 PTQ score as a function of reminding and image strength.

on how the story reminded participants of things from their lives should lead to those memories being more available for perspective taking, and the number and strength of such remindings should predict perspective taking. However, the actual pattern of results was more complicated. Although there was a trend for the strength of remindings to predict perspective taking, the *number* of remindings only had an effect in the memory condition. One interpretation of this pattern is that the activation of autobiographical memory is primarily a function of the text and that our reading orientation manipulation had little effect on this process. Instead, asking participants to focus on memory may have merely made the activated autobiographical episodes more available for subsequent report. That is, the reading orientation manipulation affected what participants reported during the sentence categorization phase, not any components of perspective taking. Following this interpretation, remindings (and the associated perspective taking) would also occur in the imagery condition, but because participants were focused on imagery rather than reminders, they may have failed to connect them to the perspective-taking process.

A somewhat different description of the obtained interaction is that when participants reported no remindings in the memory condition, it was because the story made no contact to their lives (and there was little perspective taking). In other words, self-relevance, as discussed in Chapter 5, was low. In contrast, in the imagery condition, participants may have reported no remindings because they were focused on images and did not take note of any remindings that occurred. In both conditions, though, there was a tendency for the reported strength of those remindings to be related to perspective taking.

The main result in this study is largely correlational: We measured both number of remindings and degree of perspective taking as they varied endogenously across participants. Our preferred interpretation is that in the memory condition, the increase in remindings led to an increase in perspective taking. In particular, the remindings, according to our theory, provide the foundation for perspective-taking analogies. However, it is also possible that both measures were affected by some third variable rather than being causally related to each other. For example, interest in the story could have affected both without necessarily requiring a causal relation between remindings and perspective taking. More generally, both remindings and perspective taking can vary across stories and individuals for a wide range of reasons. Stronger evidence for the importance of prior experience requires an experimental manipulation of available autobiographical episodes; this approach was used in Experiment 3.

Experiment 3: Priming Prior Experience

In a third experiment, we used a different approach to manipulating the knowledge that might be used for constructing a perspective-taking analogy. Rather than measuring the extent to which personal knowledge and experience were spontaneously used during reading, we attempted to prime readers to think about relevant experiences in their own lives. Our hypothesis was that when readers have actively recalled situations that they experienced that might be analogous to the story-world situation, they should more easily see the similarity relation between the story and their prior experiences and more readily construct an analogy. In other words, the expectation is that readers who were reminded of analogous experiences should be more likely to take the perspective of the story character.

The experiment had the following design: We identified two stories, "Celia Behind Me" (Huggan, 1943/1995) and "Good Night Air" (Mellet, 1997), that we believed could be understood in terms of common experiences. In "Celia," the protagonist expresses regret from a childhood instance of bullying; in "Air" the protagonist feels frustration with his life situation. We then designed two autobiographical retrieval exercises, one involving bullying and one involving feeling trapped by a social obligation. A critical aspect of this manipulation is that it did not require participants to have had experiences that are closely related to the stories; rather, the rationale for the retrieval exercises was that what matters is being able to find some element of similarity. In other words, we wanted participants to find personal experiences that would be seen as analogous (not necessarily identical) to the situation in the story world. Different groups of readers performed one of the two retrieval exercises and then read one of the two stories. Our prediction was that more perspective taking should occur when the retrieval exercise matched the content of the story. As a control, we also constructed a lexical retrieval exercise that did not entail recalling any autobiographical experiences.

Several previous studies have demonstrated an effect of "episodic simulation" on measures that may be related to perspective taking. As described in Chapters 3 and 5, the process of episodic simulation entails constructing representations of scenarios by recombining elements of past experience (see also Schacter et al., 2007). This process can be used both for reconstructing prior episodes and for imagining scenarios that might occur in the future. We hypothesize that episodic reconstruction can be used in building analogies between the story world and the reader's prior experience and is thus often central to perspective taking. Vollberg et al. (2021) had participants engage in episodic simulation by asking them to imagine or simulate the details of an event that might take place ten to thirty years in the future. Subsequently, they expressed greater empathy for individuals in negative scenarios. A comparable effect was observed when participants recalled details from a viewed video. Similarly, Gregory et al. (2021) found that episodic simulation of a negative scenario increased ratings of personal distress. Gaesser and Schacter (2014) also found that simulating a previous episode in which participants engaged in a helping behavior increased the self-reported intention to help in a future context. These results are broadly consistent with our hypothesis that the retrieval of relevant prior episodes (in the course of episodic simulation) might foster perspective taking.

Experiment 3: Priming Prior Experience

Method

Materials
The two stories we used were "Celia Behind Me" (Huggan, 1943/1995) and "Good Night Air" (Mellet, 1997). In "Celia," the narrator describes a series of episodes in which she participated in the bullying of another girl and her remorse after a particularly egregious event. In "Air," the narrator describes an unpleasant home life in which he feels compelled to care for his ailing and ungrateful mother while his wife is unhelpful and uncaring. "Celia" was 3,157 words and 38 paragraphs; "Air" was 2,007 words and 73 paragraphs.

Procedure
The study was conducted online. There were three priming conditions: "Celia," "Air," and Control. For the "Celia" and "Air" priming conditions, participants read the retrieval task instructions shown in Box 7.1. Following the instructions, they were asked to list on a piece of paper in point form: details of the spatiotemporal context of the event; the precise and detailed sequence of events in the retrieved episode; and emotional and evaluative reactions of themselves and others at the time. A minimum of a minute was taken for each question (but participants could take longer). The listed details were not recorded, but for each question, participants entered the number of details that they were able to list.

Following the retrieval task, participants rated the retrieved episode on the "strength" items shown in Box 7.2. For each item, they moved a slider to indicate the extent to which they agreed with the statement. The slider was labeled "strongly disagree" on the left, "strongly agree" on the right, and "neither agree nor disagree" in the middle. The slider began in the middle, and participants could move it one way or the other before clicking on a button to go on to the next item. The software recorded a value from 0–100 to indicate the selected position.

In the control condition there was no retrieval task, but to make the task comparable, participants were asked to do several lexical knowledge tasks: They listed the number of words they could think of starting with "am…," words that end with "…ate," and synonyms for "pretty." As in the retrieval tasks, participants were given a minute for each question and entered the number of words listed on the computer. They also responded to comparable "strength" items shown in Box 7.3.

After completing the strength scales, participants read one of the two stories. There were six between-participant groups determined by the

> **Box 7.1   Priming tasks in Experiment 3**
>
> ### "CELIA BEHIND ME"
> All humans are flawed, and everyone at some point in life says or does something that is unkind, consciously or unconsciously. For example, children can sometimes be very mean, as can siblings, friends, or employers. It can involve trivial actions, like making a cutting remark, or be more significant, like deliberately excluding someone from some social event, spreading rumours about someone, or "ratting" someone out. In extreme cases, meanness takes the malicious form of bullying. We may be deliberately mean to someone because of deeply felt animosity or because we feel the need to "get back" at someone we think deserves it. However, it can also be purely passive: We fail to do something or say something we know we should do, like offering a hand or word of encouragement or coming to the defence of someone in need. Sometimes we are in a group of people who are being mean, and it's easier to just go along with it. The problem with being mean is that people's feelings are hurt. For this exercise, we would like you to try and remember some instance from your past when you were unkind in as much detail as possible.
>
> ### "GOOD NIGHT AIR"
> At some point in our lives, all of us have felt trapped in an undesirable situation, at the mercy of circumstances beyond our control. Such situations can arise in personal, family, or work settings. For example, we might be stuck with a demanding boss, unpleasant co-workers, coerced to attend a tedious family function, or need to be pleasant with an unlikeable acquaintance. Sometimes we may sense that these situations are isolated and short-lived, or we may understand that they are trivial in the grand scheme of things. However, sometimes they last for longer periods of time and point to deeper issues. Whether serious or trivial, short or long-lived, such situations can be unpleasant and sometimes stressful. We might handle them calmly and stoically, but we might also feel emotions such as helplessness, frustration, or impatience. We might wish that we could react in some way to make a statement or express our unhappiness but fear the consequences of doing so. For this exercise, we would like you to try to recall in as much detail as possible some episode from your past when you felt trapped.

combination of three priming conditions and two stories. We refer to the priming conditions as related (e.g., "Celia" priming task followed by "Celia" story), unrelated (e.g., "Celia" priming task followed by "Air" story), or control. Following the story, participants completed the PTQ using the same slider scale.

Experiment 3: Priming Prior Experience 197

Box 7.2 Strength items for retrieval tasks in Experiment 3

I was easily able to recall an episode and with many details.
Recalling this episode generated a lot of emotion.
I still sometimes think about that episode.
The memory of the episode was very vivid.
My emotions at the time the episode occurred were very intense.
I often think about this event.
This event happened in the recent past.
I am certain about the order of events.
I am confident about the accuracy of my memory.

Box 7.3 Strength items for control task in Experiment 3

I was easily able to think of words for the "am…" task.
I was easily able to think of words for the "…ate" task.
I was easily able to think of words for the synonym task.
Thinking of words was challenging.
I sometimes use the words I came up with in conversation or writing.
I know the precise meaning of all the words I came up with.
The tasks made me wish I had a larger vocabulary.
I could have thought of more words if I had more time.
I worked very hard at thinking of words.

Participants

Participants were 151 paid volunteers recruited from the Testable Minds participant panel (www.testable.org). Data from two participants were not used because their mean reading time was less than 0.1 s/word, suggesting that they did not read the story carefully. Data from three further participants were not used because the questionnaire rating response was exactly 50 over half the time, suggesting that they often did not move the slider to make a response. The participants were distributed across the six conditions as follows: Celia/control, thirty-six; Celia/related, twenty; Celia/unrelated, nineteen; Air/control, thirty-six; Air/related, seventeen; Air/unrelated, eighteen. (A programming error led to twice as many participants in the control prime condition than had originally been intended. This lack of balance did not affect the analysis of the results.)

Results

Figure 7.4 shows the perspective-taking questionnaire scores for the two stories and the different prime conditions. As can be seen, more perspective taking occurred in the related prime conditions than in the unrelated prime condition, with intermediate perspective taking in the control condition. Perspective taking was also greater for "Air" than for "Celia." This interpretation was supported by the fit of linear models. A model that included the effect of story was superior to a null model, $\lambda_{adj} > 1000$. Adding a contrast between the related and unrelated prime improved the

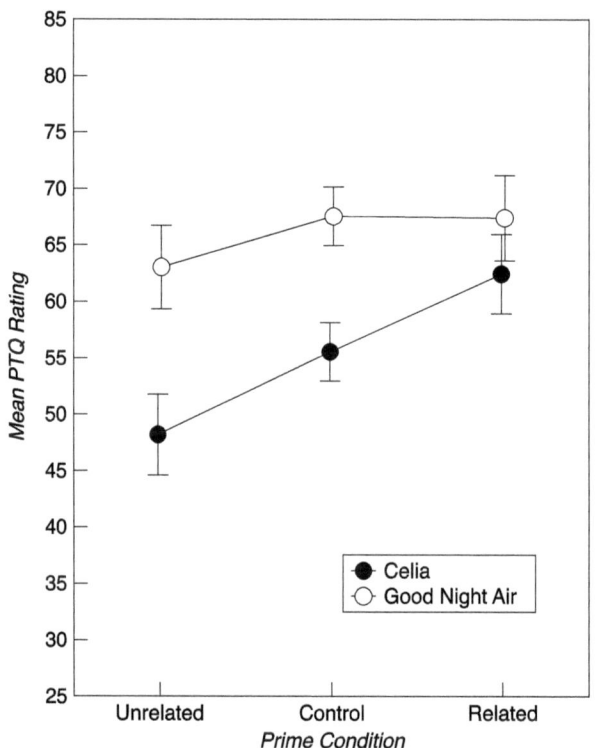

Figure 7.4 Mean PTQ score as a function of story and prime condition.
Note. Error bars indicate the standard error of the mean.

model, λ_{adj} = 12.26, indicating clear evidence for a difference between related and unrelated prime conditions. Although the priming effect was numerically weaker with "Air," there was no evidence that this prime effect interacted with story, λ_{adj} = .94.

We hypothesized that the effect of autobiographical retrieval should be related to how successful that retrieval was. In particular, the strength of the recall should be important when the recall is related to the story, with greater strength leading to more perspective taking. This should not be true for recollections in the unrelated condition. As a simple measure of recollection strength, we averaged the nine rating scale responses for each participant. The relationship to the PTQ score is shown in Figure 7.5. Our expectation was confirmed: There was good evidence for a relationship between intensity and perspective taking in the related condition, λ_{adj} = 25.83, but none in the unrelated condition, λ_{adj} = .37.

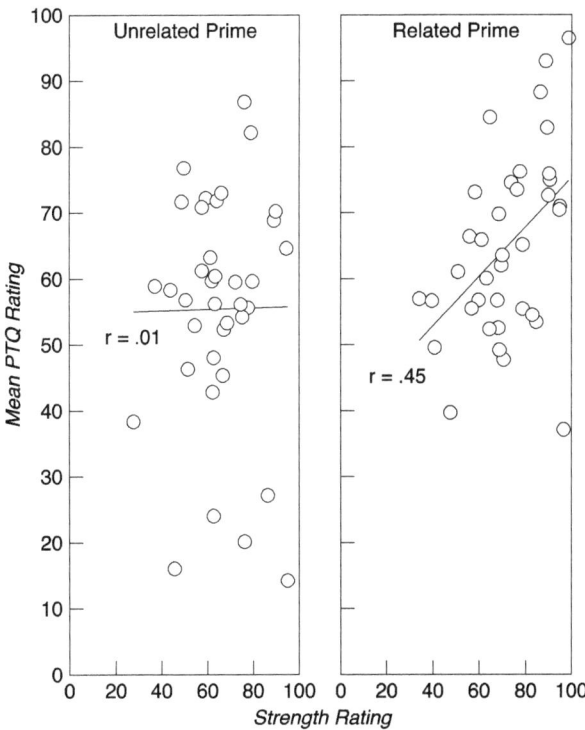

Figure 7.5 Relation between PTQ and retrieval strength.

Discussion

The present results provide good support for the importance of prior experiences for perspective taking. Our interpretation is that performing the priming task makes those prior episodes and other episodes of that type more salient (in the sense discussed in Chapter 5). In effect, our priming manipulation may have been comparable to what interested readers might do spontaneously. However, critically, the availability of those experiences was experimentally manipulated in this study, making it less likely that the variations across conditions in both were caused by interest or some other third variable. The effect of retrieval strength, and its specificity to the related prime condition (as shown in Figure 7.4), would seem to be compelling evidence for this interpretation.

Although we obtained a priming effect across both stories, the effect appeared to be weaker for "Air." There are several possible reasons for this. One is that our analysis of the kinds of experiences relevant to perspective taking in this instance was incorrect. We had conjectured that the idea of social obligation and how such obligations might be emotionally burdensome would form a good basis for perspective-taking analogies. However, perhaps this was a poor choice for our participant population, and they may have had, on average, relatively little experience with such situations. However, it is not the case that participants simply failed to take the character's perspective, since the overall PTQ score for the story was actually greater than in "Celia." Perhaps the text activated relevant autobiographical episodes that made sense to the participants but were often unrelated to our priming theme. For example, emotions generated by the tensions of close family life or the protagonist's problematic marriage may have been more relevant to the readers.

Originally, we included the control prime condition (consisting of a simple lexical knowledge task) because we were concerned that simply asking people to retrieve autobiographical experiences might prime all experiences, leading to greater perspective taking even for unrelated stories. Something like this effect was suggested by the work of Sheldon et al. (2019; see also Vollberg et al., 2021). They found that an induction task in which participants attempted to remember details from a video led to more details being retrieved during a subsequent autobiographical memory task even though the video had little to do with the memories that were retrieved. In other words, practicing remembering details seemed to have a general effect on an unrelated autobiographical retrieval task. If this type of effect had occurred, we might have expected perspective taking to be higher in both the related and unrelated prime condition than in the control, contrary to what we found. Instead, our interpretation is that the facilitation of perspective taking requires that the prior retrieval be related to the analogies that might be formed. In this interpretation, however, one might wonder why the unrelated prime condition showed in fact less perspective taking than the control. The relative lack of perspective taking in the unrelated condition may have occurred because retrieving unrelated experiences interfered with finding more suitable analogies.

We suspect that the priming effects observed here are likely to be found only with relatively brief short stories. In a longer work, the material itself should be sufficient to activate suitable prior experiences. Indeed, it is difficult to imagine that a brief priming task such as that used here would last for the days or weeks needed to read a full-length novel. Further, a longer work of fiction would generally include a wide array of life experiences, each of which would be a potential basis for a perspective-taking analogy. It seems likely that the effect of priming one of these would have minimal impact across the entire reading experience. On the other hand, it is notable that Dixon et al. (2011) found that a short critique read initially had an effect on the evaluation of a novel even after participants finished reading the entire work. Thus, it is conceivable that getting readers started "on the right foot" could have a lasting effect.

Summary and Conclusions

In this chapter, we presented three experiments that provide some empirical support for our analysis of perspective taking. In Experiment 1, cultural background had the predicted effect on perspective taking. In Experiment 2, the strength of remindings while reading a text seemed to be related to perspective taking, and the number of remindings predicted perspective taking when participants were told to focus on the relation to prior experience. In Experiment 3, an experimental manipulation of the availability of relevant prior episodes affected perspective taking. Together, these results provide evidence that the availability of relevant prior experience is a good predictor of perspective taking. While this evidence does not necessarily prove the details of the analogical processes we envision (involving, for example, the identification of corresponding patterns of evaluations and justification), it does seem to suggest something at least comparable. In particular, we argue that what is needed to explain the evidence presented here is some mental representation capable of relating personal knowledge and experience of the reader to analogous experiences of the character.

The present research extends previous results demonstrating that perspective taking is related to homophily. For example, de Graaf (2014) found that participants were more likely to relate a story to themselves (and, presumably, more likely to take the perspective of the protagonist) when the character was superficially similar to the reader. Similarly, Eyal and Rubin (2003), in a study of the perception of aggression among television characters, found a relationship between homophily and identification. However, the present research demonstrates that homophily is in fact not needed for perspective taking. Instead, the results demonstrate that it can be promoted by the availability of simply analogous experience. The results of Experiments 2, and Experiment 3 in particular, suggest that perspective taking is not limited to those individuals who are similar to the character. Instead, they support the view that any individual can take the perspective of a character if an analogy of some form can be found to connect to their own experiences. Thus, in our view, what matters is not the nature of the prior experience per se but the analogy that is used to connect to the character.

CHAPTER 8

Conclusions

We begin this chapter with a restatement of our theory of perspective taking and a summary of how the material we have covered contributed to that theory. Next, we discuss how our theory relates to a question we raised in Chapter 1: Are there real-life benefits of taking of a character's perspective? The chapter concludes with a reflection on future empirical directions.

A Theory of Perspective Taking As a Process of Analogical Inferencing

The main goal of our book was to explore in detail a new theory of perspective taking based on well-understood cognitive processes. The inspiration for that goal arose in the course of reviewing research on the topic in both literary studies and psychology, which revealed the need for disciplinary cross-fertilization; decades' worth of research on real-life perspective taking produced valuable findings that we believed could help advance our understanding of how the phenomenon functions in the context of reading literature. Recurring concepts in that research, such as evaluation, personal memories, knowledge, cognitive abilities, and analogy, were clearly pivotal but not developed into a coherent theory of perspective taking. On the basis of that body of work, we arrived at our basic insight: Taking a target's perspective requires bridging the self–other gap by making an analogical connection between the target's situation and one's own personal knowledge and experience. Most of the book involves an attempt to draw out what this must mean in terms of cognitive processing and what the implications must be for perspective taking in life and literature.

We began this book with a delineation of the problem of interest: psychological (as opposed to perceptual) perspective taking. While this is an appropriate step in a work of this sort, it also required a careful consideration of what a perspective is and what constitutes perspective taking. In Chapter 2, as a step beyond an intuitive or metaphorical understanding of these terms and building on the psychological understanding of the term, we described a perspective as a coherent interpretation of some set of evaluations. Further, we argued that perspective *taking* required a personal connection between the reader or perceiver and the perspective-taking target. Thus, perspective taking cannot be reduced to simply agreement or understanding. On the basis of our definition of "perspective," we specified that readers must not only perceive that some character evaluations cohere but also be able to understand the correspondence between a character's evaluations and their own.

In Chapters 3 and 4, we delineated how this approach is related to a variety of associated concepts. Mentalizing theories often explain the self–other relation in terms that implicitly require at least some simple form of analogy. However, they leave unexplained the processes that make that relation more personal. We argued that the missing link is the recruitment of personal knowledge and experience to construct analogies and the use of such analogies to elaborate on the denizens of the story world. In literary studies, theories of the reader–character interaction include identification, empathy, and transportation. In our analysis, all of these concepts are dependent on perspective taking and follow from understanding it as an analogical connection between the reader and the text. For example, identification is the recognition of the analogical mapping between the reader and the character; empathy should be understood as emotional perspective taking; and transportation is the elaborative processing that can underlie perspective taking.

A critical question that we attempted to address in Chapter 4 is how perspective taking is related to the text. Specifically, the chapter reviewed empirical evidence regarding the claim that particular stylistic features lead the reader to take a character's perspective. Based on our review of this evidence, we concluded that there is little compelling evidence that what we have termed "first-order" textual features – for example, narrative mode, mental and perceptual access, and free-indirect speech – in and of themselves lead to perspective taking. Rather, we argued, perspective taking is more reliably related to the cognitive processing of more subtle aspects of the text that we refer to as "second-order" textual features. These are textual properties that lead readers to elaborate the text based on personal knowledge and experience, which, in turn, provides the basis for perspective-taking analogies. (As we noted in that chapter, related processes may apply to elaboration in real life.) Properties of the text that we hypothesize promote elaboration include showing versus telling styles, evaluative gaps, embodied language, and narratorial implicatures. Although we believe that this conceptualization is the more promising avenue for future research, we do not at this juncture have a simple recipe for how different texts produce or do not produce perspective taking.

While the notion that perspective taking involves an analogical connection between the reader and the target is intuitive, we go beyond this intuition to lay out precisely what the nature of the analogy is and how it can be constructed. In particular, and drawing on previous research on analogy, we argue that a perspective-taking analogy involves corresponding justification structures in the reader and the character: In both cases, evaluations are justified in some way by prior experiences. Building the analogy requires identifying these correspondences. As discussed in Chapter 5, understanding this process depends on two critical concepts: The first is an abstract notion of similarity that we refer to as a similarity plane; finding a similarity plane effectively means finding a common manner of description. The second is a deeper sense of what counts as personal knowledge and experience, including generalized experience, reconstructed experience, and experience by proxy. Based on our definition of perspective as a subset of character evaluations that are perceived as coherent, a reader must be able to find analogous correspondences to some coherent set of character evaluations and justifications in order for perspective taking to occur. In this sense, the process of perspective taking is not the result of engaging with characters but the driving force. The same is true, we argue, in real-life perspective taking: In order to take a target's perspective, one must find a common description that applies to both the target's and the perceiver's circumstances and evaluations, and identify those correspondences.

In addition to describing this analogy structure, we laid out several detailed hypotheses concerning prototypical dynamics of perspective taking, including evaluation-driven analogies and event-driven analogies. In event-driven processing, readers notice some form of similarity between the events in the story world and events from their experience, and then work forwards from those antecedents to identify correspondingly similar evaluations justified by those events. In evaluation-driven processing, readers notice similarity between evaluations of the character and those from their own lives and then work backwards to find comparable justifying prior events. In both cases, inference and elaboration are used to fill out representations of the story world or of their experiences. Through this retrieval and analogical mapping, the reader elaborates on the story world and forms personal connections with characters.

This way of thinking of perspective taking makes it clear that it is not all or none but rather that it varies quantitatively and qualitatively. Quantitatively, the strength of perspective taking would depend both on the number of analogically matching evaluations that can be subsumed under a coherent interpretation and on the strength of those analogies. Qualitatively, perspective taking can vary with the nature of the reader experiences that are recruited and the nature of the similarity relations used to construct those analogies. The emotional and cognitive effects of perspective taking thus can be very different depending on the nature of those relationships. Moreover, these quantitative and qualitative properties are not static but develop over time. On this understanding, perspective taking is not a stable, homogenous state but rather a constructive process that unfolds over the course of the reading in a piecemeal fashion, constituted by a blend of each reader's unique responses.

One of the important functions for a theory of perspective taking is not simply explaining how it can occur but also explaining the conditions in which it might not. On our interpretation, perspective taking is effortful, disconcertingly complex and error-prone, and subject to the distorting influence of numerous psychological and contextual factors. This is true for real-life perspective taking, and we can assume that readers of fiction face the same challenges. In Chapter 6, we outlined some of the relevant variables, including interest in the story, reader motivation, reader experience and skill, and various cognitive capacities. We outlined how perspective taking can go awry during the process of building analogies and in integrating those analogies. Moreover, many of these issues interact with the nature of the text, and the text can pose its own hurdles to perspective taking, including multiple perspectives, multiple perspective-taking targets, and changing and unreliable perspectives. Our review of the challenges to perspective taking was neither exhaustive nor deep but hopefully served to highlight the complexity of the problem.

In keeping with this foundation on empirical evidence, we also provided new studies of our own in Chapter 7. These provided support for the critical role of personal knowledge and experience in perspective taking: Experiment 1 demonstrated the effect of culture and genre knowledge; Experiment 2 found an effect of explicitly noted reminders on perspective taking; and Experiment 3 showed that activating relevant autobiographical experiences enhanced perspective taking.

What Are the Benefits of Perspective Taking?

Effects on General Social Cognition

An important but controversial claim is that reading fiction, particularly high-quality literary fiction, enhances social-cognitive abilities, including perspective taking (Mar et al., 2006; Kidd & Castano, 2013; Kidd et al., 2016). This claim is effectively that "practicing" perspective taking in the context of reading literature generalizes to real-life perspective taking. In a broad sense, this claim is consistent with the present theoretical approach because we assume that there are common components to fictional and real-life perspective taking. Thus, in principle, skill with a common component should support perspective taking both in literature and in real life. Mar (2018a) suggested that frequent reading of stories with social content engages social-cognitive processes, and this might result in the strengthening and practice of these mental processes in real life. However, the claim rests on the assumption that the relevant processes are amenable to the additional training that might follow from reading fiction and that the improvement generalizes to new real-life situations. As we outlined in Chapter 3 with respect to the exercise of neural mechanisms, we find this hypothesis unlikely: The components of perspective taking are diverse (e.g., autobiographical memory retrieval, similarity assessment, analogical inference) and used in many real-life contexts, and even avid readers spend only a fraction of their waking hours reading fiction. Thus, the increment in the exercise of these components due to fiction reading may not be large. Moreover, this "practice hypothesis" would seem to minimize the many variables that differ between literature and real life. Indeed, some authors have noted how experience with fictional social interactions might negatively affect social interactions in real social contexts (Woolfolk Cross, 1983; Currie, 2016). Despite these conceptual hurdles, the intuitive appeal of the hypothesis remains. In this section, we briefly review the evidence on the impact of fictional reading on social cognition and discuss some of the methodological issues.

In an important early study, Mar et al. (2006) found a positive correlation between a measure of exposure to text, the Author Recognition Test (ART), and a measure of social cognition, the Reading the Mind in the Eyes Test (RMET). The ART measures one's exposure to text in an objective manner by assessing the extent to which one can distinguish actual author names from foils. Stanovich and West (1989) demonstrated that this tool has a substantial correlation with other indices of how much people read, such as self-reports, number of magazine subscriptions, and having a favorite author, as well as indices of reading achievement. Other studies have found relationships with real-world reading (West et al., 1993) and knowledge acquisition (Stanovich & Cunningham, 1993). Thus, there is some reason to think this tool provides a useful measure of how much people read, despite its limited face validity (i.e., knowing author names is not the same as having read the books). A range of previous research has found that similar approaches are useful in the context of understanding readers' processing of text (e.g., Dixon et al., 2015b). Mar et al. (2006) used an analogous approach to distinguish exposure to fiction and exposure to nonfiction.

An important dependent variable in the Mar et al. (2006) study was the RMET. This test consists of thirty-six facial photographs cropped to show only the eyes, and participants are asked to choose from four adjectives the one that best describes what the person is thinking or feeling. The test was originally developed to test for psychopathologies such as Asperger syndrome (Baron-Cohen et al., 2001). However, even in neurotypical populations, variations in performance have been presumed to assess the extent to which an individual can understand the perspective of others from limited perceptual information, and thus they are a useful predictor of social cognition. (Note, however, that Black [2019] found evidence that in neurotypical populations performance is at ceiling for many items on the test and that it has little power to distinguish levels of perspective-taking ability.) The results of Mar et al. (2006) can be interpreted as evidence that reading fiction improves one's ability to interact with others in social contexts in which perspective taking is important.

An obvious problem with this interpretation, noted by the authors themselves, is that the direction of causation is ambiguous: It is possible that individuals with greater interpersonal social skills are precisely those individuals who are attracted to reading fiction (Hogan, 2013). Mar et al. (2009) countered this argument by controlling for several of the more obvious confounds. They found that the relationship between the ART and the RMET remained even after controlling for the personality trait of openness and for a measure of transportation as an individual difference. These results provide at least some converging support for an interpretation that reading fiction was the cause of the RMET effect.

However, strong evidence for such a causal effect of reading literature requires an experimental manipulation of exposure to literature. Such evidence was reported by Kidd and Castano (2013): In their research, a brief reading session using literary stories improved performance on the

RMET relative to reading popular, more mundane, fiction. This striking result is sometimes (e.g., Kidd & Castano, 2019) but not always replicated (e.g., Panero et al., 2016). Other researchers have also provided some modest experimental evidence for improved theory of mind with the reading of literary fiction (Djikic et al., 2013; Black & Barnes, 2015; Pino & Mazza, 2016).

There are several conceptual problems with the interpretation of the Kidd and Castano (2013) effect that literary but not popular fiction promotes perspective taking. First, from our theoretical position, there is no reason to believe that popular fiction should not involve perspective taking just as much as or more than literary sources. For example, the materials we used in Experiments 1 and 2 in Chapter 7 were from the popular tradition. Indeed, Fong et al. (2013) found that reading romance produced better RMET performance, and Bal and Veltkamp (2013) found the same result for some popular fiction. Similarly, Chlebuch et al. (2020) used the same stories as Kidd and Castano but found no differences between literary and nonfiction passages. Second, the short-term effects they found would seem to require a different mechanism from the results found by Mar et al. (2006). Mar et al. found a relationship between the RMET and exposure to print, presumably acquired over years of reading. This long-term effect may depend on the incremental acquisition of social-cognitive skills from fiction, perhaps through social support mechanisms (Mar et al., 2009). In contrast, the short-term effects may be mediated by alerting or attentional priming that promotes perspective taking in the immediate context. For example, it could be that reading fiction simply puts readers in a "people mode," leading them to be more attentive to characters' mental states (Black & Barnes, 2015, p. 39). Eekhof et al. (2022) argued that it is naïve to assume that the social-cognitive benefits of any single reading could be long term.

Other critiques of the Kidd and Castano (2013) result have focused on the RMET as a measure of social cognition. Djikic et al. (2013) argued that it only assesses visually based inferences, and their results showed little relation between RMET scores and self-reported measures of empathy. Hogan (2013) and Langkau (2020) pointed out that because the RMET is not based on narrative, it "does not test our ability to empathize on the basis of verbal evidence" (p. 13). Koopman (2015) cogently argued that RMET results tell us very little about real-life attitudes and behavior. Similarly, Black and Barnes (2015) claimed that the ability to correctly identify the emotion that corresponds to RMET pictures is only a very small part of social cognition in general (which includes, e.g., the ability to reason about complex moral situations, detect deception, and react appropriately to emotions in real-life situations). Consistent with these concerns, Mumper and Gerrig (2017) found, in a meta-analysis, that across studies, effects of reading on RMET scores were small; more consistent effects were found with indices of trait empathy, such as the Interpersonal Reactivity Index (Davis, 1983b).

On balance, we do not believe one can draw a firm conclusion from the research on generalized effects on social cognition. Although experimentally induced, short-term effects on perspective taking do seem to be possible, these effects may be small or limited to particular materials, situations, or measures. Although the long-term relationship between reading fiction and real-life perspective taking may be more robust, its interpretation in terms of causal mechanisms is ambiguous. It remains unclear whether fiction reading leads to better perspective taking, whether facility in real-life perspective taking leads to reading more fiction, or whether both variables are determined by some other personal or situational factor. In our view, a core problem with this research is that perspective taking is a complex process with different components that apply in different contexts. Thus, one would not necessarily expect to see consistent, general effects, even if some of those components were enhanced by reading fiction.

Effects on Specific Social Cognition

In contrast to the debatable effects of reading on social cognition generally, there would seem to be much clearer effects of perspective taking in literature on specific prosocial attitudes. This has been noted anecdotally in a number of contexts. For example, *Uncle Tom's Cabin* (Stowe, 1891/2021) arguably changed attitudes about slavery (Kane, 2013), *A Christmas Carol* (Dickens, 1843/1992) apparently changed attitudes about charity (Standiford, 2008), and *Black Beauty* "is credited with having the greatest effect on the treatment of animals of any publication in history" (Anonymous, n.d.). For example, it is said to have led to legislation for the protection of horses and the abandonment of "bearing reins" and changed attitudes about the treatment of horses and animals generally (Moss, 1961; Unti, 1998). Multiple works may also have cumulative effects if they have a consistent perspective. For example, there is some evidence that children's books affect perceptions of socially acceptable emotions (Tsai et al., 2007).

Effects of fiction on attitude change have often been investigated in the context of transportation and persuasion. For example, in a seminal study,

Green and Brock (2000) found that individuals who reported more transportation were more likely to report an attitude consistent with the events of a story. Other researchers have found similar effects (e.g., Appel & Richter, 2007; de Graaf et al., 2009). We conjecture that these effects might be due, at least in part, to perspective taking rather than immersion per se. For example, de Graaf et al. found that persuasive effects were related to emotional reactions rather than the sense of being in the story world. Indeed, the transportation scale developed by Green and Brock (2000) includes a number of items that could conceivably be related to perspective taking rather than phenomenal immersion. Given such considerations, it seems appropriate that future research on attitude change in the context of literary texts consider whether perspective taking is a critical mediating variable.

However, our theoretical framework makes it clear that the link between perspective taking (and transportation) and real-world action or attitude change may not always be straightforward: Constructing a perspective-taking analogy associated with a character's evaluation does not mean that the reader will adopt such an evaluation. Indeed, as we discussed in Chapter 5, a reader may have a "direct" evaluation of a story-world situation that conflicts with that of the character. This evaluation would need to be suppressed in order to develop an analogical connection to the character. To take a particular case, suppose a reader, before encountering *Black Beauty*, believed that animals, and horses in particular, did not harbor human-like emotions or thoughts. Such a reader might nonetheless successfully take the perspective of Black Beauty when reading the story by forming analogies with their own experience and inhibiting their prior beliefs while doing so. For example, early in the book, the first-person narrator describes his thoughts while frolicking with other colts; it would be straightforward to form an analogy to childhood playground experience in this case. However, in order to do so, the reader's prior belief that horses do not have human-like thoughts would need to be inhibited. After finishing the book, though, this suppression would no longer be needed, and there is no reason, based on our logic, to believe that this process would necessarily lead to long-lasting attitude change. Indeed, in the absence of suppression, the original evaluation may be even stronger (cf. Macrae et al., 1994).

The ideas posited in discussions of transportation do not easily explain how an analogical character evaluation comes to supplant the suppressed direct evaluation, at least in this example. First, Appel and Richter (2010) hypothesized that transportation is related to increased realism, perhaps allowing the events of the story to become confused with real memories. This seems implausible in this instance given that the protagonist is a horse. Second, Green and Brock (2000) and others have argued that when readers are transported they are less likely to engage in the "cognitive elaboration" or counter-arguing that might occur when encountering a direct persuasive message in a nonfiction text. (Note that this use of "elaboration" is different from our use of elaborative processing in perspective taking as described in Chapter 4.) This seems tantamount to the suppression of a direct evaluation that we described earlier as part of perspective taking. Although we agree that something of this sort likely occurs, we do not think by itself it explains why a character's evaluation is retained after reading is completed. Finally, transportation is associated with emotional reactions (e.g., de Graaf et al., 2009). However, this would not seem to be specific to fiction, since direct persuasion can also have emotional content. Further, claiming that emotional involvement with the character makes the emotional attitude of the character more compelling strikes us as circular.

Instead, we hypothesize that perspective taking is associated with attitude change because of the extensive construction of similarity that forms the basis of a perspective-taking analogy. In taking the character's perspective in *Black Beauty*, for example, readers would generate multiple analogies, all of which are based on a supposition that horses and people are similar at some level of description. Because these descriptions of similarity are, to some extent, abstract, they would not necessarily conflict with the reader's prior belief that horses do not have human-like thoughts and feelings. Thus, we argue that some sense of similarity between horses and humans may persist after finishing the text. Although this representation of similarity would not directly supplant the reader's prior beliefs, it may undermine it in a more subtle fashion. In particular, it may make the reader more amenable to arguments that, say, horses have feelings that should be considered, even if they are not the same as human feelings. We suspect that the construction of similarity may have the same function in other texts that have persuasive effects. In this way, the work of constructing analogies may generate the foundation for more lasting attitude change.

Future Empirical Directions

In this book, we have described a wide range of processes and variables related to perspective taking. Chapter 7 outlines evidence related to one critical process, the use of personal knowledge and experience in perspective taking. Further work in this vein might examine other variables related to the availability of relevant experience. For example, age might index the number and variety of experiences a reader might have; background related to the story world should have an effect (cf. Green, 2004; de Graaf, 2014); and the familiarity of the story-world situation should matter. Here, we describe how several other predictions of our account could be investigated.

First, we have argued at many points in this book that the process of perspective taking is complex and effortful. Mental work needs to be done, for example, in identifying similarity, searching for relevant personal knowledge and experience, and constructing analogical inferences. This is a strong prediction that is easy to test: Perspective taking should be hampered if readers have to concurrently perform a second, demanding task (cf. Besner, 1987), if resources are required for demanding encoding operations (e.g., Masson & Sala, 1978), or if readers are not focused on the task (e.g., Schad et al., 2012; Dixon et al., 2015a). A variety of research in related tasks is consistent with this prediction (e.g., Davis et al., 1996; Lin et al., 2010). A further expectation is that perspective taking should vary with individual difference measures that index cognitive capacity. Such measures often combine reading with a secondary task to assess the spare capacity that is available (e.g., Unsworth & McMillan, 2013). Presumably, that capacity could be used to perform the work of perspective taking. Ryskin et al. (2015) found such an effect with visual perspective taking, for example.

Related to the potential for individual differences based on cognitive capacity, another avenue is to investigate individual differences in comprehension style. As we noted in Chapter 4, Schneider and Dixon (2009) found that some readers read more slowly and more accurately, and they referred to these as "careful" readers. Careful readers were more likely to maintain a coherent spatial representation of the story world, which we might think of as a form of elaboration. We conjecture that such careful readers may also elaborate other aspects of the story world based on personal knowledge and experience. If true, then we would predict that careful readers would also engage in more perspective taking. In order to test this prediction, one would need a workable index of reading "care," presumably based on a composite of comprehension accuracy and reading speed.

In our discussion of the textual variables related to perspective taking, we argued that first-order features (such as narrative mode or the use of free-indirect speech) do not consistently evoke perspective taking. Instead, second-order features that produce elaborative processing may be more important. Evidence for such effects was obtained by Kotovych et al. (2011) but much more work could be done. For example, one could manipulate the text to add or remove textual gaps that might be filled with information from personal knowledge and experience, texts could be constructed that varied showing versus telling narrative styles, or embodied descriptions could be added or deleted in a text. According to our analysis of these features in Chapter 4, all of these manipulations should affect the degree of perspective taking.

Another approach to assessing the importance of elaborative processing would be to measure the elaborations directly. Suh and Trabasso (1993) developed a convergent methodology for determining when inferences were generated during reading, and it might be possible to apply a related technique to the elaborative inferences that support perspective taking. The first step would be to analyze a text in order to identify what types of elaborations might be generated based on personal knowledge and experience. The second step would be to collect think-aloud protocols while participants are reading the text. According to the Suh and Trabasso (1993) procedure, participants would read each sentence one at a time and then describe their understanding of the sentence in the context of the story and anything else that came into their minds. The protocols would be assessed in terms of whether the expected elaborative inference was mentioned. Finally, the third step would be to assess the elaborative inference generation online, while reading. In this case, probe words would be presented while participants are reading the text, and they would be asked to decide if the probe was related to the story. The expectation is that probes related to the elaborative processing of the story would generate faster responses than suitable control probes. For both of these effects, we would predict that the magnitude of the effect should vary with the extent to which the participant takes the perspective of the character.

As we argued in Chapter 6, constructing a perspective-taking analogy requires information about the target and their situation. Thus, one might anticipate that not having that information available could be detrimental to perspective taking. One could imagine a study in which information about a character's background or situation is either provided or not provided, and we would predict variation in perspective taking with that information. However, such a manipulation would need to be carefully done. In particular, if it is possible for the reader to infer the missing information, they are likely to do so based on their own knowledge and experience, and such inferences might then be associated with greater rather than lesser perspective taking. (We made a related argument about the information provided by mental access in Dixon et al., 2020.) One possibility is to conduct control studies in which readers are explicitly asked to infer the missing information to see if such inferences are normally possible.

Closing Remarks

The main goal of this book was to advance our understanding of perspective taking and, in particular, how it is achieved by readers of fictional narratives. Our analogical inferencing theory captures the essential processing mechanism that is implicit, but undeveloped, in previous theories and exposes the multiple mechanisms that come into play in the reading of fiction and, we believe, in simple, daily interactions as well. However, the complexity of our account has led to an extended debate between the two authors: Is perspective taking common or is it rare? If it is common, how do the effort and complexity go unnoticed? And if it is rare, why does it figure so prominently in accounts of reading enjoyment? One of us noted that in selecting experimental materials, our intuitive judgment was that many short stories did not seem to generate much in the way of perspective taking and afforded little opportunity to build analogies. In particular, short fiction often takes the form of schematic vignettes that provide little information about characters. Further, some longer works seem to thwart perspective taking, exposing so many fluctuations in characters' development that only some portion of evaluations seemed conducive to analogy formation. At the same time, though, the other coauthor argued that perspective taking seems to be commonplace among many types of fiction, and, in some cases, it is arguably the perspective taking that makes the works popular.

We offer two types of solutions to this puzzle: First, it may be the case that much of the cognitive processing required by perspective taking is often subsumed under more general efforts at comprehension and understanding. In effect, texts may be written so that in order to understand the import of the story, one must do the work required to take a character's perspective. In this view, the effort and complexities of taking a perspective are unnoticed because they are part of the typical work of creating a mental representation of the character and the story world. For many types of stories, then, perspective taking would be natural because it is part of comprehension.

Second, if strong perspective taking is rare, it may still be important even though commonly incomplete or partial. Framing reader–character interactions in terms of self-referential, constructive processing implies that literature affects readers differentially. The appeal of fiction resides to a great extent in the invitation to co-construct the characters and interpret them in a personal way, and perspective taking is a function of the way in which we construct those characters. This view shifts attention from the product to the process. As we noted in a number of places, perspective taking is not a unitary or stable process but rather a dynamic, piecemeal one that can obtain to varying degrees and in various ways. Thus, despite being a common phenomenon, perspective taking may be minimal or fleeting under many circumstances. What matters is not whether readers align themselves fully with any character but rather the process of seeking deeper connections in the service of understanding characters who have large, perhaps even disconcerting, differences from the reader.

During the act of reading a fictional text, readers experience a steady stream of reactions, interpretations, and emotions. Perhaps even more interesting is what happens afterwards: The experience of the text changes as readers continue to have thoughts about the text, accumulated recollections and reactions are distilled and modified, and memory traces of the text combine with readers' own experiences (cf. van den Broek & Helder, 2017). This may be similar to how we process people in real life: The most intriguing people are often those we do not fully understand and about whom we keep thinking. In that sense, not taking a character's perspective, or only taking it sporadically and weakly during the initial encounter, might not diminish but perhaps even enhance the reading experience. The kaleidoscope of perspectival fragments accumulated during reading may create a sense of enigma that lingers in the reader's mind, where it can undergo its own development. This dynamic, offline process may help readers reassess their own experiences and achieve greater self-knowledge. Perhaps the best fiction depicts ambiguous characters for the very purpose of provoking a sense of unease, an awareness of our own limited experience, in the hopes of stimulating continued rumination and ongoing perspective-taking processing. The appeal of fiction may reside to a great extent in the invitation to make the characters our own.

References

Abacioglu, C. S., Volman, M., & Fischer, A. H. (2020). Teachers' multicultural attitudes and perspective taking abilities as factors in culturally responsive teaching. *British Journal of Educational Psychology*, *90*(3), 736–752.

Ackermann, E. (1996). Perspective-taking and object construction: Two keys to learning. In Y.B. Kafai & M. Resnick (Eds.), *Constructionism in practice* (pp. 25–37). Lawrence Erlbaum.

Adams, D. (1995). *The hitch hiker's guide to the galaxy omnibus*. Random House.

Akaike, H. (1973). Information theory and an extension of the maximum likelihood principle. In B. N. Petrov & F. Csaki (Eds.), *Second international symposium on information theory* (pp. 267–281). Académiai Kiadó.

Alba, J. W., & Hasher, L. (1983). Is memory schematic? *Psychological Bulletin*, *93*(2), 203.

Alber, J., Jumpertz, J., & Mayer, A. (2020). How professional readers process unnatural narratives. *Scientific Studies of Literature*, *10*(2), 193–213.

Alexander, P. A., Dumas, D., Grossnickle, E. M., List, A., & Firetto, C. M. (2016). Measuring relational reasoning. *The Journal of Experimental Education*, *84*(1), 119–151.

Anderson, J. R., & Milson, R. (1989). Human memory: An adaptive perspective. *Psychological Review*, *96*(4), 703.

Angelotti, M., Behnke, R. R., & Carlile, L. W. (1975). Heart rate: A measure of reading involvement. *Research in the Teaching of English*, *9*(2), 192–199.

Anonymous. (n.d.). "Black Beauty." *Novels for students*. www.encyclopedia.com/arts/educational-magazines/black-beauty.

Anonymous. (1994). The epic of Gilgamesh. In M. A. Caws & C. Prendergast (Eds.), *World reader* (pp. 97–140). Harper Collins. (Original work published circa 1200 BCE.)

Anonymous. (2006). Beowulf (S. Heaney, trans.). In S. Lawall (Ed.), *The Norton anthology of Western literature* (pp. 1174–1247). W. W. Norton. (Original work published circa 850 BCE.)

Appel, M., & Richter, T. (2007). Persuasive effects of fictional narratives increase over time. *Media Psychology*, *10*(1), 113–134.

Appel, M., & Richter, T. (2010). Transportation and need for affect in narrative persuasion: A mediated moderation model. *Media Psychology*, *13*(2), 101–135.

Apperly, I. A. (2012). What is "theory of mind"? Concepts, cognitive processes and individual differences. *Quarterly Journal of Experimental Psychology*, *65*(5), 825–839. https://doi.org/10.1080/17470218.2012.676055.

Apperly, I. A., Samson, D., & Hunphreys, G. W. (2009). Studies of adults can inform accounts of theory of mind development. *Developmental Psychology*, *45*(1), 190–201.

Aristotle. (2013). *Poetics* (A. Kenny, trans.). Oxford University Press. (Original work published circa 335 BCE.)

Asturias, M. A. (1997). The legend of el cadejo (H. St. Martin, trans.). In R. González Echevarría (Ed.), *The Oxford book of Latin American short stories* (pp. 243–246). Oxford University Press. (Original work published in 1930.)

Atwood, M. (2010). *Oryx and Crake*. Vintage Canada.

Aujla, H., Crump, M. J. C., Cook, M. T., & Jamieson, R. K. (2019). The semantic librarian: A search engine built from vector-space models of semantics. *Behavior Research Methods*, *51*, 2405–2418.

Axelrad, E. (1993). Repeated recall as a measure of subjective response to literature. Unpublished Master's thesis, University of Toronto.

Baddeley, A. (2000). The episodic buffer: A new component of working memory? *Trends in Cognitive Science*, *4*(11), 417–423.

Bailey, K., & Im-Bolter, N. (2020). My way or your way? Perspective taking during social problem solving. *Journal of Applied Developmental Psychology*, *66*, 1–9.

Baker, C., Saxe, R., & Tenenbaum, J. (2011). Bayesian theory of mind: Modeling joint belief-desire attribution. *Proceedings of the Cognitive Science Society*, *33*.

Bal, M. (1983). The narrating and the focalizing: A theory of the agents in narrative. *Style*, *17*(2), 234–269.

Bal, P. M., & Veltkamp, M. (2013). How does fiction reading influence empathy? An experimental investigation on the role of emotional transportation. *PLOS ONE*, *8*(1), e55341. https://doi.org/10.1371/journal.pone.0055341.

Bálint, K., & Tan, E. S. (2019). Absorbed character engagement: From social cognition responses to the experience with fictional constructions. In A. Taylor & J. Riis (Eds.), *Screening characters* (pp. 209–229). Routledge.

Ballatore, A., & Natale, S. (2016). E-readers and the death of the book: Or, new media and the myth of the disappearing medium. *New Media & Society*, *18*(10), 2379–2394.

Barceló, E. (2021). *El eco de la piel* (*The echo of the skin*). Roco Bolsillo. (Original work published in 1989.)

Barlassina, L., & Gordon, R. M. (2017). Folk psychology as mental simulation. In E. N. Zalta (Ed.), *Stanford Encyclopedia of Philosophy*. The Metaphysics Research Lab, Stanford University.

Barnes, J. L. (2018). Imaginary engagement, real-world effects: Fiction, emotion, and social cognition. *Review of General Psychology*, *22*(2), 125–134.

Barnes-Holmes, Y., McHugh, L., & Barnes-Holmes, D. (2004). Perspective-taking and theory of mind: A relational frame account. *The Behavior Analyst Today*, *5*(1), 15–25.

Baron-Cohen, S., Leslie, A. M., & Frith, U. (1985). Does the autistic child have a "theory of mind"? *Cognition, 21*(1), 37–46.

Baron-Cohen, S., Wheelwright, S., Hill, J., Raste, Y., & Plumb, I. (2001). The "reading the mind in the eyes" test revised version: A study with normal adults, and adults with Asperger syndrome or high-functioning autism. *The Journal of Child Psychology and Psychiatry and Allied Disciplines, 42*(2), 241–251.

Barsalou, L. W. (1983). Ad hoc categories. *Memory & Cognition, 11*(3), 211–227.

Barsalou, L. W. (2008). Grounded cognition. *Annual Review of Psychology, 59*, 617–645. https://doi.org/10.1146/annurev.psych.59.103006.093639.

Bartlett, F. C. (1932). *Remembering: A study in experimental and social psychology*. Cambridge University Press.

Bates, D., Maechler, M., Bolker, B., & Walker, S. (2015). Fitting linear mixed-effects models using lme4. *Journal of Statistical Software, 67*(1), 1–48. https://doi.org/10.18637/jss.v067.i01.

Batson, C. D. (1991). *The altruism question: Toward a social-psychological answer*. Lawrence Erlbaum.

Batson, C. D. (1995). Immorality from empathy-induced altruism: When compassion and justice conflict. *Journal of Personality and Social Psychology, 68*(6), 1042–1054.

Batson, C.D., Early, S., & Salvarani, G. (1997). Perspective taking: Imagining how another feels versus imagining how you would feel. *Personality and Social Psychology Bulletin, 23*, 751–758.

Batson, C. D., Chang, J., Orr, R., & Rowland, J. (2002). Empathy, attitudes and action: Can feeling for a member of a stigmatized group motivate one to help the group? *Personality and Social Psychology Bulletin, 28*, 1656–1666.

Batson, C. D., Lishner, D. A., Cook, J., & Sawyer, S. (2005). Attitudes and attraction: A new test of the attraction, repulsion, and similarity-dissimilarity asymmetry hypotheses. *British Journal of Social Psychology, 27*, 15–25.

Batson, C. D., Batson, J. G., Griffitt, C. A., Barrientos, S., Brandt, J. R., Sprengelmeyer, P., & Bayly, M. J. (1989). Negative-state relief and the empathy-altruism hypothesis. *Journal of Personality and Social Psychology, 56*(6), 922–933.

Bavidge, M., & Ground, I. (2009). Do animals need a theory of mind? In I. Leudar & A. Costall (Eds.), *Against theory of mind* (pp. 167–188). Palgrave.

Benjamin, W. (2019). *The storyteller essays: The crisis of the novel* (L. Tess, trans.). New York Review of Books. (Original work published in 1930.)

Bennett, W. J. (1993). *The book of virtues: A treasury of great moral stories*. Simon and Schuster.

Berns, G. S., Blaine, K., Prietula, M. J., & Pye, B. E. (2013). Short- and long-term effects of a novel on connectivity in the brain. *Brain Connect, 3*(6), 590–600.

Berscheid, E., & Walster, E. H. (1969). *Interpersonal attraction*. Addison Wesley.

Besner, D. (1987). Phonology, lexical access in reading, and articulatory suppression: A critical review. *The Quarterly Journal of Experimental Psychology, 39*(3), 467–478.

Beyard-Tyler, K. C., & Sullivan, H. J. (1980). Adolescent reading preferences for type of theme and sex of character. *Reading Research Quarterly, 16*(1), 104–120.

Black, J. B., Turner, T. J., & Bower, G. H. (1979). Point of view in narrative comprehension, memory, and production. *Journal of Verbal Learning and Verbal Behavior, 18*(2), 187–198.

Black, J. E. (2019). An IRT analysis of the reading the mind in the eyes test. *Journal of Personality Assessment, 101*(4), 425–433.

Black, J. E., & Barnes, J. L. (2015). The effects of reading material on social and non-social cognition. *Poetics, 52*, 32–43.

Black, J. E., Barnes, J. L., Oately, K., Tamir, D. I., Dodell-Feder, D., Richter, T., & Mar, R. A. (2021). Stories and their role in social cognition. In D. Kuiken & A. M. Jacobs (Eds.), *Handbook of empirical literary studies* (pp. 229–250). De Gruyter.

Bluck, S., & Habermas, T. (2000). The life story schema. *Motivation and Emotion, 24*(2), 121–147.

Boccacio, G. (1972). *The Decameron* (G. H. McWilliam, trans.). Penguin Books. (Original work published in 1353.)

Bonowitz, E. B., van Schijndel, T. J. P., Friel, D., & Schultz, L. (2012). Children balance theories and evidence in exploration, explanation, and learning. *Cognitive Psychology, 64*, 215–234.

Booth, W. (1961). *The rhetoric of fiction.* University of Chicago Press.

Boroojerdi, B., Phipps, M., Kopylev, L., Wharton, C. M., Cohen, L. G., & Grafman, J. (2001). Enhancing analogic reasoning with rTMS over the left prefrontal cortex. *Neurology, 56*(4), 526–528.

Borowski, T. (1980). Het record (The record) (L. Stembor, trans.). In J. Kott & L. Stembor (Eds.), *Hierheen naar de gaskamer, dames en heren (Here to the gas chamber, ladies and gentlemen).* De Arbeiderspers.

Bortolussi, M., & Dixon, P. (1996). The effects of formal training on literary reception. *Poetics, 23*(6), 471–487.

Bortolussi, M., & Dixon, P. (2003). *Psychonarratology: Foundations for the empirical study of literary response.* Cambridge University Press.

Bortolussi, M., & Dixon, P. (2015). Transport: Challenges to the metaphor. In L. Zunshine (Ed.), *The Oxford handbook of cognitive literary studies* (pp. 525–540). Oxford University Press.

Bortolussi, M., Dixon, P., & Linden, C. (2018). Putting perspective taking in perspective. *Review of General Psychology, 22*(2), 178.

Bortolussi, M., Dixon, P., & Sopčák, P. (2010). Gender and reading. *Poetics, 38*(3), 299–318.

Botterill, G. (1996). Folk psychology and theoretical status. In P. Carruthers & P. K. Smith (Eds.), *Theories of theories of mind* (pp. 105–118). Cambridge University Press.

Bower, G. H. (1981). Mood and memory. *American Psychologist, 36*(2), 129–148.

Bower, G. H. (1992). How might emotions affect learning? In S.-Å. Christiansen (Ed.), *The handbook of emotion and memory: Research and theory* (pp. 3–31). Lawrence Erlbaum.

Bower, G. H., & Gilligan, S. G. (1979). Remembering information related to one's self. *Journal of Research in Personality*, *13*(4), 420–432.

Brewer, M. B. (1988). A dual process model of impression formation. In T. K. Srull & R. S. Wyer (Eds.), *Advances in social cognition, volume I* (pp. 1–36). Lawrence Erlbaum.

Brown, N. R., & Shi, L. (November 2019). Me, you, and Harry Potter: On the organization and retrieval of personal-event memories, vicarious-event memories, and fictional-event memories. Presentation at the meeting of the Psychonomic Society, Montréal, Canada.

Brunyé, T. T., Ditman, T., Mahoney, C. R., Augustyn, J. S., & Taylor, H. A. (2009). When you and I share perspectives: Pronouns modulate perspective taking during narrative comprehension. *Psychological Science*, *20*(1), 27–32.

Buccino, G., Lui, F., Canessa, N., Patteri, I., Lagravinese, G., Benuzzi, F. . . . Rizzolatti, G. (2004). Neural circuits involved in the recognition of actions performed by nonconspecifics: An fMRI study. *Journal of Cognitive Neuroscience*, *16*(1), 114–126.

Buck, R. (1984). *The communication of emotion*. Guilford Press.

Buckner, R. L., & Carroll, D. C. (2007). Self-projection and the brain. *Trends in Cognitive Science*, *11*(2), 49–57. https://doi.org/10.1016/j.tics.2006.11.004.

Buckner, R. L., Andrew-Hann, J. R., & Schacter, D. L. (2008). The brain's default network. *Annals of the New York Academy of Sciences*, *1124*, 1–38.

Burke, M. (2006). Emotion: Stylistic approaches. In K. Brown (Ed.), *Encyclopedia of language and linguistics* (pp. 127–129). Elsevier.

Burke, M. (2011). *Literary reading, cognition and emotion: An exploration of the oceanic mind*. Routledge.

Busselle, R., & Bilandzic, H. (2008). Fictionality and perceived realism in experiencing stories: A model of narrative comprehension and engagement. *Communication Theory*, *18*(2), 255–280.

Busselle, R., & Bilandzic, H. (2009). Measuring narrative engagement. *Media Psychology*, *12*(4), 321–347.

Byrne, D. (1971). *The attraction paradigm*. Academic Press.

Cakal, H., Halabi, S., Cazan, A.-M., & Eller, A. (2021). Intergroup contact and endorsement of social change motivations: The mediating role of intergroup trust, perspective-taking, and intergroup anxiety among three advantaged groups in Northern Cyprus, Romania, and Israel. *Group Processes & Intergroup Relations*, *24*(1), 48–67.

Calarco, N., Fong, K., Rain, M., & Mar, R. A. (2017). Absorption in narrative fiction and its possible impact on social abilities. In F. Hakemulder, M. M. Kuijpers, E. S. Tan, K. Bálint, & M. M. Doicaru (Eds.), *Narrative absorption* (pp. 293–313). John Benjamins.

Camerer, C. F., Loewenstein, G., & Weber, M. (1989). The curse of knowledge in economic settings: An experimental analysis. *Journal of Political Economy*, *97*, 1232–1254.

Capote, T. (2013). *In cold blood*. Random House Digital. (Original work published in 1966.)

Caracciolo, M. (2013). Patterns of cognitive dissonance in readers' engagement with characters. *Enthymema, 8*, 21–37.
Caracciolo, M. (2014). Beyond other minds: Fictional characters, mental simulation, and "unnatural" experiences. *Journal of Narrative Theory, 44*(1), 29–53.
Carlson, S. M., & Moses, L. J. (2001). Individual differences in inhibitory control and children's theory of mind. *Child Development, 72*(4), 1032–1053.
Carpendale, J. I., & Chandler, M. J. (1996). On the distinction between false belief understanding and subscribing to an interpretive theory of mind. *Child Development, 68*, 1686–1706.
Carpenter, J. M., Green, M. C., & Fitzgerald, K. (2018). Mind-reading motivation. *Scientific Study of Literature, 8*(2), 211–238.
Carroll, N. (2001). *Beyond aesthetics: Philosophical essays*. Cambridge University Press.
Carroll, N. (2013). The paradox of suspense. In E. S. Tan & G. Diteweg (Eds.), *Suspense* (pp. 81–102). Routledge.
Carruthers, P. (1996). Simulation and self-knowledge: A defence of theory-theory. In P. Carruthers & P. K. Smith (Eds.), *Theories of theories of mind* (pp. 22–38). Cambridge University Press.
Cervone, D., & Tripathi, R. (2009). The moral functioning of the person as a whole: On moral psychology and personality science. In D. Narvaez (Ed.), *Personality, identity, and character: Explorations in moral psychology* (pp. 30–51). Cambridge University Press.
Chafe, W. L. (1980). Integration and involvement in speaking, writing, and oral literature. In D. Tannen (Ed.), *Spoken and written language: Exploring orality and literacy* (pp. 35–54). Ablex.
Chapman, A. (2011). Taking the perspective of the other seriously? Understanding historical argument. *Educar em Revista, 42*, 95–106.
Chatman, S. (1978). *Story and discourse: Narrative structure in fiction and film*. Cornell University Press.
Chatman, S. (1986). Characters and narrators: Filter, center, slant, and interest-focus. *Poetics Today, 7*, 189–204.
Cherryh, C. J. (1982). *The pride of Chanur*. Penguin Books.
Cherryh, C. J. (1984). *Forty thousand in Gehenna*. DAW Books.
Chiavarino, C., Apperly, I. A., & Humphreys, G. W. (2012). Understanding intentions: Distinct processes for mirroring, representing, and conceptualizing. *Current Directions in Psychological Science, 21*(5), 284–289.
Chlebuch, N., Goldstein, T. R., & Weisberg, D. S. (2020). Fact or fiction? Clarifying the relationship between reading and the improvement of social skills. *Scientific Study of Literature, 10*(2), 167–192.
Chow, H. M., Mar, R. A., Xu, Y., Liu, S., Wagage, S., & Braun, A. R. (2015). Personal experience with narrated events modulates functional connectivity within visual and motor systems during story comprehension. *Human Brain Mapping, 36*(4), 1494–1505.
Christie, A. (1997). *The murder of Roger Ackroyd*. HarperCollins. (Original work published in 1926.)

Christie, A. (2011). *Murder on the Orient Express.* Harper. (Original work published in 1934.)
Churchland, P. M. (1991). Folk psychology and the explanation of human behavior. In J. D. Greenwood (Ed.), *The future of folk psychology* (pp. 51–69). Cambridge University Press.
Citron, F. M. M., Cacciari, C., Funcke, J. M., Hsu, C.-T., & Jacobs, A. M. (2019). Idiomatic expressions evoke stronger emotional responses in the brain than literal sentences. *Neuropsychologia, 131,* 233–248.
Cohen, J. (1999). Favorite characters of teenage viewers of Israeli serials. *Journal of Broadcasting & Electronic Media, 43*(3), 327–345.
Cohen, J. (2001). Defining identification: A theoretical look at the identification of audiences with media characters. *Mass Communication and Society, 4,* 253–277.
Cohen, J. (2006). Audience identification with media characters. In J. Bryant & P. Vorderer (Eds.), *Psychology of entertainment* (pp. 183–197). Lawrence Erlbaum.
Cohn, D. (1978). *Transparent minds: Narrative modes for presenting consciousness in fiction.* Princeton University Press.
Conrad, J. (2006). *Heart of darkness.* Project Gutenberg. (Original work published in 1899.)
Converse, B. A., Lin, S., Keysar, B., & Epley, N. (2008). Mood to get over yourself: Mood affects theory-of-mind use. *Emotion, 8*(5), 725–730.
Coplan, A. (2004). Empathetic engagement with narrative fictions. *The Journal of Aesthetics and Art Criticism, 62*(2), 141–152.
Creer, S. D., Cook, A. E., & O'Brien, E. J. (2019). Can readers fully adopt the perspective of the protagonist? *Quarterly Journal of Experimental Psychology, 73*(5), 1–12.
Cupchik, G. C., Oatley, K., & Vorderer, P. (1998). Emotional effects of reading excerpts from short stories by James Joyce. *Poetics, 25,* 363–377.
Currie, G. (1995). The moral psychology of fiction. *Australasian Journal of Philosophy, 73*(2), 250–259.
Currie, G. (2016). Does fiction make us less empathic? *Teorema, 35*(3), 47–68.
Currie, G. (2020). Does reading fiction boost empathy? Psychological approaches. In M. C. Scott (Ed.), *Empathy and the strangeness of fiction* (pp. 1–18). Edinburgh University Press.
Currie, G., & Ravenscroft, I. (2002). *Recreative minds: Imagination in philosophy and psychology.* Clarendon.
Dalai Lama, H. H., & Cutler, H. C. (1998). *The art of happiness.* Easton.
Davie, J., & Reinhardt, T. (2007). *Seneca: Dialogues and essays* (J. Davie, trans.). Oxford University Press.
Dávila, A. (2013). Detrás de la rejas (Behind bars). In Sobrejano-Morán (Ed.), *Tornasol: Guía para la interpretación de textos literarios y cine* (*Tornasol: Guide to the interpretation of literary texts and cinema*) (pp. 51–62). Panda.
Davis, M. H. (1980). A multidimensional approach to individual differences in empathy. *JSAS Catalog of Selected Documents in Psychology, 10,* 85.

Davis, M. H. (1983a). The effects of dispositional empathy on emotional reactions and helping: A multidimensional approach. *Journal of Personality and Social Psychology, 51*, 167–184.

Davis, M. H. (1983b). Measuring individual differences in empathy: Evidence for a multidimensional approach. *Journal of Personality and Social Psychology, 44*(1), 113.

Davis, M. H. (1994). *Empathy: A social psychological approach*. Brown and Benchmark.

Davis, M. H. (2006). Empathy. In J. E. Stets & J. H. Turner (Eds.), *Handbook of the sociology of emotion* (pp. 443–466). Springer.

Davis, M. H., Conklin, L., Smith, A., & Luce, C. (1996). Effect of perspective taking on the cognitive representation of persons: A merging of self and other. *Journal of Personality and Social Psychology, 70*(4), 713–726. https://doi.org/10.1037/0022-3514.70.4.713.

Day, A., Howells, K., Mohr, P., Schall, E., & Gerace, A. (2008). *The development of CBT programmes for anger: The role of interventions to promote perspective-taking skills*. Cambridge University Press.

de Graaf, A. (2014). The effectiveness of adaptation of the protagonist in narrative impact: Similarity influences health beliefs through self-referencing. *Human Communication Research, 40*(1), 73–90.

de Graaf, A. (2017). Children adopt the traits of characters in a narrative. *Child Development Research, 2017*, 1–16.

de Graaf, A., Hoeken, H., Sanders, J., & Beentjes, H. (2009). The role of dimensions of narrative engagement in narrative persuasion. *Communications, 34*(4), 385–405. https://doi.org/10.1515/COMM.2009.024.

de Graaf, A., Hoeken, H., Sanders, J., & Beentjes, J. W. J. (2012). Identification as a mechanism of narrative persuasion. *Communication Research, 39*(6), 802–823.

de Maupassant, G. (1903). In the moonlight. In G. de Maupassant (Ed.), *The complete short stories* (pp. 51–54). P. F. Collier.

de Mulder, H. N. M., Hakemulder, F., van den Berghe, R., Klaassen, F., & van Berkum, J. J. A. (2017). Effects of exposure to literary narrative fiction: From book smart to street smart. *Scientific Study of Literature, 7*(1), 129–169.

de Waal, F. B. (2008). Putting the altruism back into altruism: The evolution of empathy. *Annual Review of Psychology, 59*, 279–300.

de Waal, F. (2016). *Are we smart enough to know how smart animals are?* W. W. Norton.

de Waal, F., Wright, R., Korsgaard, C. M., Kitcher, P., & Singer, P. (2006). *Primates and philosophers: How morality evolved*. Princeton University Press.

Decety, J., & Cowell, J. M. (2014). Friends or foes: Is empathy necessary for moral behavior? *Perspectives on Psychological Science, 9*, 525–537.

Decety, J., & Jackson, P. L. (2006). A social-neuroscience perspective on empathy. *Current Directions in Psychological Science, 15*(2), 54–58.

Decety, J., & Jackson, P. L. (2004). The functional architecture of human empathy. *Behavioral and Cognitive Neuroscience Reviews, 3*(2), 71–100.

Deighton, L. (1989). *Spy hook*. Grafton Books.

Dennett, D. C. (1987). *The intentional stance*. MIT Press.
Dennett, D. C. (1981). Making sense of ourselves. *Philosophical Topics*, *12*(1), 63–81.
Devine, R. T., & Hughes, C. (2013). Silent films and strange stories: Theory of mind, gender, and social experiences in middle childhood. *Child Development*, *84*(3), 989–1003.
Dickens, C. (1992). *A Christmas carol*. Project Gutenberg. (Original work published in 1843.)
Dimberg, U., & Thunberg, M. (1998). Rapid facial reactions to emotional facial expressions. *Scandinavian Journal of Psychology*, *39*(1), 39–45.
Dixon, P., & Bortolussi, M. (1996). Literary communication: Effects of reader-narrator cooperation. *Poetics*, *23*(6), 405–430.
Dixon, P., & Bortolussi, M. (2001). Text is not communication: A challenge to a common assumption. *Discourse Processes*, *31*(1), 1–25.
Dixon, P., & Bortolussi, M. (2019). Readers' processing of perceptual perspective and stance. *Discourse Processes*, *56*(7), 513–529.
Dixon, P., Bortolussi, M., & Khangura, M. (2015a). Mind wandering, non-contingent processing, and recall in reading. *Discourse Processes*, *52*(5–6), 517–531. https://doi.org/10.1080/0163853X.2015.1039471.
Dixon, P., Bortolussi, M., & Mullins, B. (2015b). Judging a book by its cover. *Scientific Study of Literature*, *5*(1), 2–15.
Dixon, P., Bortolussi, M., & Mullins, B. (July 2011). Effects of extratextual information on the evaluation of novels. Presentation at the meeting of the Society for Text and Discourse, Poitiers, France.
Dixon, P., Saadat, S., & Bortolussi, M. (2020). Reader reactions to psychological perspective: Effects of narratorial stance. *Scientific Study of Literature*, *10*(2), 214–227.
Djikic, M., Oatley, K., & Moldoveanu, C. (2013). Reading other minds: Effects of literature on empathy. *Scientific Study of Literature*, *3*(1), 28–47.
Dodell-Feder, D., & Tamir, D. I. (2018). Fiction reading has a small positive impact on social cognition: A meta-analysis. *Journal of Experimental Psychology: General*, *147*(11), 1713–1727. https://doi.org/10.1037/xge0000395.
Dore, R. A., Smith, E. D., & Lillard, A. S. (2017). Children adopt the traits of characters in a narrative. *Child Development Research*, *2017*, 1–16.
Dostoyevsky, F. (1996). *Notes from underground*. Project Gutenberg. (Original work published in 1864.)
Dostoevsky, F. (2012). *The eternal husband*. Melville House. (Original work published in 1870.)
Dunbar, K. (2001). The analogical paradox: Why analogy is so easy in naturalistic settings, yet so difficult in the psychological laboratory. In D. Gentner, K. J. Holyoak, & B. N. Kokinov (Eds.), *The analogical mind: Perspectives from cognitive science* (pp. 313–334). MIT Press.
Dunbar, R. I. M. (2006). Brains, cognition and the evolution of culture. In S. C. Levinson & P. Jaisson (Eds.), *Evolution and culture* (pp. 169–179). MIT Press.
Dymond, R. F. (1950). Personality and empathy. *Journal of Consulting Psychology*, *14*, 343–350.

Dziobek, I., Rogers, K., Fleck, S., Bahnemann, M., Heekeren, H. R., Wolf, O. T., & Convit, A. (2008). Dissociation of cognitive and emotional empathy in adults with Asperger syndrome using the multifaceted empathy test (MET). *Journal of Autism and Developmental Disorders, 38*, 464–473.

Eekhof, L. S., van Krieken, K., & Willems, R. M. (2022). Reading about minds: The social-cognitive potential of narratives. *Psychonomic Bulletin & Review, 29*(5), 1703–1718.

Eekhof, L. S., van Krieken, K., Sanders, J., & Willems, R. M. (2023). Engagement with narrative characters: The role of social-cognitive abilities and linguistic viewpoint. *Discourse Processes*, Advance online publication. https://doi.org/10.1080/0163853X.2023.2206773.

Egan, C., Cristino, F., Payne, J. S., Thierry, G., & Jones, M. W. (2020). How alliteration enhances conceptual–attentional interactions in reading. *Cortex, 124*, 111–118.

Eisenberg, N. (1988). Empathy and sympathy: A brief review of the concepts and empirical literature. *Anthrozoös: A Multidisciplinary Journal of the Interactions of People and Animals, 2*(1), 15–17.

Eisenberg, N., & Strayer, J. (1987). Empathy and its development. In N. Eisenberg & J. Strayer (Eds.), *Critical issues in the study of empathy*. Cambridge University Press.

Eisenberg, N., Murphy, B., & Shepard, S. (1997). The development of empathic accuracy. In W. Ickes (Ed.), *The communication of emotion* (pp. 73–116). Guilford Press.

Eisenberg, N., Fabes, R. A., Murphy, B., Karbon, M., Maszk, P., Smith, M. . . . Suh, K. (1994). The relations of emotionality and regulation to dispositional and situational empathy-related responding. *Journal of Personality and Social Psychology, 66*(4), 776.

Eliot, G. (2000). *Middlemarch*. Random House. (Original work published in 1872.)

Elke, S., & Wiebe, S. A. (2017). Proactive control in early and middle childhood: An ERP study. *Developmental Cognitive Neuroscience, 26*, 28–38.

Ellison, K. (2021, January 17). Five things worth knowing about empathy. *Washington Post*. www.washingtonpost.com/health/empathy-what-to-know/2021/01/15/b3c7665c-4ea4-11eb-bda4-615aaefd0555_story.htmlge.

Epley, N., & Caruso, E. M. (2009). Perspective taking: Misstepping into others' shoes. In K. D. Markman, W. M. P. Klein, & J. A. Suhr (Eds.), *Handbook of imagination and mental simulation* (pp. 295–309). Psychology Press.

Epley, N., Morewedge, C. K., & Keysar, B. (2004). Perspective taking in children and adults: Equivalent egocentrism but differential correction. *Journal of Experimental Social Psychology, 40*(6), 760–768.

Epley, N., Savitsky, K., & Gilovich, T. (2002). Empathy neglect: Reconciling the spotlight effect and the correspondence bias. *Journal of Personality and Social Psychology, 83*, 300–312.

Epley, N., Keysar, B., van Boven, L., & Gilovich, T. (2004). Perspective taking as egocentric anchoring and adjustment. *Journal of Personality and Social Psychology, 87*(3), 327–339. https://doi.org/10.1037/0022-3514.87.3.327.

Escalas, J. E. (2007). Self-referencing and persuasion: Narrative transportation versus analytical elaboration. *Journal of Consumer Research*, *34*(4), 421–429.
Eyal, K., & Rubin, A. M. (2003). Viewer aggression and homophily, identification, and parasocial relationships with television characters. *Journal of Broadcasting & Electronic Media*, *47*(1), 77–98.
Eyal, T., & Epley, N. (2010). How to seem telepathic: Enabling mind reading by matching construal. *Psychological Science*, *2*(5), 700–705.
Fadiga, L., Fogassi, L., Pavesi, G., & Rizzolatti, G. (1995). Motor facilitation during action observation: A magnetic stimulation study. *Journal of Neurophysiology*, *73*, 2608–2611.
Faulkner, W. (1990). *As I lay dying*. Vintage Books. (Original work published in 1930.)
Fernandes, C., Gonçalves, A. R., Pasion, R., Ferreira-Santos, F., Barbosa, F., Martins, I. P., & Marques-Teixeira, J. (2019). Age-related decline in emotional perspective-taking: Its effect on the late positive potential. *Cognitive, Affective, & Behavioral Neuroscience*, *19*(1), 109–122.
Fiske, S. T. (1993). Social cognition and social perception. *Annual Review of Psychology*, *44*, 155–194.
Flaubert, G. (1972). *Madame Bovary* (L. Bair, trans.). Bantam Books. (Original work published in 1857.)
Fodor, J. A. (1987). *Psychosemantics: The problem of meaning in the philosophy of mind*. MIT Press.
Fong, K., Mullin, J. B., & Mar, R. A. (2013). What you read matters: The role of fiction genre in predicting interpersonal sensitivity. *Psychology of Aesthetics, Creativity, and the Arts*, *7*(4), 370.
Forgas, J. P. (1992). Affect in social judgments and decisions: A multiprocess model. In M. P. Zanna (Ed.), *Advances in experimental social psychology* (pp. 227–275). Academic Press.
Forster, E. M. (1927). *Aspects of the novel*. Harcourt, Brace.
Fowler, A. (1982). *Kinds of literature: An introduction to theory of genres and modes*. Harvard University Press.
Fowler, R. (1982). How to see through language: Perspective in fiction. *Poetics*, *11*(3), 213–235.
Franklin, D. R. J., & Mewhort, D. J. K. (2015). Memory as a hologram: An analysis of learning and recall. *Canadian Journal of Experimental Psychology*, *69*(1), 115.
Frick, A. (2018). Perspective taking. In M. H. Bornstein (Ed.), *The SAGE encyclopedia of lifespan human development* (pp. 1627–1628). Sage.
Frischkorn, G. T., Von Bastian, C. C., Souza, A. S., & Oberauer, K. (2022). Individual differences in updating are not related to reasoning ability and working memory capacity. *Journal of Experimental Psychology: General*, *151*(7), 1341–1357.
Fuentes, C. (1991). *The death of Artemio Cruz* (A. MacAdam, trans.). Farrar, Straus and Giroux. (Original work published in 1962.)
Fuyama, M., & Hidaka, S. (2016). Describing temporal changes of absorption with reader's physical measures. *Cognitive Studies: Bulletin of the Japanese Cognitive Science Society*, *23*(2), 135–152.

Gaesser, B., & Schacter, D. L. (2014). Episodic simulation and episodic memory can increase intentions to help others. *Proceedings of the National Academy of Sciences*, *111*(12), 4415–4420.

Gaiman, N. (2009). *Neverwhere: A novel*. Harper Collins.

Galdós, B. P. (1923). *Doña Perfecta* (M. J. Serrano, trans.). Harper & Brothers. (Original work published in 1876.)

Galinsky, A., & Ku, G. (2004). The effects of perspective-taking on prejudice: The moderating role of self-evaluation. *Personality and Social Psychology Bulletin*, *30*, 594–604.

Galinsky, A. D., & Moskowitz, G. B. (2000). Perspective-taking: Decreasing stereotype expression, stereotype accessibility, and in-group favoritism. *Journal of Personality and Social Psychology*, *78*(4), 708. https://doi.org/10.1037//0022-3514.78.4.708.

Galinsky, A. D., Want, C. S., & Ku, G. (2008). Perspective-takers behave more stereotypically. *Journal of Personality and Social Psychology*, *95*(2), 404–419.

Gallese, V., Fadiga, L., Fogassi, L., & Rizzolatti, G. (1996). Action recognition in the premotor cortex. *Brain*, *119*(2), 593–609.

Galper, R. E. (1976). Turning observers into actors: Differential causal attributions as a function of "empathy." *Journal of Personality and Social Psychology*, *10*, 328–335.

Gentner, D. (1983). Structure-mapping: A theoretical framework for analogy. *Cognitive Science*, *7*, 155–170.

Gentner, D., Holyoak, K. J., & Kikinow, B. N. (Eds.). (2001). *The analogical mind: Perspectives from cognitive science*. MIT Press.

Gerace, A., Day, A., Casey, S., & Mohr, P. (2015). Perspective taking and empathy: Does having similar past experience to another person make it easier to take their perspective? *Journal of Relationships Research*, *6*(10), 1–14.

Gernsbacher, M. A., Goldsmith, H. H., & Robertson, R. R. W. (1992). Do readers mentally represent characters' emotional states? *Cognition & Emotion*, *6*(2), 89–111.

Gerrig, R. J. (1989). Reexperiencing fiction and non-fiction. *The Journal of Aesthetics and Art Criticism*, *47*(3), 277–280.

Gerrig, R. J. (1993). *Experiencing narrative worlds*. Yale University Press.

Gerrig, R. J. (2005). The scope of memory-based processing. *Discourse Processes*, *39*(2–3), 225–242.

Gerrig, R. J., & Allbritton, D. W. (1990). The construction of literary character: A view from cognitive psychology. *Style*, *24*(3), 380–391.

Gibbs, R. W., Jr. (2006a). *Embodiment and cognitive science*. Cambridge University Press.

Gibbs, R. W., Jr. (2006b). Metaphor interpretation as embodied simulation. *Mind & Language*, *21*(3), 434–458.

Gick, M. L., & Holyoak, K. J. (1983). Schema induction and analogical transfer. *Cognitive Psychology*, *15*(1), 1–38.

Gilman, C. P. (1997). *The yellow wallpaper and other stories*. Dover Publications. (Original work published in 1892.)

Glenberg, A. M., & Kaschak, M. P. (2002). Grounding language in action. *Psychonomic Bulletin & Review*, *9*(3), 558–565.
Glover, S., & Dixon, P. (2004). Likelihood ratios: A simple and flexible statistic for empirical psychologists. *Psychonomic Bulletin & Review*, *11*, 791–806. https://doi.org/10.3758/bf03196706.
Goldman, A. (1995). Interpretation psychologized. In M. Davis & T. Stone (Eds.), *Folk psychology* (pp. 74–99). Blackwell.
Goldman, A. (2006). *Simulating minds: The philosophy, psychology, and neuroscience of mindreading*. Oxford University Press.
Goldman, A. (1993a). The psychology of folk psychology. *Behavioural and Brain Sciences*, *16*, 15–28.
Goldman, A. (1993b). *Philosophical applications of cognitive science*. Westview.
Gordon, R. M. (1986). Folk psychology as simulation. *Mind and Language*, *1*, 158–171.
Gordon, R. M. (1995). Simulation without introspection or inference from me to you. In T. Stone & M. Davies (Eds.), *Mental simulation* (pp. 53–67). Blackwell.
Gordon, R. M. (1996). "Radical" simulationism. In P. Carruthers & P. K. Smith (Eds.), *Theories of theories of mind* (pp. 11–21). Cambridge University Press.
Gottschall, J. (2012). *The storytelling animal: How stories make us human*. Houghton Mifflin Harcourt.
Gowdy, B. (1997). We so seldom look on love. In M. Atwood & R. Weaver (Eds.), *The new Oxford book of Canadian short stories* (pp. 357–366). Oxford University Press.
Graesser, A. C., Singer, M., & Trabasso, T. (1994). Constructing inferences during narrative text comprehension. *Psychological Review*, *101*(3), 371–395.
Graesser, A. C., Bowers, C., Olde, B., & Pomeroy, V. (1999a). Who said what? Source memory for narrator and character agents in literary short stories. *Journal of Educational Psychology*, *91*(2), 284.
Graesser, A. C., Bowers, C., Olde, B., White, K., & Person, N. K. (1999b). Who knows what? Propagation of knowledge among agents in a literary story world. *Poetics*, *26*(3), 143–175.
Green, M. C. (2004). Transportation into narrative worlds: The role of prior knowledge and perceived realism. *Discourse Processes*, *38*(2), 247–266.
Green, M. C., & Brock, T. C. (2000). The role of transportation in the persuasiveness of public narratives. *Journal of Personality and Social Psychology*, *79*(5), 701–721.
Green, M. C., Brock, T. C., & Kaufman, G. F. (2004). Understanding media enjoyment: The role of transportation into narrative worlds. *Communication Theory*, *14*(4), 311–327.
Gregory, A. J. P., Rioux, M., Gaesser, B., Sheldon, S., & Bartz, J. A. (April 2021). Episodic simulation as a mechanism driving empathic responding. Poster presented at the meeting of the Society for Affective Science.
Grezes, J., & Decety, J. (2001). Functional anatomy of execution, mental simulation, observation, and verb generation of actions: A meta-analysis. *Human Brain Mapping*, *12*(1), 1–19.

Grice, H. P. (1975). Logic and conversation. In P. Cole & J. Morgan (Eds.), *Syntax and semantics* (vol. 3, pp. 41–58). Academic Press.

Grimm, J. L. K., & Grimm, W. K. (1982). The Bremen town band (D. Luke, trans.). In D. Luke (Ed.), *Brothers Grimm: The robber bridegroom* (pp. 35–39). Penguin Books. (Original work published in 1819.)

Gurguryan, L., & Sheldon, S. (2019). Retrieval orientation alters neural activity during autobiographical memory recollection. *NeuroImage, 199*, 534–544.

Hakemulder, F. (2000). *The moral laboratory: Experiments examining the effects of reading literature on social perception and moral self-knowledge*. John Benjamins.

Hakemulder, J., & Koopman, E. (2010). Readers closing in on immoral characters' consciousness. Effects of free indirect discourse on response to literary narratives. *Journal of Literary Theory, 4*(1), 41–62.

Halasz, L. (1968). Experimental research into the effect mechanism of literary works. *Pszichologiai Tanulmanyok, 11*, 411–427.

Hamsun, K. (2012). *Hunger*. Tebbo. (Original work published in 1890.)

Happé, F. G. E. (1994). An advanced test of theory of mind: Understanding of story characters' thoughts and feelings by able autistic, mentally handicapped, and normal children and adults. *Journal of Autism and Developmental Disorders, 24*, 129–154.

Harash, A. (2021). The model of failed foregrounding. *Psychology of Aesthetics, Creativity, and the Arts, 16*(4), 594–609.

Harding, D. W. (1961). Psychological processes in the reading of fiction. *British Journal of Aesthetics, 2*(2), 133–147. https://doi.org/10.1093/bjaesthetics/2.2.133.

Harker, J. E. (2010). The limits of the mind: Cognition and narrative form in the modernist novel. Unpublished doctoral dissertation, University of California, Berkeley.

Harris, P. (2000). *Understanding children's worlds: The work of the imagination*. Blackwell.

Harrison, C. (2017). *Cognitive grammar in contemporary fiction*. John Benjamins.

Hayawaka, S. I. (1990). *Language in thought and action*. Harcourt Brace.

Heal, J. (1986). Replication and functionalism. In J. Butterfield (Ed.), *Language, mind, and logic* (pp. 135–150). Cambridge University Press.

Heal, J. (1996). Simulation, theory and content. In P. Carruthers & P. K. Smith (Eds.), *Theories of theories of mind* (pp. 75–89). Cambridge University Press.

Heinlein, R. A. (1961). *Stranger in a strange land*. Putnam Books.

Helson, R., Jones, C., & Kwan, V. S. Y. (2002). Personality change over 40 years of adulthood: Hierarchical linear modeling analyses of two longitudinal samples. *Journal of Personality and Social Psychology, 83*(3), 752.

Hemingway, E. (2002). *To have and have not*. Simon and Schuster. (Original work published in 1937.)

Hidi, S., & Baird, W. (1986). Interestingness: A neglected variable in discourse processing. *Cognitive Science, 10*(2), 179–194.

Hintzman, D. L. (1986). "Schema abstraction" in a multiple-trace memory model. *Psychological Review, 93*(4), 411.

Hodges, S. D. (2005). Is how much you understand me in your head or mind? In B. F. Malle & S. D. Hodges (Eds.), *Other minds: How humans bridge the divide between self and others* (pp. 298–309). Guilford Publications.

Hodges, S. D., Kiel, K. J., Kramer, A. D. I., Veach, D., & Villanueva, R. (2010). Giving birth to empathy: The effects of similar experience on empathic accuracy, empathic concern, and perceived empathy. *Personality and Social Psychology Bulletin, 36*(3), 398–409.

Hoeken, H., & Fikkers, K. M. (2014). Issue-relevant thinking and identification as mechanisms of narrative persuasion. *Poetics, 44*, 84–99.

Hoeken, H., Kolthoff, M., & Sanders, J. (2016). Story perspective and character similarity as drivers of identification and narrative persuasion. *Human Communication Research, 42*(2), 292–311.

Hoffman, M. (1979). Development of moral thought, feeling and behaviour. *American Psychologist, 34*(10), 958–966.

Hoffman, M. (1984). Interaction of affect and cognition in empathy. In C. Izard, J. Kagan, & R. B. Zajonc (Eds.), *Emotions, cognitions, and behavior* (pp. 103–131). Cambridge University Press.

Hoffner, C. (1996). Children's wishful identification and parasocial interaction with favorite television characters. *Journal of Broadcasting and Electronic Media, 40*(3), 389–402.

Hofstadter, D. R. (2001). Epilogue: Analogy at the core of cognition. In D. Gentner, K. J. Holyoak, & B. N. Kokinov (Eds.), *The analogical mind: Perspectives from cognitive science* (pp. 499–538). MIT Press.

Hogan, P. C. (2003). *The mind and its stories: Narrative universals and human emotion*. Cambridge University Press.

Hogan, P. C. (2011). *The Cambridge encyclopedia of the language sciences*. Cambridge University Press.

Hogan, P. C. (2013). Art and value: An essay in three voices. *SubStance, 42*(131), 61–79.

Holyoak, K. J. (1982). An analogical framework for literary interpretation. *Poetics, 11*(2), 105–126.

Holyoak, K. J., & Thagard, P. (1989). Analogical mapping by constraint satisfaction. *Cognitive Science, 13*, 295–355.

Holyoak, K. J., Gentner, D., & Kokinov, B. N. (2001). Introduction: The place of analogy in cognition. In D. Gentner, K. J. Holyoak, & B. N. Kokinov (Eds.), *The analogical mind*. MIT Press.

Hoorn, J. (1996). Psychophysiology and literary processing: ERPs to semantic and phonological deviations in reading small verses. In R. J. Kreuz & M. S. MacNealy (Eds.), *Empirical approaches to literature and aesthetics* (pp. 339–358). Ablex.

Howard, L. (2019). *Shades of twilight*. Pocket Books.

Hoyos, C., Horton, W. S., Simms, N. K., & Gentner, D. (2020). Analogical comparison promotes theory-of-mind development. *Cognitive Science, 44*(9), e12891.

Huggan, I. (1995). Celia behind me. In M. Atwood & R. Weaver (Eds.), *The new Oxford book of Canadian short stories* (pp. 307–313). Oxford University Press. (Original work published in 1943).

Hüln, P., Schmidt, W., & Shönert, J. (Eds.). (2009). *Point of view, perspective, and focalization: Modeling mediation in narrative.* De Gruyter.

Huttenlocher, P. R., & Dabholkar, A. S. (1997). Regional differences in synaptogenesis in human cerebral cortex. *Journal of Comparative Neurology, 387*(2), 167–178.

Hutto, D. D. (2008). *Folk psychological narratives: The socio-cultural basis of understanding reasons.* MIT Press.

Hutto, D. D. (2011). Understanding fictional minds without theory of mind. *Style, 45*(2), 276–282.

Ichheiser, G. (1949). Misunderstandings in human relations: A study in false social perception. *American Journal of Sociology, 55,* Part 2, viii, 70.

Ickes, W. (1993). Empathic accuracy. *Journal of Personality, 61,* 587–610.

Ickes, W. (2003). *Everyday mind reading: Understanding what other people think and feel.* Prometheus Books.

Ickes, W., & Simpson, J. A. (1997). Managing empathic accuracy in close relationships. In W. Ickes (Ed.), *Empathic accuracy* (pp. 218–250). Guilford Press.

Igl, N. (2016). The double-layered structure of narrative discourse and complex strategies of perspectivization. In N. Igl & S. Zeman (Eds.), *Perspectives on narrativity and narrative perspectivization* (pp. 91–114). John Benjamins.

Ingarden, R. (1973a). *The literary work of art: An investigation on the borderlines of ontology, logic, and theory of literature, 3rd ed.* (G. Grabowics, trans.). Northwestern University Press. (Original work published in 1931.)

Ingarden, R. (1973b). *The cognition of the literary work of art* (R. A. Crowley & K. R. Olson, trans.). Northwestern University Press. (Original work published in 1931.)

Iser, W. (1978). *The act of reading.* Johns Hopkins University Press. (Original work published in 1976.)

Jabali, E. H. (2015). The effects of perspective-taking on perceptual learning. *International Letters of Social and Humanistic Sciences, 48,* 123–132.

Jellema, T., Baker, C. I., Wicker, B., & Perrett, D. I. (2000). Neural representation for the perception of the intentionality of actions. *Brain and Cognition, 44*(2), 280–302.

Johnson, D. R. (2012). Transportation into a story increases empathy, prosocial behavior, and perceptual bias toward fearful expressions. *Personality and Individual Differences, 52*(2), 150–155. https://doi.org/10.1016/j.paid.2011.10.005.

Johnson, D. R. (2013). Transportation into literary fiction reduces prejudice against and increases empathy for Arab-Muslims. *Scientific Studies of Reading, 3*(1), 77–92.

Johnson, D. J., Oliveira, O. S., & Barnett, G. A. (1989). Communication factors related to closer international ties: An extension of a model in Belize. *International Journal of Intercultural Relations, 13*(1), 1–18.

Johnson, M. K., Hashtroudi, S., & Lindsay, D. S. (1993). Source monitoring. *Psychological Bulletin, 114*(1), 3.

Johnson, D. R., Cushman, G. K., Borden, L. A., & McCune, M. S. (2013). Potentiating empathic growth: Generating imagery while reading fiction increases empathy and prosocial behavior. *Psychology of Aesthetics, Creativity, and the Arts, 7*(3), 306–312.

Jolliffe, D., & Farrington, D. P. (2006). Development and validation of the basic empathy scale. *Journal of Adolescence, 29*(4), 393–408.

Jones, E. E., & Nisbett, R. E. (1971). *The actor and the observer: Divergent perceptions of the causes of behavior.* General Learning Press.

Jumpertz, J., & Tary, W. (2020). An empirical study of readers' identification with a narrator. *Anglistik: International Journal of English Studies, 31*(1), 111–128.

Just, M. A., & Carpenter, P. A. (1992). A capacity theory of comprehension: Individual differences in working memory. *Psychological Review, 99*, 122–149.

Just, M. A., Carpenter, P. A., & Keller, T. A. (1996). The capacity theory of comprehension: New frontiers of evidence and arguments. *Psychological Review, 103*(4), 773–780.

Kafka, F. (1995). *The complete stories.* Schocken.

Kahneman, D., & Tversky, A. (1973). On the psychology of prediction. *Psychological Review, 80*(4), 237–251.

Kane, K. (2013). Lincoln and a key to *Uncle Tom's Cabin*. *Connecticut Explored, 11*(1).

Kaufman, G. F., & Libby, L. K. (2012). Changing beliefs and behavior through experience-taking. *Journal of Personality and Social Psychology, 103*(1), 1–19. https://doi.org/10.1037/a0027525.

Kayser, W. (1954). *Entstehung und krise des modernen romans (Emergence and crisis of the modern novel).* Metzler.

Keen, S. (2007). *Empathy and the novel.* Oxford University Press.

Kidd, D. C., & Castano, E. (2013). Reading literary fiction improves theory of mind. *Science, 342*(6156), 377–380.

Kidd, D., & Castano, E. (2016). Different stories: How levels of familiarity with literary and genre fiction relate to mentalizing. *Psychology of Aesthetics, Creativity, and the Arts, 11*(4), 474–486. https://doi.org/10.1037/aca0000069.

Kidd, D., & Castano, E. (2019). Reading literary fiction and theory of mind: Three preregistered replications and extensions of Kidd and Castano (2013). *Social Psychological and Personality Science, 10*(4), 522–531. https://doi.org/10.1177/1948550618775410.

Kidd, D., Ongis, M., & Castano, E. (2016). On literary fiction and its effects. *Scientific Study of Literature, 6*(1), 42–58.

Kim, T., & Biocca, F. (1997). Telepresence via television: Two dimensions of telepresence may have different connections to memory and persuasion. *Journal of Computer-Mediated Communication, 3*(2), JCMC325.

Kintsch, W., & Greene, E. (1978). The role of culture-specific schemata in the comprehension and recall of stories. *Discourse Processes, 1*(1), 1–13.

Klein, S. B., & Loftus, J. (1988). The nature of self-referent encoding: The contributions of elaborative and organizational processes. *Journal of Personality and Social Psychology, 55*(1), 5–11.

Kohlberg, L. (1976). Moral stages and moralization: The cognitive-developmental approach. In T. Lickona (Ed.), *Moral development and behavior: Theory, Research and Social Issues* (pp. 31–53). Holt, Rinehart and Winston.

Kohlmeier, J. (2005). The power of a woman's story: A three-step approach to historical significance in high school world history. *The International Journal of Social Education: Official Journal of the Indiana Council for the Social Studies, 20*, 64–75.

Kolodner, J. (1993). *Case-based reasoning*. Morgan Kaufmann.

Konrath, S. H., O'Brien, E. H., & Hsing, C. (2011). Changes in dispositional empathy in American college students over time: A meta-analysis. *Personality and Social Psychology Review, 15*, 180–198.

Koopman, E. (2015). Empathic reactions after reading: The role of genre, personal factors and affective responses. *Poetics, 50*, 1–44.

Koopman, E. (2016). Effects of "literariness" on emotions and on empathy and reflection after reading. *Psychology of Aesthetics, Creativity, and the Arts, 10*(1), 82–98.

Kotovych, M., Dixon, P., Bortolussi, M., & Holden, M. (2011). Textual determinants of a component of literary identification. *Scientific Study of Literature, 1*(2), 260–291. https://doi.org/10.1075/ssol.1.2.05kot.

Krawczyk, D. (2017). *Reasoning: The neuroscience of how we think*. Academic Press.

Kuhn, T. (1962). *The structure of scientific revolutions*. University of Chicago Press.

Kuiken, D., Miall, D. S., & Sikora, S. (2004a). Forms of self-implication in literary reading. *Poetics Today, 25*(2), 171–203.

Kuiken, D., Phillips, L., Gregus, M., Miall, D. S., Verbitsky, M., & Tonkonogy, A. (2004b). Locating self-modifying feelings within literary reading. *Discourse Processes, 38*(2), 267–286.

Kuzmičová, A. (2012). Presence in the reading of literary narrative: A case for motor enactment. *Semiotica, 189*(1), 23–48. https://doi.org/10.1515/semi.2011.071/html.

Kuzmičová, A., & Bálint, K. (2019). Personal relevance in story reading: A research review. *Poetics Today, 40*(3), 429–451.

Kuzmičová, A., Mangen, A., Støle, H., & Begnum, A. C. (2017). Literature and readers' empathy: A qualitative text manipulation study. *Language and Literature, 26*(2), 137–152.

LaBerge, D., & Samuels, S. J. (1974). Toward a theory of automatic information processing in reading. *Cognitive Psychology, 6*(2), 293–323.

Lamm, C., Batson, C. D., & Decety, J. (2007). The neural substrate of human empathy: Effects of perspective-taking and cognitive appraisal. *Journal of Cognitive Neuroscience, 19*(1), 42–58.

Landauer, T. K., & Dumais, S. T. (1997). A solution to Plato's problem: The latent semantic analysis theory of acquisition, induction, and representation of knowledge. *Psychological Review, 104*(2), 211-240.

Langkau, J. (2020). The empathic skill fiction can't teach us. *Philosophical Psychology, 33*(3), 313–331. https://doi.org/10.1080/09515089.2020.1731446.

Lanser, S. (1981). *The narrative act*. Princeton University Press.

Larsen, S. F., & Seilman, U. (1988). Personal remindings while reading literature. *Text*, *8*(4), 411–430.

László, J., & Larsen, S. F. (1991). Cultural and text variables in processing personal experiences while reading literature. *Empirical Studies of the Arts*, *9*(1), 23–34.

Launay, J., Pearce, E., Wlodarski, R., van Duijn, J. C., & Dunbar, R. I. M. (2015). Higher-order mentalizing and executive functioning. *Personality and Individual Differences*, *86*, 6–14.

Laurence, M. (1997). The mask of the bear. In M. Atwood & R. Weaver (Eds.), *The new Oxford book of Canadian short stories* (pp. 76–91). Oxford University Press.

Laurence, M. (2010). *A bird in the house*. New Canadian Library.

Le Carré, J. (2001). *Tinker, tailor, soldier, spy*. Penguin Books. (Original work published in 1974.)

Le Carré, J. (2006). *Smiley's people*. Penguin Canada. (Original work published in 1969.)

Le Carré, J. (2008). *The night manager*. Penguin Books. (Original work published in 1993.)

Le Guin, U. K. (1980). *The beginning place*. Bantam Books.

Le Guin, U. K. (1990). *Tehanu*. Atheneum.

Le Guin, U. K. (2008). *The lathe of heaven*. Simon and Schuster. (Original work published in 1971.)

Le Guin, U. K. (2012). *A wizard of Earthsea*. Houghton Mifflin Harcourt. (Original work published in 1968.)

Leacock, S. (1911). My financial career. In *Literary lapses* (pp. 9–14). John Lane. (Original work published in 1910.)

Leech, G. N., & Short, M. H. (1981). *Style in fiction: A linguistic introduction to English fictional prose*. Longman.

LeFevre, J. A., & Dixon, P. (1986). Do written instructions need examples? *Cognition and Instruction*, *3*, 1–30.

Lepman, J. (1969). *A bridge of children's books: The inspiring autobiography of a remarkable woman*. Brockhampton Press.

Leslie, A. M., & Thaiss, L. (1992). Domain specificity in conceptual development: Neuropsychological evidence from autism. *Cognition*, *43*, 225–251.

Leslie, A. M., Friedman, O., & German, T. P. (2004). Core mechanisms in "theory of mind." *Trends in Cognitive Sciences*, *8*, 528–533.

Leudar, I., & Costall, A. (Eds.). (2009). *Against theory of mind*. Palgrave Macmillan.

Lewis, D. (1966). An argument for the identity theory. *Journal of Philosophy*, *63*, 17–25.

Li, S.-C., Lindenberger, U., Hommel, B., Aschersleben, G., Prinz, W., & Baltes, P. B. (2004). Transformations in the couplings among intellectual abilities and constituent cognitive processes across the life span. *Psychological Science*, *15*(3), 155–163.

Liebes, T., & Katz, E. (1990). *The export of meaning: Cross-cultural readings of "Dallas."* Oxford University Press.

Lin, S., Keysar, B., & Epley, N. (2010). Reflexively mindblind: Using theory of mind to interpret behavior requires effortful attention. *Journal of Experimental Social Psychology*, *46*(3), 551–556.

Lindsay, D. S., Hagen, L., Read, J. D., Wade, K. A., & Garry, M. (2004). True photographs and false memories. *Psychological Science*, *15*(3), 149–154.

Loftus, E. F., Miller, D. G., & Burns, H. J. (1978). Semantic integration of verbal information into a visual memory. *Journal of Experimental Psychology: Human Learning and Memory*, *4*(1), 19-31.

Lubbock, P. (1921). *The craft of fiction*. Viking Press.

Mack, M. (Ed.). (1997). *The Norton anthology of world masterpieces: Expanded edition in one volume*. W. W. Norton.

Macrae, C. N., Bodenhausen, G. V., Milne, A. B., & Jetten, J. (1994). Out of mind but back in sight: Stereotypes on the rebound. *Journal of Personality and Social Psychology*, *67*(5), 808.

Maio, G. R., & Esses, V. M. (2001). The need for affect: Individual differences in the motivation to approach or avoid emotions. *Journal of Personality*, *69*(4), 583–614.

Mandler, J. M. (1984). *Stories, scripts, and scenes: Aspects of schema theory*. Lawrence Erlbaum.

Mar, R. A. (2004). The neuropsychology of narrative: Story comprehension, story production and their interrelation. *Neuropsychologia*, *42*(10), 1414–1434.

Mar, R. A. (2011). The neural bases of social cognition and story comprehension. *Annual Review of Psychology*, *62*, 103–134.

Mar, R. A. (2018a). Evaluating whether stories can promote social cognition: Introducing the social processes and content entrained by narrative (SPaCEN) framework. *Discourse Processes*, *5/6*, 454–479.

Mar, R. A. (2018b). Stories and the promotion of social cognition. *Current Directions in Psychological Science*, *27*, 257–262.

Mar, R. A., & Oatley, K. (2008). The function of fiction is the abstraction and simulation of social experience. *Perspectives on Psychological Science*, *3*(3), 173–192.

Mar, R. A., Oatley, K., & Peterson, J. B. (2009). Exploring the link between reading fiction and empathy: Ruling out individual differences and examining outcomes. *Communications*, *34*(4), 407–428.

Mar, R. A., Oatley, K., Hirsh, J., de la Paz, J., & Peterson, J. B. (2006). Bookworms versus nerds: Exposure to fiction versus non-fiction, divergent associations with social ability, and the simulation of fictional social worlds. *Journal of Research in Personality*, *40*(5), 694–712.

Margolin, U. (1990). The what, the when, and the how of being a character in literary narrative. *Style*, *24*(3), 453–486.

Margolin, U. (2009). Focalization: Where do we go from here? In P. Hühn, W. Schmid, & J. Schönert (Eds.), *Point of view, perspective, and focalization: Modelling mediation in narrative* (vol. 17, pp. 41–57). De Gruyter.

Margolin, U. (2014). Narrator. In P. Huhn, J. C. Meister, J. Pier, & W. Schmid (Eds.), *Handbook of narratology*, 2nd ed. (vol. 1, pp. 646–667). De Gruyter.

Masson, M. E. J., & Sala, L. S. (1978). Interactive processes in sentence comprehension and recognition. *Cognitive Psychology*, *10*(2), 244–270.
Matute, A. M. (1989a). Sin of omission (M. S. Doyle, trans.). In *The heliotrope wall and other stories* (pp. 68–71). Columbia University Press.
Matute, A. M. (1989b). Very happy (M. S. Doyle, trans.). In *The heliotrope wall and other stories* (pp. 37–42). Columbia University Press.
Maylor, E. A., Moulson, J. M., Muncer, A., & Taylor, L. A. (2002). Does performance on theory of mind tasks decline in old age? *British Journal of Psychology*, *93*(4), 465–485.
McClelland, D. C., & Winter, D. G. (1969). *Motivating economic achievement*. Free Press.
McClelland, J. L., & Rumelhart, D. E. (1985). Distributed memory and the representation of general and specific information. *Journal of Experimental Psychology: General*, *114*(2), 159.
McKennan, R. A. (1965). *The Chandalar Kutchin: Technical paper no. 17*. Arctic Institute of North America.
McKoon, G., & Ratcliff, R. (1992). Inference during reading. *Psychological Review*, *99*(3), 440.
Mead, G. H. (1934). *Mind, self, and society from the standpoint of a social behaviorist*. University of Chicago Press.
Mellet, V. (1997). Good night air (K. S. Leonard, trans.). In K. S. Leonard (Ed.), *Cruel fictions, cruel realities: Short stories by Latin American women writers* (pp. 83–88). Latin American Literary Review Press.
Melville, H. (1991). *Moby Dick, or the whale*. Project Gutenberg. (Original work published in 1851.)
Meskin, A., & Weinberg, J. M. (2003). Emotions, fiction, and cognitive architecture. *British Journal of Aesthetics*, *43*(1), 18–34.
Mewhort, D. J. K., & Johns, E. E. (2005). Sharpening the echo: An iterative-resonance model for short-term recognition memory. *Memory*, *13*, 300–307. https://doi.org/10.1080/09658210344000242.
Miall, D. S., & Kuiken, D. (1994). Foregrounding, defamiliarization, and affect: Response to literary stories. *Poetics*, *22*(5), 389–407.
Michlmayr, M. (2002). Simulation theory versus theory theory. Unpublished doctoral dissertation, Leopold-Franzens-Universität Innsbruck.
Mikolov, T., Chen, K., Corrado, G., & Dean, J. (2013). Efficient estimation of word representations in vector space. arXiv preprint arXiv:1301.3781.
Miller, J., Brookie, K., Wales, S., Wallace, S., & Kaup, B. (2018). Embodied cognition: Is activation of the motor cortex essential for understanding action verbs? *Journal of Experimental Psychology: Learning, Memory, and Cognition*, *44*(3), 335.
Miller, P. J., Hoogstra, L., Mintz, J., Fung, H., & Williams, K. (1993). Troubles in the garden and how they get resolved: A young child's transformation of his favorite story. *Memory and Affect in Development: The Minnesota Symposia on Child Psychology*, *26*, 87–114.
Miller, S. A. (2009). Children's understanding of second-order mental states. *Psychological Bulletin*, *135*(5), 749–773.

Milligan, K., Astington, J. W., & Dack, L. A. (2007). Language and theory of mind: Meta-analysis of the relation between language ability and false-belief understanding. *Child Development*, *78*, 622–646.

Molix, L., & Nichols, C. P. (2012). The importance of perspective taking and respect for dignity in understanding radicalization. *Analyses of Social Issues and Public Policy*, *12*(1), 320–323.

Monterroso, A. (2013). El eclipse (The eclipse). In A. Sobejano-Morán (Ed.), *Tornasol: Guía para la interpretación de textos literarios y cine (Tornasol: Guide to the interpretation of literary texts and cinema)* (p. 6). Panda Publications.

Moors, A., Ellsworth, P. C., Scherer, K. R., & Frijda, N. H. (2013). Appraisal theories of emotion: State of the art and future development. *Emotion Review*, *5*(2), 119–124.

Morrow, D. G., Greenspan, S. L., & Bower, G. H. (1987). Accessibility and situation models in narrative comprehension. *Journal of Memory and Language*, *26*(2), 165–187.

Morton, A. (1980). *Frames of mind: Constraints on the common-sense conception of the mental*. Oxford University Press.

Moss, A. W. (1961). *Valiant crusade: The history of the RSPCA*. Cassell.

Mukařovský, J. (2014). Standard language and poetic language. In J. Chovanec (Ed.), *Chapters from the history of Czech functional linguistics* (pp. 41–53). Masarykova Univerzita. (Original work published in 1932.)

Mulcahy, M., & Gouldthorp, B. (2016). Positioning the reader: The effect of narrative point-of-view and familiarity of experience on situation model construction. *Language and Cognition*, *8*(1), 96–123.

Mullins, B., & Dixon, P. (2007). Narratorial implicatures: Readers look to the narrator to know what is important. *Poetics*, *35*(4–5), 262–276. https://doi.org/10.1016/j.poetic.2007.08.002.

Mumper, M. L., & Gerrig, R. J. (2017). Leisure reading and social cognition: A meta-analysis. *Psychology of Aesthetics, Creativity, and the Arts*, *11*(1), 109.

Munro, A. (1996). The office. In A. Munro (Ed.), *Selected short stories*. Random House.

Murdock, B. B. (1982). A theory for the storage and retrieval of item and associative information. *Psychological Review*, *89*(6), 609–626.

Myers, M. W., & Hodges, S. D. (2008). Making it up and making do: Simulation, imagination, and empathetic accuracy. In K. Markham, W. Klein, & J. Suhr (Eds.), *Handbook of imagination and mental simulation* (pp. 281–294). Psychology Press.

Naaeke, A., Kurylo, A., Grabowski, M., Linton, D., & Radford, M. (2011). Insider and outsider perspective in ethnographic research. *Proceedings of New York State Communication Association*, *2010*, article 9.

Narvaez, D. (2002). Does reading moral stories build character? *Educational Psychology Review*, *14*(2), 155–171.

Nichols, S., Stich, S., Lslie, A., & Klein, D. (1996). Varieties of off-line simulation. In P. Carruthers & P. K. Smith (Eds.), *Theories of theories of mind* (pp. 39–74). Cambridge University Press.

Nickerson, R. S. (1999). How we know – and sometimes misjudge – what others know: Imputing one's own knowledge to others. *Psychological Bulletin, 125*, 737–759.

Niederhoff, B. (2014). Perspective: Point of view. In P. Huhn, J. C. Meister, J. Pier, & W. Schmid (Eds.), *Handbook of narratology* (vol. 2, pp. 692–705). De Gruyter.

Nijhof, A. D., & Willems, R. M. (2015). Simulating fiction: Individual differences in literature comprehension revealed with fMRI. *PLOS ONE, 10*(2).

Nilsen, E. S., & Graham, S. A. (2009). The relations between children's communicative perspective-taking and executive functioning. *Cognitive Psychology, 58*(2), 220–249.

Norton, M. I., Monin, B., Cooper, J., & Hogg, M. A. (2003). Vicarious dissonance: Attitude change from the inconsistency of others. *Journal of Personality and Social Psychology, 85*(1), 47–62.

Nussbaum, M. C. (2001). *Upheavals of thought: The intelligence of emotions.* Cambridge University Press.

O'Brien, E. J., & Cook, A. E. (2016). Coherence threshold and the continuity of processing: The RI-Val model of comprehension. *Discourse Processes, 53*, 326–338.

O'Connor, F. (1955). *A good man is hard to find and other stories.* Houghton Mifflin Harcourt.

Oatley, K. (1999). Meeting of minds: Dialogue, sympathy, and identification in reading fiction. *Poetics, 26*, 439–454.

Oatley, K. (2002). Emotions and the story worlds of fiction. In M. C. Green, J. J. Strange, & T. C. Brock (Eds.), *Narrative impact: Social and cognitive foundations* (pp. 39–69). Lawrence Erlbaum.

Oatley, K. (2016). Fiction: Simulation of social worlds. *Trends in Cognitive Sciences, 20*(8), 618–628.

Oatley, K., Keltner, D., & Jenkins, J. M. (2006). *Understanding emotions.* Blackwell.

Ohreen, D. (2015). Gaining perspective on perspective taking. *Business Ethics Journal Review, 5*(7), 40–46.

Onishi, K. H., & Baillargeon, R. (2005). Do 15-month-old infants understand false beliefs? *Science, 308*, 255–258.

Ortega y Gasset, J. (1925). Ideas sobre la novela [Ideas about the novel]. In *Obras completas III (Complete works III)* (pp. 387–419). Revista de Occidente.

Palencik, J. T. (2008). Emotions and the force of fiction. *Philosophy and Literature, 32*(2), 258–277.

Palmer, A. (2004). *Fictional minds.* University of Nebraska Press.

Panero, M. E., Weisberg, D. S., Black, J., Goldstein, T. R., Barnes, J. L., Brownell, H., & Winner, E. (2016). Does reading a single passage of literary fiction really improve theory of mind? An attempt at replication. *Journal of Personality and Social Psychology, 111*(5), e46–e54. https://doi.org/10.1037/pspa0000064.

Pearl, S. (2007). *Books for children of the world: The story of Jella Lepman.* Pelican.

Perfetti, C. (2007). Reading ability: Lexical quality to comprehension. *Scientific Studies of Reading, 11*(4), 357–383.

Perner, J. (1996). Simulation as explicitation of predication-implicit knowledge about the mind: Arguments for a simulation-theory mix. In P. Carruthers & P. K. Smith (Eds.), *Theories of theories of mind* (pp. 90–104). Cambridge University Press.

Peters, S. L., & Sheldon, S. (2021). Common and distinct neural systems support the generation retrieval phase of autobiographical memory and personal problem solving. *Behavioural Brain Research, 397*, 112911.

Petty, R. E., & Cacioppo, J. T. (1986). The elaboration likelihood model of persuasion. In L. Berkowitz (Ed.), *Advances in experimental social psychology* (vol. 19, pp. 123–205). Academic Press.

Pexman, P. M., Muraki, E., Sidhu, D. M., Siakaluk, P. D., & Yap, M. J. (2019). Quantifying sensorimotor experience: Body–object interaction ratings for more than 9,000 English words. *Behavior Research Methods, 51*(2), 453–466.

Piaget, J. (1932). *The moral reasoning of the child.* Kegan, Paul, Trench, Trubner.

Piaget, J. (1959). *Judgment and reasoning in the child.* Littlefield, Adams.

Pino, M. C., & Mazza, M. (2016). The use of "literary fiction" to promote mentalizing ability. *PLOS ONE, 11*(8), e0160254.

Platt, M. L. (2020). *The leaders brain: Enhance your leadership, build stronger teams, make better decisions, and inspire greater innovation with neuroscience.* Wharton School Press.

Porter, K. A. (1975). Rope. In S. Cahill (Ed.), *Women and fictions: Short stories by and about women* (pp. 78–84). New American Library. (Original work published in 1928.)

Pouillon, J. (1946). *Temps et roman (Time and the novel).* Gallimard.

Premack, D., & Woodruff, G. (1978). Does the chimpanzee have a theory of mind? *Behavioral and Brain Sciences, 1*(4), 515–526.

Preston, S. D., & de Waal, F. B. M. (2002). Empathy: Its ultimate and proximate bases. *Behavioural and Brain Sciences, 25*, 1–72.

Prince, G. (1987). *Dictionary of narratology.* University of Nebraska Press.

Pronin, E., Gilovich, T., & Ross, L. (2004). Objectivity in the eye of the beholder: Divergent perceptions of bias in self versus others. *Psychological Review, 111*(3), 781–799.

Proust, M. (2009). *Swann's way: Remembrance of things past, volume one.* Project Gutenberg. (Original work published in 1922.)

Pulvermüller, F., Shtyrov, Y., & Ilmoniemi, R. (2005). Brain signatures of meaning access in action word recognition. *Journal of Cognitive Neuroscience, 17*(6), 884–892.

R Core Team. (2022). R: A language and environment for statistical computing. R Foundation for Statistical Computing. www.R-project.org.

Radford, C. (1975). How can we be moved by the fate of Anna Karenina? *Proceedings of the Aristotelian Society (Supplementary), 49*, 67–80.

Raichle, M. E., MacLeod, A. M., Snyder, A. Z., Powers, W. J., Gusnard, D. A., & Shulman, G. L. (2001). A default mode of brain function. *Proceedings of the National Academy of Sciences, 98*(2), 676–682.

Raney, A. A. (2006). The psychology of disposition-based theories of media enjoyment. In J. Bryant & P. Vorderer (Eds.), *The psychology of entertainment* (pp. 137–150). Lawrence Erlbaum.

Regan, D. T., & Totten, J. (1975). Empathy and attribution: Turning observers into actors. *Journal of Personality and Social Psychology, 32*(5), 850–856.

Reik, T. (1948). *Listening with the third ear: The inner experience of a psychoanalyst.* Farrar, Strauss.

Renninger, A., & Hidi, S. E. (2016). *The power of interest for motivation and engagement.* Routledge.

Richardson, B. (2015). *Unnatural narrative.* Ohio State University Press.

Richardson, D. R., Hammock, G. S., Smith, S. M., Gardner, W., & Signo, M. (1994). Empathy as a cognitive inhibitor of interpersonal aggression. *Aggressive Behavior, 20,* 275–289.

Richland, L. E., & Morrison, R. G. (2010). Is analogical reasoning just another measure of executive functioning? *Frontiers in Human Neuroscience, 4,* e00180.

Riffaterre, M. (1981). Interview: Michael Riffaterre. *Diacritics, 11*(4), 12–16.

Rimmon-Kenan, S. (1983). *Narrative fiction: Contemporary poetics.* Methuen.

Rinck, M., & Bower, G. H. (1995). Anaphora resolution and the focus of attention in situation models. *Journal of Memory and Language, 34*(1), 110–131.

Rizzolatti, G., & Arbib, M. A. (1998). Language within our grasp. *Trends in Neurosciences, 21*(5), 188–194.

Robards, K. (2011). *One summer.* Dell.

Robbe Grillet, A. (1963). *Pour un nouveau roman (For a new novel).* Les Editions du Minuit.

Rogers, E. M., & Bhowmik, D. K. (1970). Homophily-heterophily: Relational concepts for communication research. *Public Opinion Quarterly, 34,* 523–538.

Rokeach, M. (1979). Some unresolved issues in theories of beliefs, attitudes, and values. In M. M. Page (Ed.), *Nebraska symposium on motivation* (pp. 261–304). University of Nebraska Press.

Ross, B. H., & Kilbane, M. C. (1997). Effects of principle explanation and superficial similarity on analogical mapping in problem solving. *Journal of Experimental Psychology: Learning, Memory, and Cognition, 23*(2), 427.

Rothbart, M. K., & Posner, M. I. (1985). Temperament and the development of self-regulation. In L. Hartlage & C. F. Telzrow (Eds.), *The neuropsychology of individual differences: A developmental perspective* (pp. 93–123). Plenum.

Rowling, J. K. (1997). *Harry Potter and the philosopher's stone.* Bloomsbury.

Ruby, P., & Decety, J. (2001). Effect of subjective perspective taking during simulation of action: A PET investigation of agency. *Nature Neuroscience, 4*(5), 546–550.

Ruby, P., & Decety, J. (2004). How would you feel versus how do you think she would feel? A neuroimaging study of perspective-taking with social emotions.

Journal of Cognitive Neuroscience, 16(6), 988–999. https://doi.org/10.1162/0898929041502661.

Ryskin, R. A., Benjamin, A. S., Tullis, J., & Brown-Schmidt, S. (2015). Perspective-taking in comprehension, production, and memory: An individual differences approach. *Journal of Experimental Psychology: General, 144*(5), 898–915. https://doi.org/dx.doi.org/10.1037/xge0000093.

Salem, S., Weskott, T., & Holler, A. (2017). Does narrative perspective influence readers' perspective-taking? An empirical study on free indirect discourse, psycho-narration and first-person narration. *Glossa: A Journal of General Linguistics, 2*(1), 1–18.

Salinger, J. D. (1951). *The catcher in the rye*. Little, Brown.

Samson, D., Apperly, I. A., Chiavarino, C., & Humphreys, G. W. (2004). Left temporoparietal junction is necessary for representing someone else's belief. *Nature Neuroscience, 7*(5), 499–500.

Sanford, A. J., & Emmott, C. (2012). *Mind, brain, and narrative*. Cambridge University Press.

Sato, M., Sakai, H., Wu, J., & Bergen, B. K. (2012). Towards a cognitive science of literary style: Perspective-taking in processing omniscient versus objective voice. *Proceedings of the Annual Meeting of the Cognitive Science Society, 34*.

Scapin, G., Loi, C., Hakemulder, F., Bálint, K., & Konijn, E. (2023). The role of processing foregrounding in empathic reactions in literary reading. *Discourse Processes*, 1–21. https://doi.org/10.1080/0163853X.2023.2198813.

Schacter, D. L., & Addis, D. R. (2007). The cognitive neuroscience of constructive memory: Remembering the past and imagining the future. *Philosophical Transactions of the Royal Society of London B, 362*(1481), 773–786.

Schacter, D. L., Addis, D. R., & Buckner, R. L. (2007). Remembering the past to imagine the future: The prospective brain. *Nature Reviews Neuroscience, 8*(9), 657–661. https://doi.org/10.1038/nrn2213.

Schacter, D. L., Addis, D. R., Hassabis, D., Martin, V. C., Spreng, N. R., & Szpunar, K. K. (2012). The future of memory: Remembering, imagining, and the brain. *Neuron Review, 76*, 677–694.

Schad, D. J., Nuthmann, A., & Engbert, R. (2012). Your mind wanders weakly, your mind wanders deeply: Objective measures reveal mindless reading at different levels. *Cognition, 125*, 179–194. https://doi.org/j.cognition.2012.07.004.

Scheler, M. (1954). *The nature of sympathy*. Routledge.

Schmid, W. (2003). Narrativity and eventfulness. In T. Kindt & H.-H. Müller (Eds.), *What is narratology? Questions and answers regarding the status of a theory* (pp. 17–33). De Gruyter.

Schneider, D. W., & Dixon, P. (2009). Visuospatial cues for reinstating mental models in working memory during interrupted reading. *Canadian Journal of Experimental Psychology, 63*(3), 161–172. https://doi.org/10.1037/a0014867.

Schneider, R. (2001). Toward a cognitive theory of literary character: The dynamics of mental-model construction. *Style, 35*(4), 607–640.

Scholl, B. J., & Leslie, A. M. (1999). Modularity development and theory of mind. *Mind & Language*, *14*(1), 131–153.

Schooler, J. W., Reichle, E. D., & Halpern, D. V. (2004). Zoning out while reading: Evidence for dissociations between experience and metaconsciousness. In D. T. Levin (Ed.), *Thinking and seeing: Visual metacognition in adults and children* (pp. 203–226). MIT Press.

Seilman, S., & Larsen, S. F. (1989). Personal resonance to literature: A study of remindings while reading. *Poetics*, *18*(1–2), 165–177.

Sevillano, V., Aragones, J. I., & Schultz, P. W. (2007). Perspective taking, environmental concern, and the moderating role of dispositional empathy. *Environment and Behavior*, *39*(5), 685–705.

Shanker, S. (2009). The roots of mindblindness. In I. Leudar & A. Costall (Eds.), *Against theory of mind* (pp. 685–703). Palgrave Macmillan.

Sharrock, W., & Coulter, J. (2009). "Theory of mind": A critical commentary continued. In I. Leudar & A. Costall (Eds.), *Against theory of mind* (pp. 56–88).

Sheldon, S., Gurguryan, L., Madore, K. P., & Schacter, D. L. (2019). Constructing autobiographical events within a spatial or temporal context: A comparison of two targeted episodic induction techniques. *Memory*, *27*(7), 881–893.

Shelley, C. (2003). *Multiple analogies in science and philosophy*. John Benjamins.

Shelley, M. W. (1993). *Frankenstein; or, the modern Prometheus*. Project Gutenberg. (Original work published in 1818.)

Shepard, L. (1987). *Life during wartime*. Bantam Books.

Shiffrin, R. M., & Steyvers, M. (1997). A model for recognition memory: REM-retrieving effectively from memory. *Psychonomic Bulletin & Review*, *4*(2), 145–166. https://doi.org/10.3758/BF03209391.

Siegal, M. (2011). Theory of mind and language acquisition. In P. H. Hogan (Ed.), *The Cambridge encyclopedia of the language sciences* (pp. 862–863). Cambridge University Press.

Sillars, A. L. (1998). (Mis)understanding. In B. H. Spitzberg & W. R. Cupach (Eds.), *The dark side of close relationships* (pp. 73–102). Lawrence Erlbaum.

Simas, E. N., Clifford, S., & Kirkland, J. H. (2019). How empathic concern fuels political polarization. *American Political Science Review*, *114*(1), 258–269.

Singer, M. (1980). The role of case-filling inferences in the coherence of brief passages. *Discourse Processes*, *3*(3), 185–201.

Singer, T. (2006). The neuronal basis and ontogeny of empathy and mind reading: Review of literature and implications for future research. *Neuroscience and Biobehavioral Reviews*, *30*, 855–863.

Singer, T., Seymour, B., O'Doherty, J., Kaube, H., Dolan, R. J., & Frith, C. D. (2004). Empathy for pain involves the affective but not sensory components of pain. *Science*, *303*(5661), 1157–1162.

Singer, T., Seymour, B., O'Doherty, J. P., Stephan, K. E., Dolan, R. J., & Frith, C. D. (2006). Empathic neural responses are modulated by the perceived fairness of others. *Nature*, *439*(7015), 466–469.

Singh, R., & Soo Yan, H. (2000). Attitudes and attraction: A new test of the attraction, repulsion and similarity-dissimilarity asymmetry hypotheses. *British Journal of Social Psychology, 39*(2), 197–211.

Skitka, L., & Morgan, S. G. (2009). The double-edged sword of a moral state of mind. In D. Narvaez (Ed.), *Personality, identity, and character: Explorations in moral psychology* (pp. 355–374). Cambridge University Press.

Slade, L., & Ruffman, T. (2005). How language does (and does not) relate to theory of mind: A longitudinal study of syntax, semantic, working memory and false beliefs. *British Journal of Developmental Psychology, 23*, 117–141.

Slater, M. D., & Rouner, D. (2002). Entertainment-education and elaboration likelihood: Understanding the processing of narrative persuasion. *Communication Theory, 12*(2), 173–191.

Smith, A. (1759). *The theory of moral sentiments*. Hafner.

Sodian, B., & Frith, U. (1993). The theory-of-mind deficit in autism: Evidence from deception. In S. Baron-Cohen, H. Tager-Flusberg, & D. J. Cohen (Eds.), *Understanding other minds: Perspectives from autism* (pp. 158–177). Oxford University Press.

Sommer, R. (2013). Other stories, other minds: The intercultural potential of cognitive approaches to narrative. In L. Bernaerts, D. D. Geest, L. Herman, & B. Vervaeck (Eds.), *Stories and minds: Cognitive approaches to literary narrative* (pp. 155–174). University of Nebraska Press.

Spark, M. (1999). *The prime of Miss Jean Brodie*. Harper Collins. (Original work published in 1962.)

Speer, N. K., Reynolds, J. R., Swallow, K. M., & Zacks, J. M. (2009). Reading stories activates neural representations of visual and motor experiences. *Psychological Science, 20*(8), 989–999.

Spence, I., & Efendov, A. (2001). Target detection in scientific visualization. *Journal of Experimental Psychology: Applied, 7*(1), 13–26. https://doi.org/10.1037//1076-898X.7.1.13

Spilich, G. J., Vesonder, G. T., Chiesi, H. L., & Voss, J. F. (1979). Text processing of domain-related information for individuals with high and low domain knowledge. *Journal of Verbal Learning and Verbal Behavior, 18*(3), 275–290.

Spreng, R. N., McKinnon, M. C., Mar, R. A., & Levine, B. (2009). The Toronto empathy questionnaire: Scale development and initial validation of a factor-analytic solution to multiple empathy measures. *Journal of Personality Assessment, 91*(1), 62–71.

Standiford, L. (2008). *The man who invented Christmas: How Charles Dickens's A Christmas Carol rescued his career and revived our holiday spirits*. Crown.

Stanovich, K. E., & West, R. F. (1989). Exposure to print and orthographic processing. *Reading Research Quarterly, 24*, 402–433.

Stanovich, K. E., & Cunningham, A. E. (1993). Where does knowledge come from? Specific associations between print exposure and information acquisition. *Journal of Educational Psychology, 85*(2), 211.

Stanzel, F. K. (1981). Teller-characters and reflector-characters in narrative theory. *Poetics Today, 2*(2), 5–15.

Stich, S. P., & Nichols, S. (1992). Folk psychology: Simulation or tacit theory? *Mind and Language*, *7*, 35–71.
Stockwell, P., & Mahlberg, M. (2014). War, worlds and cognitive grammar. *Cognitive Grammar in Literature*, *17*, 17–34.
Stockwell, P., & Mahlberg, M. (2015). Mind-modelling with corpus stylistics in *David Copperfield*. *Language and Literature*, *24*(2), 129–147.
Stone, T., & Davies, M. (1996). The mental simulation debate: A progress report. In P. Carruthers & P. K. Smith (Eds.), *Theories of theories of mind* (pp. 119–137). Cambridge University Press.
Storms, M. D. (1973). Videotape and the attribution process: Reversing actors' and observers' points of view. *Journal of Personality and Social Psychology*, *27*(2), 165.
Stowe, H. B. (2021). *Uncle Tom's cabin: Or, life among the lowly*. Project Gutenberg. (Original work published in 1891.)
Suh, S. Y., & Trabasso, T. (1993). Inferences during reading: Converging evidence from discourse analysis, talk-aloud protocols, and recognition priming. *Journal of Memory and Language*, *32*(3), 279–300.
Sujan, M., Bettman, J. R., & Baumgarnter, H. (1993). Influencing consumer judgments using autobiographical memories: A self-referencing perspective. *Journal of Marketing Research*, *30*(4), 422–436.
Sukenick, R. (1969). *The death of the novel and other stories*. Dial Press.
Surtees, A. D. R., & Apperly, I. A. (2012). Egocentrism and automatic perspective taking in children and adults. *Child Development*, *85*(2), 452–460.
Tal-Or, N., & Cohen, J. (2010). Understanding audience involvement: Conceptualizing and manipulating identification and transportation. *Poetics*, *38*(4), 402–418.
Tamir, D. I., Bricker, A. B., Dodell-Feder, D., & Mitchell, J. P. (2016). Reading fiction and reading minds: The role of simulation in the default network. *Social Cognitive and Affective Neuroscience*, *11*(2), 215–224.
Tan, E. S. (1994). Story processing as an emotion episode. In H. van Oostendorp & R. Zwaan (Eds.), *Naturalistic text comprehension* (pp. 165–187). Praeger.
Thagard, P., & Shelley, P. (2001). Emotional analogies and analogical inference. In D. Gentner, K. J. Holyoak, & B. N. Kokinov (Eds.), *The analogical mind* (pp. 335–362). MIT Press.
Todd, A. R., Hanko, K., Galinsky, A. D., & Mussweiler, T. (2011). When focusing on differences leads to similar perspectives. *Psychological Science*, *22*(1), 134–141.
Todd, A. R., Forstmann, M., Burgmer, P., & Galinsky, A. D. (2018). Anxious and egocentric: How specific emotions influence perspective taking. *Journal of Experimental Psychology*, *144*(2), 374–391.
Tolkien, J. R. R. (2008). *The fellowship of the ring*. Harper Collins. (Original work published in 1937.)
Tolstoy, L. (1998). *Anna Karenina* (C. Garnett, trans.). Project Gutenberg. (Original work published in 1878.)
Tomasino, B., Fink, G. R., Sparing, R., Dafotakis, M., & Weiss, P. H. (2008). Action verbs and the primary motor cortex: A comparative TMS study of silent

reading, frequency judgments, and motor imagery. *Neuropsychologia, 46*(7), 1915–1926.

Treisman, A. M., & Gelade, G. (1980). A feature-integration theory of attention. *Cognitive Psychology, 12*(1), 97–136.

Tsai, J. L., Louie, J. Y., Chen, E. E., & Uchida, Y. (2007). Learning what feelings to desire: Socialization of ideal affect through children's storybooks. *Personality and Social Psychology Bulletin, 33*(1), 17–30.

Tsunemi, K., & Kusumi, T. (2011). The effect of perceptual and personal memory retrieval on story comprehension. *Psychologia, 54*(3), 119–134.

Tversky, A. (1977). Features of similarity. *Psychological Review, 84*, 327–352.

Tversky, A., & Kahneman, D. (1974). Judgment under uncertainty: Heuristics and biases. *Science, 185*, 1124–1130.

Twenge, J. M., Campbell, W. K., & Freeman, E. C. (2012). Generational differences in young adults' life goals, concern for others, and civic orientation, 1966–2009. *Journal of Personality and Social Psychology, 102*(5), 1045–1062.

Umiltà, M. A., Escola, L., Intskirveli, I., Grammont, F., Rochat, M., Caruana, F. … Rizzolatti, G. (2008). When pliers become fingers in the monkey motor system. *Proceedings of the National Academy of Sciences, 105*(6), 2209–2213.

Unsworth, N., & McMillan, B. D. (2013). Mind wandering and reading comprehension: Examining the roles of working memory capacity, interest, motivation, and topic experience. *Journal of Experimental Psychology: Human Learning and Memory, 39*(3), 832–842. https://doi.org/10.1037/a0029669.

Unti, B. (1998). Sewill, Anna. In M. Bekoff (Ed.), *Encyclopedia of animal rights and animal welfare* (p. 313). Greenwood Press.

Uspensky, B. (1973). *Poetics of composition: The structure of the artistic text and typology of a compositional form* (V. Zavarin & S. Wittig, trans.). University of California Press.

Uzer, T., Lee, P. J., & Brown, N. R. (2012). On the prevalence of directly retrieved autobiographical memories. *Journal of Experimental Psychology: Learning, Memory, and Cognition, 38*(5), 1296.

van den Broek, P., & Helder, A. (2017). Cognitive processes in discourse comprehension: Passive processes, reader-initiated processes, and evolving mental representations. *Discourse Processes, 54*, 360–372.

van den Broek, P., Risden, K., & Husebye-Hartmann, E. (1995). The role of readers' standards of coherence in the generation of inferences during reading. In R. F. Lorch & E. J. O'Brien (Eds.), *Sources of coherence in reading* (pp. 353–373). Lawrence Erlbaum.

van Krieken, K. (2018). How reading narratives can improve our fitness to survive: A mental simulation model. *Narrative Inquiry, 28*(1), 139–160.

van Krieken, K., Hoeken, H., & Sanders, J. (2017). Evoking and measuring identification with narrative characters: A linguistic cues framework. *Frontiers in Psychology, 8*, 1190. https://doi.org/10.3389/fpsyg.2017.01190.

van Lissa, C. J., Caracciolo, M., Van Duuren, T., & Van Leuveren, B. (2016). Difficult empathy: The effect of narrative perspective on readers' engagement with a first-person narrator. *Diegesis, 5*(1), 42–63.

van Overwalle, F., & Baetens, K. (2009). Understanding others' actions and goals by mirror and mentalizing systems: A meta-analysis. *Neuroimage, 48*(3), 564–584.
van Peer, W. (1997). Toward a poetics of emotion. In M. Hjort & S. Laver (Eds.), *Emotion and the arts* (pp. 215–224). Oxford University Press.
van Peer, W., & Vander Maat, H. P. (2001). Narrative perspective and the interpretation of characters' motives. *Language and Literature, 10*(3), 229–241.
van Peer, W., Hakemulder, J., & Zyngier, S. (2007). Lines on feeling: Foregrounding, aesthetics and meaning. *Language and Literature, 16*(2), 197–213.
Vermeule, B. (2011). *Why do we care about literary characters?* Johns Hopkins University Press.
Vischer, R. (1994). On the optical sense of form: A contribution to aesthetics (H. F. Mallgrave, trans.). In H. F. Mallgrave & E. Ikonomou (Eds.), *Empathy, form, and space: Problems in German aesthetics, 1873–1893* (pp. 89–123). Getty Center for the History of Art and the Humanities.
Vitz, P. C. (1990). The use of stories in moral development: New psychological reasons for an old education model. *American Psychologist, 45*, 709–720.
Vollberg, M. C., Gaesser, B., & Cikara, M. (2021). Activating episodic simulation increases affective empathy. *Cognition, 209*, ArtID 104558.
Walton, K. (1987). Fearing fictions. *Journal of Philosophy, 75*, 5–27.
Walton, K. (1997). Spelunking, simulation, and slime: On being moved by fiction. In M. Hjort (Ed.), *Emotion and the arts* (pp. 37–49). Oxford University Press.
Waltz, J. A., Knowlton, B. J., Holyoak, K. J., Boone, K. B., Mishkin, F. S., de Menezes Santos, M. . . . Miller, B. L. (1999). A system for relational reasoning in human prefrontal cortex. *Psychological Science, 10*(2), 119–125.
Wang, C. S., Tai, K., Ku, G., & Galinsky, A. D. (2014). Perspective-taking increases willingness to engage in intergroup contact. *PLOS ONE, 9*(1).
Webster. (1989). Empathy. In *Webster's ninth new collegiate dictionary* (p. 1099). Merriam Webster.
Weingartner, K. M., & Klin, C. M. (2005). Perspective taking during reading: An on-line investigation of the illusory transparency of intention. *Memory & Cognition, 33*(1), 48–58.
Wellman, H., Cross, D., & Watson, J. (2001). Meta-analysis of theory of mind development: The truth about false-belief. *Child Development, 72*(3), 655–684.
West, R. F., Stanovich, K. E., & Mitchell, H. R. (1993). Reading in the real world and its correlates. *Reading Research Quarterly, 28*(1), 35–50.
Whalen, D. H., Zunshine, L., & Holquist, M. I. (2012). Theory of mind and embedding of perspective: A psychological test of a literary "sweet spot." *Scientific Study of Literature, 2*(2), 301–315.
Wharton, C. M., Grafman, J., Flitman, S. S., Hansen, E. K., Brauner, J., Marks, A., & Honda, M. (2000). Toward neuroanatomical models of analogy: A positron emission tomography study of analogical mapping. *Cognitive Psychology, 40*(3), 173–197.

Wharton, E. (2012). *The custom of the country*. Vintage Books. (Original work published in 1913.)
White, S., Hill, E., Happé, F., & Frith, U. (2009). Revisiting the strange stories: Revealing mentalising impairments in autism. *Cognition, 89*, 25–41.
Wierzbicka, A. (1996). *Semantics: Primes and universals*. Oxford University Press.
Willems, R., & Hartung, F. (2017). Engaging regularly with fiction influences connectivity in cortical areas for language and mentalizing. https://psyarxiv.com/e7bqj/download?format=pdf.
Willis, C. (1993). *Doomsday book*. Spectra.
Willis, C. (2010). *Blackout*. Spectra.
Wimmer, H., & Perner, J. (1983). Beliefs about beliefs: Representation and constraining function of wrong beliefs in young children's understanding of deception. *Cognition, 13*, 103–128.
Wimmer, L. F., El-Salahi, L., & Ferguson, H. J. (2022). Narrativity and literariness affect the aesthetic attitude in text reading. *Empirical Studies of the Arts, 41*(1).
Wimmer, L. F., Friend, S., Currie, G., & Ferguson, H. J. (2021). Reading fictional narratives to improve social and moral cognition: The influence of narrative perspective, transportation, and identification. *Frontiers in Communication, 5*.
Wispe, L. (1986). The distinction between sympathy and empathy: To call forth a concept, a word is needed. *Journal of Personality and Social Psychology, 50*, 314–321.
Wollheim, R. (Ed.). (1974). *Identification and imagination*. Anchor/Doubleday.
Wondra, J. D., & Ellsworth, P. C. (2015). An appraisal theory of empathy and other vicarious emotional experiences. *Psychological Review, 122*(3), 411–428. https://doi.org/10.1037/a0039252.
Woolfolk Cross, D. (1983). *Mediaspeak: How television makes up your mind*. Coward-McCann.
Wu, S., & Keysar, B. (2007). The effect of culture on perspective taking. *Psychological Science, 18*(7), 600–606.
Xiong, C., Walsh, P., & Olson, R. (2021). Derek Chauvin cuffed after murder, manslaughter convictions in death of George Floyd. *Minneapolis Star Tribune*. www.startribune.com/derek-chauvin-convicted-of-murder-manslaughter-in-death-of-george-floyd/600047825.
Yamamoto, H. (1994). Seventeen syllables. In K.-K. Cheung (Ed.), *Seventeen syllables: Hisaye Yamamoto* (pp. 21–38). Rutgers University Press.
Yanal, R. J. (1996). The paradox of suspense. *The British Journal of Aesthetics, 36*(2), 146–159.
Yang, B. W., Deffler, S. A., & Marsh, E. J. (2022). A comparison of memories of fiction and autobiographical memories. *Journal of Experimental Psychology: General, 151*(5), 1089–1106.
Yule, G. (1996). *Pragmatics*. Oxford University Press.
Zaki, J. (2014). Empathy: A motivated account. *Psychological Bulletin, 140*, 1608–1647.
Zeman, S. (2016). Introduction: Perspectives on narrativity and narrative perspectivization. In N. Igl & S. Zeman (Eds.), *Perspectives on narrativity and narrative perspectivization* (pp. 1–14). John Benjamins.

Zhang, X., Fung, H. H., Stanley, J. T., Isaacowitz, D. M., & Ho, M. Y. (2013). Perspective taking in older age revisited: A motivational perspective. *Developmental Psychology*, *49*(10), 1848.
Zillmann, D. (1991). Empathy: Affect from bearing witness to the emotions of others. In J. Bryant & D. Zillmann (Eds.), *Responding to the screen: Reception and reaction processes* (pp. 135–167). Lawrence Erlbaum.
Zillmann, D. (1994). Mechanisms of emotional involvement with drama. *Poetics*, *23*, 33–51.
Zillmann, D. (2006). Empathy: Affective reactivity to others' emotional experiences. In J. Bryant & P. Vorderer (Eds.), *Psychology of entertainment* (pp. 151–181). Lawrence Erlbaum.
Zucchini, W. (2000). An introduction to model selection. *Journal of Mathematical Psychology*, *44*, 41–61.
Zunshine, L. (2006). *Why we read fiction: Theory of mind and the novel*. Ohio State University Press.
Zwaan, R. A. (2004). The immersed experiencer: Toward an embodied theory of language comprehension. *Psychology of Learning and Motivation*, *44*, 35–62.

Index

Alber, J., 168
analogy
  and literary perspective taking, 140
  and simulation, 53
  and theory of mind, 45
  and theory theory, 48
  inference, 35, 36, 39, 122, 138–140, 169
  mapping, 138
  quality, 141–142
  structure, 123, 139
  theory, 138
analogy, perspective-taking
  coherent interpretation, 162
  evaluation-driven, 144, 205
  event-driven, 142, 205
  problems with evaluation-driven analogies, 161
  problems with event-driven analogies, 160
  structure, 36, 37
anchoring and adjustment heuristic, 54
Anderson, J. R., 128
Anna Karenina, 164
Appel, M., 171, 211
Apperly, I. A., 41, 42, 44, 168, 170
Aristotle, 54
As I Lay Dying, 164
attention, 5, 15, 56
attribution, 157–159
  and perspective taking, 158
  fundamental attribution error, 157
Aujla, H., 133
Author Recognition Test, 207, 208
autobiographical memory
  and elaboration, 73, 100, 123
  and emotion, 68
  and suspense, 69
  as reconstruction, 73, 123, 124–125, 205
  constructed experience, 127–128
  cues for retrieval, 124
  errors and distortions, 125
  experience by proxy, 129–131, 205
  priming of, 193–202, 206
  retrieval, 122, 124
  retrieval, direct, 129
  retrieval, search, 129
Axelrad, E., 84

Baddeley, A., 166
Bal, M., 97
Bal, P. M., 62, 64
Barlassina, L., 52, 54
Barnes, J. L., 87, 99, 100, 209
Barnes-Holmes, Y., 166
Barsalou, L. W., 75, 104, 134
Batson, C. D., 4, 27, 32, 61, 65, 171
Bavidge, M., 60
Beginning Place, The, 103
Beowulf, 146
Berns, G. S., 77
Berscheid, E., 31
Beyard-Tyler, K. C., 116
Black Beauty, 32, 210, 211, 212
Black, J. B., 97
Black, J. E., 60, 208, 209
Blackout, 156
Book of Virtues: A Treasury of Great Moral Stories, The, 8
Bortolussi, M., 49, 86, 88, 108, 114, 131, 156
Bower, G. H., 69, 97, 131
"Bremen Town Band, The," 182
Brewer, M. B., 152
Brock, T. C., 211
Brown, N. R., 131
Brunyé, T. T., 92
Buccino, G., 72
Buck, R., 4, 60, 154
Buckner, R. L., 73, 74
Burke, M., 68
Busselle, R., 82, 87

Cakal, H., 4, 11, 18, 65
Camerer, C. F., 45
Caracciolo, M., 64

Index

Carlson, S. M., 168, 169, 170
Carpenter, J. M., 173
Carroll, N., 51, 52, 56, 69, 83
Carruthers, P., 42, 47, 51
Caruso, E. M., 173
Castano, E., 7
Catcher in the Rye, The, 158
Cervone, D., 153
Chafe, W., 156
character
    affinity with, 118–120, 157
    and reader similarity. *See*: homophily
    imaginative resistance to, 119
    information about, 152–153
    multiple perspectives, 163
    multiple perspective-taking targets, 164
    ontological status, 18–19, 80, 90
    personalization, 152
    unreliable perspectives, 163
Chatman, S., 17, 89
Chiavarino, C., 72
Chlebuch, N., 209
Chow, H. M., 106
Christmas Carol, A, 6, 21, 22, 23, 25, 30, 68, 125, 127, 134, 142, 144, 146, 149, 153, 210
Cohen, J., 64, 83, 85, 86, 100, 117, 119
Cohn, D., 111
constructive episodic simulation hypothesis, 73
Coplan, A., 56, 63, 65
Creer, S. D., 5
cultural knowledge, 154, 175, 181–186, 206
    and story comprehension, 186
    Western versus Eastern cultures, 186
Cupchik, G. C., 156, 157, 188
Currie, G., 56, 62, 63, 65, 89

Dalai Lama, H. H., 6
Davie, J., 89
Davis, M. H., 4, 33, 52, 60, 65, 83, 166, 210
de Graaf, A., 32, 82, 92, 117, 152, 178, 202
de Mulder, H. N. M., 103
de Waal, F. B., 5, 60, 64
Decety, J., 58, 60, 63, 65
default network, 73–74
    and autobiographical memory, 73
deictic center, 96
Devine, R. T., 44, 59
Dimberg, U., 74
Dixon, P., 17, 91, 94, 95, 98, 114, 156, 165, 201, 208
Djikic, M., 56, 209
Dodell-Feder, D., 66
Doña Perfecta, 85
Doomsday Book, 163
Dore, R. A., 5

Dunbar, R. I. M., 4, 45, 135
Dymond, R. F., 62

Eekhof, L. S., 94, 171, 209
Efendov, A., 83
egocentric bias, 4, 44, 46, 50, 53, 54, 78, 137, 168, 169, 170
Eisenberg, N., 58, 59, 63, 65, 66
elaboration, 14, 87, 99–101, 123, 168, 204, 212
    and autobiographical memory. *See* autobiographical memory: and elaboration
    and genre knowledge, 156
    and reader knowledge, 155
    and reading strategies, 156
    and standards of coherence, 157
    as imaginary engagement, 99
Elke, S., 169
Ellison, K., 172
Ellsworth, P. C., 130, 154
embodiment, 104–107
    and autobiographical memory, 76, 105
    and reading, 75–77
emotion, appraisal theory of, 66
empathy, 4
    accuracy, 32, 54, 106, 171
    and age, 170
    and autobiographical memory, 66, 103
    and cognition, 65–67
    and context, 172
    and mind reading, 59–62
    and sympathy, 63–65, 69
    appraisal theory of, 152
    as analogical emotion, 14, 70, 204
    definition, 67, 68
    empathic dispositions. *See* reader characteristics: empathic dispositions
    perception-action model, 74
empathy circuits, 74–75
Epley, N., 4, 5, 33, 54, 173
Escalas, J. E., 52, 131, 132
experience by proxy, 123, 129
Eyal, K., 20, 117, 202

Fadiga, L., 71
Fernandes, C., 170
Fikkers, K. M., 92
Fiske, S. T., 132
foregrounding, 107–108
Forgas, J., 69
Forty Thousand in Gehenna, 104
Fowler, A., 90
Fowler, R., 111
Frankenstein, 112
free-indirect speech, 95–96

Frick, A., 63
frontal cortex, 74

Gaesser, B., 52, 194
Galinsky, A. D., 4, 20, 26, 27, 62, 154, 174
Gallese, V., 71
Galper, R. E., 158
gaps, evaluative, 102–104
Gelade, G., 133
genre
  experimental fiction, 2
  fantasy, 32
  gothic horror, 2
  science fiction, 32
  spy and detective fiction, 2
Gentner, D., 34, 135, 139
Gerace, A., 27, 69, 154
Gernsbacher, M., 29
Gerrig, R. J., 69, 85, 99, 152, 155
Gibbs R. W., 107
Gilgamesh, 34
Glenberg, A. M., 93
Goldman, A., 27, 41, 48, 52, 53, 54, 55, 59, 60, 65, 83
Gordon, R. M., 51, 52, 56
Gottschall, J., 7
Graesser, A., 99
Graham, S. A., 170
Green, M. C., 86, 117, 211, 212
Gregory, A. J. P., 194
Grezes, J., 71
Gurguryan, L., 73

Hakemulder, J., 5, 7, 96
Harash, A., 108
Harding, D. W., 117
Harker, J. E., 167
Harris, P., 85
Harrison, C., 46
Harry Potter and the Philosopher's Stone, 23, 36, 38, 124, 126, 149
Hayawaka, S. I., 7
Heal, J., 48, 51
Heart of Darkness, 159, 163
Helson, R., 170
Hidi, S. E., 157
Hintzman, D. L., 128
Hitchhiker's Guide to the Galaxy, A, 115
Hodges, S. D., 27, 171, 173
Hoeken, H., 92, 117
Hoffman, M., 65
Hoffner, C., 82
Hogan, P. C., 10, 34, 68, 209
Holyoak, K. J., 34, 139, 141, 147
homophily, 32, 38, 92, 116–118, 122

and empathy, 32, 118
definition, 31
Hoyos, C., 41, 43, 45, 57
Hughes, C., 59
Hüln, P., 62
Hunger, 91
Huttenlocher, P. R., 169
Hutto, D. D., 41, 43, 47, 48, 57

Ickes, W., 61, 62, 171
identification, 81–85
  and elaboration, 86, 157, 212
  and perspective taking, 81, 82, 204
  as analogical inferencing, 84
  as transfer, 83
  as transformation, 82
  definitions, 81, 84
Igl, N., 112
implicatures, narratorial, 24, 108–110, 113, 205
implied author, 115
Ingarden, R., 103
inhibition, 11, 44, 78, 168, 170, 211
  and age, 169, 170
  and anxiety, 168
  and frontal lobes, 169
  and theory of mind, 170
  definition, 169
interest, 159, 173
  and elaboration, 157
Iser, W., 102, 103

Jabali, E. H., 174
Jellema, T., 72
Johnson, D. J., 31
Johnson, D. R., 7, 62, 107
Johnson, M. K., 64
Jumpertz, J., 67, 110

Kahneman, D., 45
Kaschak, M. P., 93
Kaufman, G. F., 92
Kidd, D., 7, 46, 62, 208, 209
Kintsch, W., 185
Klein, S. B., 106, 131
Kohlberg, L., 4
Kolodner, J., 139
Konrath, S. H., 172
Koopman, E., 10, 64, 107, 171, 209
Kotovych, M., 24, 95, 108, 109
Krawczyk, D., 74
Ku, G., 174
Kuiken, D., 155
Kuzmičová, A., 106, 107, 131

LaBerge, D., 167
Lamm, C., 60, 65, 75, 152
Landauer, T. K., 133
Langkau, J., 60, 62, 63, 89
Lanser, S., 17, 97
Larsen, S. F., 69, 176, 186, 187
László, J., 186
Lathe of Heaven, The, 161
Launay, J., 43, 44
Leech, G., 27, 93
Leslie, A. M., 42
Leudar, I., 43
Li, S. C., 171
Libby, L. K., 92
Liebes, T., 118
Life during Wartime, 125
Lin, S., 166
Lord of the Rings, The, 134

Madame Bovary, 130, 153
Mar, R., 7, 10, 27, 55, 56, 77, 86, 207, 208, 209
Margolin, U., 110, 111
Maylor, E. A., 170
McClelland, J. L., 127, 128
McKoon, G., 99, 103
measuring perspective taking
    construct validity, 178
    criterion validity, 177
    face validity, 177
    offline measures, 177
    online measures, 176, 187
    physiological responses, 177
    post-reading questionnaires, 177
memory resonance, 129, 147
mental access, 93–95
Meskin, A., 56
Miall, D., 107
Michlmayr, M., 62
Middlemarch, 165
Mikolov, T., 133
Miller, J., 76
Miller, P. J., 84
Milson, R., 128
mind reading. *See* theory of mind, theory theory, simulation
mirror network, 71–73
    and analogy, 72
    and mentalizing system, 72
Moby Dick, 134, 137
Moors, A., 11
moral reasoning, 5
Morrow, D. G., 97
Morton, A., 47
Moses, L. J., 170
Moskowitz, B., 154

motivation, 173, 175
    and instruction, 174
    and interest, 173
    factors affecting, 173
Muerte de Artemio Cruz, La (*The Death of Artemio Cruz*), 167
Mukařovský, J., 107
Mullins, B., 136
Mumper, M. L., 210
Murder of Roger Ackroyd, The, 109
Myers, M. W., 61, 155, 171, 173

narrative mode, 91–93
    and physical perspective, 92–93
narrator
    and perspective taking, 25, 110–116
    distance, 88, 111
    perspective of, 112
    reliability, 15, 24, 112, 149, 164, 167
    types, 111
Narvaez, D., 11
Neverwhere, 148
Nichols, S., 54, 59, 66
Nickerson, R. S., 17, 20, 27, 33, 45, 65
Niederhoff, B., 113
Night Manager, The, 105
Nijhof, A. D., 56, 76
Nilsen, E. S., 170
Norton, M. I., 31, 153
Notes from Underground, 120
Nussbaum, M., 5, 7, 67

Oatley, K., 7, 55, 56, 62, 68, 82, 83, 166
"Office, The," 24, 109
One Summer, 188
Orient Express, The, 157
Oryx and Craik, 153

Palencik, J. T., 68
Perfetti, C., 167
Perner, J., 42, 45, 51, 54
personalization, 149
perspectival dissonance, 149
perspectival resonance, 147, 148, 151, 159–162
perspective
    cues for, 90
    definition, 21, 22, 204
    properties of, 21–22
perspective taking, definition, 38, 80, 204
perspective, physical, 85, 94
    relation to psychological perspective, 17, 98
Peters, S. L., 73
Pexman, P. M., 104
Piaget, J., 4, 50
Piel (*Skin*), 32

Premack, D., 42
Preston, S. D., 64
Preston, S. L., 74
Pride of Chunur, The, 130
Prime of Miss Jean Brodie, The, 164
Prince, G., 91, 101
Pronin, E., 45
Pulvermüller, F., 76

Raichle, M. E., 73
Raney, A. A., 59
Ratcliff, R., 103
reader characteristics
  age and development, 169
  "careful" readers, 97, 156
  cognitive skills and capacities, 166
  empathic dispositions, 171, 172
  executive control, 168
  experience, 154
  inferencing ability, 169
  inhibitory control. *See* inhibition
  reading skill, 49, 166
  working memory capacity, 166, 169
Reading the Mind in the Eyes Test, 7, 94, 207, 208, 209
  criticisms, 209
Regan, D. T., 58, 158
Reik, T., 58
remindings, 16, 186–193, 206
Renninger, A., 157, 173
retrieval, as reconstruction. *See* autobiographical memory: as reconstruction
Richardson, B., 167
Richardson, D., 4
Riffaterre, M., 89
Rimmon-Kenan, S., 97, 104
Rinck, M., 97
Rizzolatti, G., 71
Rogers, E. M., 31
Rokeach, M., 31
role playing, 33, 50, 174
Rothbart, M. K., 169
Ruby, P., 71
Rumelhart, D. E., 128
Ryskin, R. A., 82, 166, 213

Salem, S., 5, 82, 83, 92, 93, 97
Sanford, A. J., 118, 119
satisficing, 54
Sato, M., 92
Scapin, G., 108
Schacter, D. L., 53, 73, 124, 126, 194
Scheler, M., 63
Schmid, W., 110
Schneider, D. W., 97, 156, 213

Schneider, R., 152
Schooler, J. W., 87
self-referencing, 131–132
Shades of Twilight, 141, 188
Shanker, S., 60
Sharrock, W., 60
Sheldon, S., 200
Shi, L., 131
Silent Films Test, 44
Sillars, A. L., 6
Simas, E. N., 172
similarity
  and homophily, 135
  and inhibition, 138
  and salience, 135–136
  as common description, 134
  as feature overlap, 135
  construction, 118, 122, 134
  semantic features, 133
  similarity plane, 136, 205
  similarity space, 132–135, 137, 160
simulation, 4, 13, 50, 83
  and autobiographical memory, 125. *See also* autobiographical memory: reconstruction
  and imagination, 52, 56
  and memory, 57
  as episodic reconstruction, 125–126
  definition, 50
  limitations of, 54
  offline, 51
  transfer metaphor, 51
  transformation metaphor, 52
Singer, M., 102
Singer, T., 75
Singh, R., 32
Skitka, L., 174
Slater, M. D., 31, 32
Smiley's People, 126, 136
Smith, A., 63
social cognition, 5, 44, 77, 94
  general effects of perspective taking, 207–210
  specific effects of perspective taking, 210–212
Sommer, R., 7, 49, 155
Speer, N. K., 76
Spence, I., 83
"Spider Woman and the Lost Two Sisters," 182
Spilich, G. J., 155
Spy Hook, 108
Stanovich, K. E., 207
Stanzel, F. K., 93
Stockwell, P., 46
Stone, T., 47, 52, 57, 83
Strange Stories Test, 44

Index

Stranger in a Strange Land, 119
Strayer, J., 59
style, showing versus telling, 101–102
Suh, S. Y., 214
Sujan, M., 132
Surtees, A. D. R., 26, 168, 170
suspense, 69
Swann's Way, 64, 105

Tal-Or, N., 67, 82, 83, 86, 87, 118, 119
Tamir, D. I., 77
Tan, E., 56, 119
Tehanu, 130
text features, 100
Thagard, P., 63, 83
The Custom of the Country, 97
The Eternal Husband, 120
The Lathe of Heaven, 24
theory of mind, 3, 4, 5, 7, 13, 41–46
   acquisition and development, 42
   and inhibitory control, 168
   and language development, 43
   and reading fiction, 3
   false-belief task, 42, 43, 45, 138, 169
   higher levels, 43
   modular view, 42
   narrative practice hypothesis, 43
theory theory, 13, 47
   nativist account, 47
Tinker, Tailor, Soldier, Spy, 160
To Have and Have Not, 130
Todd, A. R., 137, 168
Tomasino, B., 76
Totten, J., 58
transcranial magnetic stimulation, 71, 74, 76
transportation, 81, 85–88, 107
   and attention, 86
   and elaboration, 81, 87
   and need for affect, 171
   and perspective taking, 86
   and persuasion, 210
   definition, 86
Treisman, A., 133
Tsai, J. L., 210
Tsunemi, K., 105
Twenge, J. M., 172

Umiltà, M. A., 72
Uncle Tom's Cabin, 6, 210
Uspensky, B., 90

van den Broek, P., 157
Vander Maat, H. P., 158
van Krieken, K., 32, 56, 66, 82, 97
van Lissa, C. J., 11, 67, 91, 171
van Peer, W., 5, 67, 94, 108, 158
Vermeule, B., 56
Vischer, R., 63
Vollberg, M. C., 106, 194, 200

Waltz, J. A., 74
Wang, Z., 4, 116
Weingartner, K. M., 5
Whalen, D. H., 46
Wharton, C. M., 74
Wierzbicka, A., 133
Wimmer, H., 42
Wimmer, L. F., 41, 92, 94, 119
Wispe, L., 65
Wizard of Earthsea, A, 162
Wollheim, R., 83
Wondra, J. D., 64, 66, 68, 130, 152, 154
Woodruff, G., 42
working memory, 5, 74
   and theory of mind, 170
   capacity. *See* reader characteristics: working memory capacity
Wu, S., 154, 186

Yanal, R. L., 69
Yang, L., 130
Yule, G., 96

Zaki, J., 12, 59
Zeman, S., 110
Zhang, X., 170
Zillmann, D., 63, 65, 119
Zunshine, L., 3, 46

For EU product safety concerns, contact us at Calle de José Abascal, 56–1°, 28003 Madrid, Spain or eugpsr@cambridge.org.

www.ingramcontent.com/pod-product-compliance
Ingram Content Group UK Ltd.
Pitfield, Milton Keynes, MK11 3LW, UK
UKHW022347090725
460592UK00018B/176